HERBLOCK: A CARTOONIST'S LIFE

Herblock:
A Cartoonist's Life

Herbert Block

A LISA DREW BOOK

Macmillan Publishing Company
New York

Maxwell Macmillan Canada
Toronto

Maxwell Macmillan International
New York   Oxford   Singapore   Sydney

Macmillan Publishing Company   Maxwell Macmillan Canada, Inc.
866 Third Avenue   1200 Eglinton Avenue East
New York, NY 10022   Suite 200
                                      Don Mills, Ontario M3C 3N1

Macmillan Publishing Company is part of the Maxwell Communication Group of Companies.

In the photo insert following page 148, the photograph on the third page showing the author at his desk and entitled "1950s and '60s: More clutter" is credited to Ralph Morris, Life Magazine, © Time-Warner; the photograph on the fifth page above the caption "Movie and TV men . . ." is © Universal City Studios, Inc., courtesy of MCA Publishing Rights, a division of MCA Inc.

Library of Congress Cataloging-in-Publication Data

Block, Herbert, 1909–
    Herblock: a cartoonist's life / Herbert Block.
      p. cm.
    "A Lisa Drew book."
    ISBN 0-02-511895-1
    1. Block, Herbert, 1909–   . 2. Cartoonists—United States—
Biography. I. Title.
    NC1429.B625A2   1993
    741.5'092—dc20
[B]   93-10098

10 9 8 7 6 5 4 3 2
Printed in the United States of America

TO DAVE AND TESSIE

Thanks a Million

but that hardly seems enough to express my grateful appreciation to my associate Jean Rickard. The weeks and months of 24-hour days she put in on every phase of this book, from editing first rough draft to selecting type and preparing everything for publication, not only made it better, but literally made it possible.

And thanks again to Robin Meszoly, editor extraordinaire, who went over innumerable drafts, each time with fresh eyes and insights. Once more, thanks to Bob and Jane Asher, who have been more than generous in lending their skills to the manuscript, even devoting precious weekends to help make deadlines. Thanks also to Jim Hoagland for giving his expert attention to special sections and to Peter Milius for his overall view.

Special thanks to Doree Lovell for the jacket photo and for her continued support.

Alison McGrady is not only a valued assistant but a top-notch researcher. Any incorrect names, facts or figures that survived her scrutiny could not have been in material she was asked to check.

And thanks to Lynda Bonieskie, Ed Rickard, Laurie Strayer and Stephanie Rhine for their help in all aspects of this project. Friends and colleagues like these add to the happy side of any production. In the thank-you column, we've long passed the million mark and are still counting.

Contents

Contents

HERBLOCK: A CARTOONIST'S LIFE

1

Kid Stuff

W hen George Shultz, as secretary of state, was asked why he had taken some modest policy initiative, he replied that it was for the same reason a Frenchman kisses a lady's hand—you have to start somewhere.

We start here with my earliest recollection of a national political campaign, at about age six.

Seated at the family dinner table in pre–World-War-I Chicago were my father and mother and their three grade school boys. During a conversational lull when we were all preoccupied with my mother's cooking, my brother Rich came forth with a rhyme he had picked up in the schoolyard and saved for a moment of maximum appreciation:

> *Wilson in the White House, singing like a bird;*
> *Hughes in the river, floating like a turd.*

I can still see his happy pride dissolve into bewildered dismay when my father said, "You may leave the table and go to your room, Richard."

My father had no objection to the expression of political opinion. In fact, he would vote for Woodrow Wilson, and later, with complete non-partisan independence, for Robert M. La Follette (Progressive), Herbert Hoover (Republican) and Franklin D. Roosevelt (Democrat). What he found offensive was the *word*. In that time of innocence, I don't think Rich at age 11 knew what it meant any more than I did. Bill, a year older than Rich, and always more streetwise than the rest of us, might have known.

You have to think of a time when more explicit and pungent words were not part of the general vocabulary—when movies and children both were seen and not heard, and when there was nothing blue on radio or television because neither of them existed.

It was a time of hand-cranked Victrolas, autos and kitchen coffee grinders, of player pianos powered by the pumping of the feet, of washing done at tubs and hung up to dry in the back yard, of floor scrubbing, a time when the few electric appliances included fans that hummed on steamy summer days and nights.

There was no cellophane, plastic or widespread pollution—but also no penicillin, no "pill," no by-pass surgery, none of the hundreds of innovations generally described as the greatest thing since sliced bread—and no sliced bread either. Bread came in loaves that smelled good in bakeries and even better in the kitchen oven when we came home from school.

If the phone and the telegraph were the only means of instant contact, there were other forms of communication—at least six or seven newspapers in Chicago, two mail deliveries a day (without junk mail) and special delivery that was special delivery. The *Saturday Evening Post* came on Thursdays—regularly. There were also *Collier's, Youth's Companion* and such humor publications as the original *Life* magazine and *Judge*. Of special interest to my father were *Scientific American* and chemical publications, domestic and foreign.

Trolleys, and later buses, had two-man teams—motorman and conductor. Among other vehicles were some early electric autos built along vertical lines with glass windows and usually steered by elderly ladies sitting straight up, looking straight ahead and keeping a firm hand on the steering bar.

Horses were still on the streets, pulling postal wagons, milk wagons, junk wagons, ice wagons. A card in the kitchen window with large numbers printed on the sides let the iceman know whether he was to carry up 25, 50 or 100 pounds. Notes in empty milk bottles told the milkman what to leave. And on cold winter days the partially frozen cream at the top of the bottle pushed up the cardboard lid. Delicious.

The corner drugstores had soda fountains with marble-topped counters. Ice-cream sodas were served in glasses that bowled out at the top and were set in open metal containers with a handle on them. Root beer, served up in glass steins, had a head on it, and the foam left its mark around the mouth and on the nose.

Long Sunday dinners that went on into much of the afternoon seemed interminable to youngsters itching to go out and play. The dinners involved much Saturday shopping at many stores and preliminary preparations all Sunday morning—stringing beans, peeling, boning, chopping, boiling, baking and finally cooking the dinner. This literally included soup to a bowlful of nuts—to be cracked and shelled during the long after-dinner conversations.

Besides being impatient to get out and play, I wanted to draw—something for which the white tablecloth with its neat folds was not suited.

The first caricature I can recall doing was not some modest attempt at drawing a childhood schoolteacher (if I was even of school age at the time). No, it portrayed the man held to be the arch-villain of the time: Kaiser Wilhelm of Germany. Actually, doing anyone I knew was probably well beyond my talent, and the Wilhelm caricature undoubtedly derived from drawings and cartoons I had seen in the papers.

With his W-shaped mustache, squinty eyes and spiked helmet he was easy, and I did him in chalk on the sidewalk. This served a double purpose. People could see (and admire) my work; and I could feel satisfaction rather than injury when that hateful face was walked on or stomped on. I could always do the kaiser over again as long as the chalk held out.

In The War we did whatever civilians were asked to do. My brothers, young, appealing and energetic, were very successful at selling Liberty Bonds. I saved tinfoil and peach pits to contribute to the cause. The peach pits, we heard, had something to do with gas mask canisters. I never knew what the tinfoil was supposed to be for, unless the hard balls of it we accumulated were fired at the enemy just as we formed them.

In the back yard behind our apartment building, we had a small victory garden, where the vegetables nudged out the nasturtiums and other flowers of earlier days. The vegetables included rhubarb, which, we were warned, was poisonous if you ate the wrong part of the plant. This I could believe because even the right part was not an all-time favorite.

School let out early to celebrate the end of the war—twice. The first was the "false armistice" proclaimed by United Press. The second time was for real. That evening my father took the family downtown to the thick of a celebration that filled the streets. After we milled around in the happy, cheering crowd, he topped off the evening by taking us to the Palace Theater, where performers and audience were all in high spirits.

Sometime after The War, the papers carried the news that France's General Foch was coming to Chicago, where he would lay a wreath at the statue of Abraham Lincoln.

At school, the teacher decided that the class should choose someone to witness this event and report back after seeing the great war hero. In the voting, I ran second to a girl who became our designated hero-watcher. But it occurred to me that I needn't be shut out of what was, after all, a public event. I could go too and perhaps add my own eyewitness account of the occasion. So on the day of the Foch visit, I went early to Lincoln Park, long before anyone else arrived, to select a good vantage point. Alas for being a kid and a particularly diffident one. When the crowd gathered, grown-ups moved in, and by the time the general passed, the adults were about four deep in front of me. My plan for military-hero reporting was, as I'm sure the general would have pointed out, well conceived but seriously flawed in its execution.

Much more satisfactory was my role as a school crossing guard, complete with elastic snap-on safety-patrol arm band. Selection for one of these posts contributed greatly to a feeling of maturity, or at least smug importance.

Being a crossing guard meant leaving class a few minutes early and ostentatiously tiptoeing to the schoolroom door in a way calculated to be completely unobtrusive except to every person in the entire room.

Being a crossing guard also meant putting out a protective arm to hold back some beautiful young classmate while I sternly looked up and down the street and around the corners in my best imitation of a western movie lawman—then, with no car visible anywhere, declaring it okay for her to proceed. What more could life hold?

Along the way I developed crushes on two or three grade school teachers who little realized that they figured in romantic fantasies. These consisted of my performing heroic deeds while they watched in total awe. A smile and praise from them for some essay or a drawing to be posted on the schoolroom wall were enough to dream on.

I felt early—and continued to feel despite long years of excruciating shyness—that God's great gift to the world was not His only begotten Son, but girls.

I didn't mind school—actually I liked it, although this was something no red-blooded kid would say aloud. The tradition, fortified by books, cartoons and movies, was that boys hated school and were supposed to spend their hours in class longing for the old swimmin' hole.

What boys were supposed to have a special aptitude for—or what was supposed to help qualify them for their lives as males—was "manual training" (later known as "woodworking" or "shop"), an obligatory all-boy class.

S. J. Perelman once named one of his characters Manuel Dexterides. Mr. Dexterides I was not. It was apparently a requirement that every boy should turn out something he could take home to show for the instructor's efforts. A pair of bookends seemed simple enough, but they didn't quite work out, failing in symmetry and stability. Applying a bright red stain in an effort to give them a classy mahogany look made their defects stand out only more, as did a border of gold paint that smelled strongly of banana oil—my last misguided effort to make them look somehow attractive.

I finally did produce something passable, something even simpler—a cutting board. This was a plain oblong piece of wood, somewhat rounded at the corners and sanded to prevent slivers. I think the teacher was relieved that he could give this work his reluctant approval, and my mother liked it fine. She used it for years.

The boys-must-hate-school mythology did not extend to liking books, as long as they were not required reading. The public library issued yellow cards for children's books and orange cards for adults'. After a while I somehow managed to get an orange card along with my yellow one. The first book I took out on it was *Uncle Tom's Cabin,* a good heavy book from the adult section. I only got through a few pages of Mrs. Stowe's work—the first of many well-known books that I never finished reading. But I felt pretty grown-up when the librarian checked it out on my new orange card.

We lived only a few blocks from Cubs Park, and afternoons we kids often watched the progress of the games via a scoreboard set above the right-field bleachers and visible from the street. We also made some quarters and half dollars from men who parked on the nearby streets by offering to "watch your car, mister." We were conscientious in looking after these cars, although I'm not sure what I would have done if somebody had tried to drive off with one.

We were loyal Cubs fans, even if we didn't all understand the finer points of the game. And it was easy to keep track of the team standings when, as someone put it so well, there were "two leagues of eight teams each, as God intended."

We earned bleacher passes by lining up after a game, hoping to be one of those selected to clean up the stands. We were given gunny-sacks for picking up pop bottles and other debris. And depending on weather predictions, sometimes we were called on to roll out the tarpaulin across the infield. Here we took quick turns standing on the pitcher's mound and imagining ourselves as strikeout kings. Once in a while a generous gate watcher would let us into the grandstand and boxes to take the place of fans who departed when the game seemed lost. And if our Cubs rallied to win at the end, it was only fitting that we should occupy the choice seats left by those of little faith.

Meanwhile, back at the drawing board—at that time, the dining room table—I continued sketching and splashing around in watercolors. My father taught me some drawing and encouraged me. He brought home drawing materials and art books, and kept alive an interest that might otherwise have flagged.

When I was 11 he entered me in Saturday afternoon classes at the Art Institute of Chicago. He was proud when, at age 12, I won a scholarship to another term there and a little item appeared in the papers about youngest-ever scholarship winner. I won some prizes in "write-a-title" and "comic coloring" contests for kids run by the local Hearst papers. These modest accomplishments brought pictures in the papers with headlines, "BOY ARTIST WINS AGAIN." Wow.

The scholarship in Saturday classes did not interfere with my approaching graduation from grade school—a status that entitled each member of the graduating class to wear, fastened to lapel or shirt pocket, a pair of long ribbons, representing the school colors. They looked nice on the girls and made a great show as soon-to-be boy graduates ran about their errands with ribbons flying over their shoulder—heralding their passage from grade school with colors flying if not flying colors.

But the coming of graduation brought a special problem for me and a kind of mini church-state crisis at home.

There are advantages to being the youngest son. Parents who have struggled to impart All The Right Things in their earlier offspring tend to get a little tired and relax their efforts. It was that way with piano lessons, which my brothers hated and which I was spared.

But religion was something else. My mother was a born-and-raised Catholic. My father was of Jewish descent, but I never knew him or his widowed mother to take part in a religious service of any denomination. When my mother and dad married, it must have been settled that the church would be satisfied if we were brought up in The Faith. Each Sunday my mother took us to Mass, and on the Sundays before Easter we carried home palm fronds or wore a little cross of palms on our lapels.

Bill and Rich made their First Communion. But I was a religious laggard and probably banked on the fact that I could escape this as I had piano lessons.

The crunch came as graduation day approached.

In this case it meant more than the passage from grade school to high school. It meant going from knee pants to long pants.

My mother, who was the gentlest and kindest of women, decided that in the fulfillment of her Christian Duty she must take a stand. She issued a kind of Edict of Rome: No First Communion, No Long Pants.

That meant memorizing the catechism. My father had previously performed *his* parental duty by handing me, just before leaving for his office one morning, a pamphlet he suggested I read called *Dick And Jane On The Farm*. This explained in less interesting and less graphic fashion what I had already heard about in the schoolyard—that I was not, in fact, brought by the stork.

I found the catechism even less compelling than *Dick And Jane On The Farm*. I struggled to learn the words by heart, but my heart wasn't in them, and it was obvious that I was not going to make the deadline. My father finally managed to convince my mother that even if I were a delinquent from a church standpoint, she had done her best, and I should be spared the embarrassment of receiving my diploma in an unsuitable suit. Torn as she was between love and perceived duty, love won. I was fitted out in a blue suit with trousers that didn't buckle at the knee, and I could appear at graduation without feeling like buckling at the knee either.

Eventually my mother and brothers also fell away from the church. But the entire family always enjoyed great Christmases, complete with tree ornaments, old and new, and carefully hidden gifts triumphantly brought out to surprise each other. One Christmas Eve I whispered excitedly, "When do we exchange presents?," and my father whispered back that we don't exchange presents, we give them, and we would start very soon. Good.

But then there was the aftermath, the cloud that followed the bright holiday: the letters to be written to relatives. Eventually the time would come when my father had to put his foot down—no more going out to play until those thank-you letters are written.

Every year each of two aunts sent us boys handsomely boxed gold-pieces—one apiece. The gifts were welcome but the annual sameness, plus the knowledge that the aunts might compare our letters, strained our writing abilities to the limit. And we would sometimes mutter that it would be easier to send the goldpieces back. But we did manage to compose something beyond "Dear Aunt Hattie:" and "Dear Aunt Carrie:," probably ending with "And now I must close, Auntie, as it is time to close."

Whew!

2

Family Album

M y father was a chemist. I think he was also a genius.
He was good at writing and drawing, as well as mathematics. As a young man he did some cartoons and verses for newspapers and humor magazines. And before devoting full time to scientific work, he had been for a while a reporter on the *Chicago Record*.

A couple of stories have come down about young David Block, reporter around the turn of the century, when the world was less sophisticated and newspapering was more free and easy than it is today.

He was assigned to cover a political speech, but bad weather kept him from getting to it. So he wrote a speech and turned in a story quoting it as having been delivered. Too late he learned that the politician hadn't made it to the rally either, and my father waited for the roof to fall in. But it didn't. The politician was delighted to see the story about "his speech" in the paper and considered it one of his *better* speeches. Young Dave Block thus became a sort of early (but one-time-only) political ghostwriter.

The other incident took place during his courtship of Theresa Lupe, whose friends all called her Tessie—my mother. He took her to a variety show she had wanted to see, but they arrived too late for the first number and she was disappointed at missing it. He was sufficiently ardent and resourceful that he asked to see the manager. He identified himself as a newspaper reporter, but then stretched a point to say that he had come there to cover the show—the *entire* show.

The audience was somewhat surprised to see the people onstage in the second number make off into the wings right in the middle of their act and bewildered to see the folks in the first number come prancing back onto the stage to do *their* act all over again—followed, of course, by the return of the second act performers. Young Dave's date, which is to say my Mom, was impressed.

How he went from reporting to a lifetime career in chemistry and chemical engineering I don't know, except that he had always been interested in science, and his stepfather had been into pharmaceuticals and medicines. But he never lost his enthusiasm for journalism and encouraged it in the three of us. Bill and Rich were both editors of their high school paper.

Now, about the genius part.

Of course, he didn't think of himself as one and we kids didn't think of him that way either. He was Papa. He worked in his laboratory. It was not a mysterious place but one where he let us drop in and see the shelves of bottles, beakers and flasks, and where we could look through the microscope.

Papa took us to movies, vaudeville shows and baseball games, and to the *Ziegfeld Follies* (where we saw onstage such stars as Will Rogers, Fanny Brice and W. C. Fields) and later to the outdoor opera at Ravinia, just north of Chicago. He helped us with our schoolwork and examined our report cards before signing them in his strong, neat handwriting. And except for moments when reports from teachers or neighbors were not so good, there was always a good deal of laughter in our family.

Webster's defines the word "genius" as:

> (a) a great mental capacity and inventive ability; especially great and original creative ability in some art, science, etc. (b) a person having such capacity or ability.

10

The definition fit my dad perfectly.

Here is a kind of composite biog sketch from his own early summaries:

> D(avid) Julian Block, chemist and electrical engineer. b. Ft. Wayne, Indiana, Aug 13, 1874, son of Maurice Lawrence and Julia (Wolff) Block. Studied at Armour Institute in Chicago, with special courses in chemistry. Professional career began with firm of Applegren and Block, electrical engineers. In 1910 his first work on the brom-chlorine secondary cell was published. He was superintendent of the American Metalizing Co., and then Director of Block Chemical Laboratories.
>
> Research chiefly in connection with synthetic products, such as synthetic sugar, synthetic rubber dyes, oils, gums, starches and dextrines. Created method of document protection by means of fluorescent salts and violet rays, kylite diaphragm for loudspeakers, a process to prevent granular caking of salts and flour improvers.

During World War I he made possible the first commercial production of synthetic mustard oil and various dyes formerly imported from Germany, and engineered construction of the first American plant for the manufacture of aspirin. Among many successful commercial products he developed were Musterole and Rit dye soaps.

You might think there would be a lot of money in all these things. Well, yes and no. Men frequently said to him that if a person could devise a formula for thus-and-so or invent a method of doing this-and-that, there would be millions in it. And they were right. He created the formulas and inventions they asked for, but—through stock changes, company reorganizations and whatnot—the millions did not come to him. I think he often created and sold formulas just to meet expenses. If necessity is the mother of invention, in his case the need to pay bills at home, the office and laboratory was the mother of multiple inventions. And there were always more ideas where those came from.

Some creative inventors have been shrewd at business affairs. But with the exception of a few like Edison and Bell, I think most of the successful ones have been people who have come up with a single— perhaps once in a lifetime—idea and devoted everything to nurturing,

11

protecting and promoting that one precious brainchild. In my dad's case, I think the very abundance of his creations depreciated their financial value to him.

Among the hundreds of things my dad developed, a couple come to mind. One was a method of *printing* the luminescent markings on radium dial watches and clocks. The early luminous markings had been painted on by women who got a good point on their brushes by putting them to their tongues, which produced a form of radium poisoning.

He solved another sticky problem with a method of chrome plating or electroplating that made chrome stay put instead of flaking off.

He developed a "puncture-proof" tire by filling it with a light, resilient gumlike substance that rode as smoothly as air. It didn't become popular as a tire filler but had other uses in products like erasers. A minor potboiler during the Depression was a press-on patch to save sewing jobs.

He developed an early antifreeze for cars, which my brother Rich sold one winter on the boulevard drive along Chicago's lakefront while I played on the ice near shore.

Synthetic sugar (before sugar substitutes) did not seem practical except during wartime shortages. But I recall that after this was written up in the newspapers, my dad's office was rifled in a way that did not suggest common burglary. Sugar interests seemed like possible suspects.

During the flu epidemic of 1918, he rigged up at home a chemical-and-burning-mantel device that apparently served as an air purifier. However it worked and whatever its benefits, our family survived that epidemic, which took countless lives.

Unlike his French mother, who drank black coffee all day long, played poker with other ladies and smoked Sweet Caporal cigarettes (though not publicly), Papa regarded card games as a waste of time, drank only a normal amount of coffee and nothing stronger, and didn't smoke. But he was a great trencherman—a large man who looked forward from one meal to the next. Sometimes right after lunch he would ask my mother what she was preparing for dinner.

Mama loved to cook, did it marvelously well and was about as inventive in the kitchen as Papa was in the laboratory. She created pineapple upside-down cake, one of her many recipe contest award-winners.

Rich, who had a phenomenal memory, cited some of the recipes when he reminisced in a 1954 letter to her on her 75th birthday. (The name Bert refers to me.) He wrote, in part:

> Plum Street is the first address I was old enough to remember. I can recall the start of a chemical lab, over the kitchen sink. That's where Bert was born [on Plum Street, not in the sink]. I can still remember the Edison Gramophone and the Kimball Piano.
>
> I believe it was here that you won the national first prize for your slogan for the Carnation Milk Company, "Milk From Contented Cows."
>
> Then came Rosemont Street, where the patents on Rit Dye Soap for Sunbeam Chemical Company were developed. I believe it was here too that the laboratory offices were in the Continental and Commercial Bank Building and the lab itself occupied the entire top floor of the Western Electric Building. . . .
>
> It was on Olive Avenue that you won the award for the Grape-Nut Custard recipe, which is still printed on the Grape-Nut boxes today. I believe it was there also that the *Chicago Daily News* ran a Cooking Contest for each separate course of a meal and despite hundreds of thousands of entries you took first, second or third prize in every category, possibly ten contests in all.
>
> It was then that the Cooking Editor of the *Chicago Daily News* asked you to collaborate with her in the publication of a cookbook. . . .

My mother's creations, whether old favorites or newly developed recipes for contests, could not have had a more appreciative reception—by a husband with a big appetite, three growing boys and whoever else came to dinner.

Early in her marriage, putting on a spread for relatives, she roasted a suckling pig and served it with an apple in its mouth. But it looked so sweet, so much like somebody's pet, that no one could eat it.

Our all-time any-time favorite was her ravioli, which she probably learned how to make from her mother, who came to this country from

Italy. On birthdays, when we could have any menu we wanted, this was the unanimous choice. And it was a highlight of Thanksgiving and Christmas as well. It would be accompanied by the more traditional fare of fowl, stuffings, sauces and side dishes. But the ravioli got the big play.

They were piled high on a giant platter—huge pasta pillows maybe 3 inches or more wide, bulging with marvelous filling and covered with meat sauce. We wolfed them down until we were as ready to burst as the ravioli themselves, and then did a little desultory picking at the turkey and other dishes before the table was cleared for dessert—if we could manage it.

It was probably only because we were constantly in motion that we boys kept in shape. Rich used to rise about 5 a.m. to be among the first in line at the public golf course. He took along a suitcase-size lunch my mother had prepared for him and played as many rounds as time and daylight would allow. He always had a head for business. During the Depression he financed some of his sports activity by buying used golf balls, running them through a paint process and then re-selling them to the pro shops properly labeled as "repaints." During tight times the repaints had a ready market.

An excellent golfer and bridge player, Rich could perform when the stakes were high. And while he never became a professional golfer, he generally did all right on side bets. He played in his everyday suit and pants, and the golfers who wore plus fours and argyles with tassels would invite him to join them under the impression that he would be a convenient loser. Since they kept raising the stakes as the game progressed, he sometimes made out quite well. Rich was not a hustler. He just didn't see how spending his limited resources on special clothes was going to improve his game.

After various business ventures, he became president of an industrial laundry. I'm sure many of his associates and clients could not have held with my political views, but Rich happily sent copies of my books to all of them and made sure his business associations invited me to speak.

Bill was what writers of Rover Boys stories would have called fun-loving. He liked all sports and games, and would bet on almost anything. But his favorite game was baseball. He was a good first baseman, with whatever advantage a left-hander has in that position. And as a boy he was horrified to find that Mama had washed his baseball uniform to a snowy white, removing all the streaks of dirt that bore proud witness to his activity on the baselines.

From high school days, Bill was a newspaper reporter. He chafed at desk jobs when he was made an editor, and returned to the freedom of outside work and the opportunities to play cards or kid around with other reporters in the pressrooms. Bill was a mentor to many who started out as Chicago reporters, including John Chancellor. They appreciated his showing them the ropes and helping them along the way. When I finally met famed Chicago columnist Mike Royko in 1990, he greeted me with the magic words "I knew your brother Bill."

From early days the family went to the movies frequently. And as far as we kids were concerned, some of my father's earliest and least important jobs were among his greatest successes. Movie houses were sometimes the victims of "stink bombs." In need of a good chemist, the theater managers called on my dad, who came up with formulas that neutralized the odors and cleared the air. In return, they gave him passes to the various chains of Chicago movies houses. Passes to the movies—Mabel Normand, Wallace Reid, Pearl White, Charlie Chaplin, Mary Pickford, Douglas Fairbanks! That's my Pop!

3

The Car

The family experience with autos did not antedate the invention of the engine, but it did go back to a time before driver's licenses were required, when cars were kept in garages and there were real "Gasoline Alleys." During the day these clean alleys came alive with the cries of scissor grinders, fruit peddlers and "rags and old bottles" men.

The number of different cars manufactured was astonishing. Our local pay-by-the-month garage had a printed list of them beginning with Anderson and Apperson and running down columns of type. Many had distinctive design features that kids sitting at curbside could identify from a distance.

Our first car was a used 1917 Oakland. My father saw it, liked it and bought it. With no previous instruction other than how to start and stop, he drove it home.

My mother had been terrified of cars because of an early experience. A dashing and well-to-do cousin of my dad had visited and taken the family out for a drive in his sporty car. He drove at the highest speed he could until it stalled on a railroad track. Mama finally got accustomed to riding as a passenger without calling out at every crossing. It was she who noticed that when we came to a dead stop at intersections, the other drivers had less trouble starting again because, as she put it, "Dave, they seem to do something with that thing on the floor." My father then learned about the uses of the gear shift, an item not included in the salesman's short course.

An early recollection of our life with a car is of my father driving down Michigan Avenue when a traffic cop, stationed on an island in the middle of the street, held up his hand and blew his whistle to STOP. The brake pedal apparently was not working properly and our car slowed but did not come to a halt. However, my father, being a law-abiding citizen, did not want to ignore the cop's order. So he turned the car sharply to the left and kept circling the safety island, with the policeman on foot making smaller inside circles while shouting and waving at us. The general effect was like something out of a Keystone comedy.

Another auto-and-cop incident many years later comes to mind, and perhaps contains a lesson. On one of my visits home after leaving Chicago, the family, with my father at the wheel, was taking me to the train depot. Delays made it look more and more as if we might miss the train. When my dad pulled up at the station to let me out, a mounted policeman called to him to get that car out of there. The one thing uppermost in my father's mind was my need to make the train, and he shouted back at the cop to get himself and his horse the hell on their way. Policeman and horse both registered surprise. The cop, apparently figuring that he must have crossed some powerful Chicago politician, galloped away. There is a lot to be said for spontaneous indignation.

My own experience in driving began with a lesson from Bill after the family had moved to the suburbs. Our house was on a lane that curved between two thoroughfares. With Bill's guidance, I eased out onto one of these roads and followed his directions to turn here, turn there, through the town, until we finally arrived back at the other end of our little lane. Filled with confidence as I went into the homestretch, I made the turn at a pretty good clip but neglected to brake or straighten the wheels sufficiently. We continued turning onto and across a neighbor's lawn and through the bushes in front of his house, when Bill pulled the emergency brake just inches from the house itself. My father paid for the damages, but Bill lost interest in trying to teach me.

Driving requirements must have remained lax, or we were unaware of them. Later, when I moved to Cleveland, a girl I knew there simply went out and bought a car and began driving it. She asked me if I would like to drive. Of course I would. I drove us to West Virginia through hill country and back, only mildly aware of all those other cars honking their horns and glaring at us.

Driving never became, as they say, second nature to me. Probably not even third nature. Long before there were things like automatic shifts I decided that cars and I probably had different natures.

4

School and the Non-Athlete

High school opened up the world of publications—a weekly 4-page paper and a monthly magazine that would actually print what you wrote and drew. On the first "drawing for publication," I made the lines about a quarter of an inch thick to be sure they would reproduce when scaled down. I did cartoons and a column for the weekly. But Herbert Davidson, then feature editor of the *Chicago Daily News,* picked up some of my columns to run in weekly selections of stuff from school papers. When I went to see him, he also encouraged the cartoons.

The high school of some 4,000 students had an art department and a journalism class. The journalism teacher, who also taught English and was faculty adviser to the school paper, was excellent. She began by training us to read the daily papers—not just look at headlines but *read* the stories.

Of course I signed up for the art class. At one of the first sessions, when the teacher gave us some instruction, this 12-year-old freshman took the occasion to show his wide experience by saying, "At the Art

Institute, they always taught us that'' (whatever it was they taught us). She said that, well, she would like us to try what she suggested. Now if I run into some kid who is attempting to be very impressive, I try to recall that incident when I was lucky the teacher and entire class did not just rise up and kill me. Actually, nobody paid any attention. It was an informal class where we all enjoyed ourselves, and I admired the work of some slightly older kids.

The art teacher encouraged imagination and individuality. She must have had quite an iris garden because one season she continually produced fresh irises for us to draw and paint. When the time came to embody the flower into a design of some kind, I did a poster in which the iris stems were entwined with the fuse of a bomb. She thought the Down-With-Irises poster was all right and promised to give us more variety in drawing subjects.

This was more relaxed than a history of art class in which I got lost in some early, obscure church decorations. When the teacher called on me for the title of one of these gold-halo works, a friend sitting behind me whispered, ''Madonna Of The Happy Doorknobs.'' I was saved by the classroom bell.

This friend, Bill Loarie, was a colleague on the school paper, and we both spent a good deal of time breaking ourselves up and nearly breaking up study periods by reading P. G. Wodehouse and Robert Benchley. Loarie declared Wodehouse to be a literary master, which I thought a pardonable exaggeration, but a judgment that has since been endorsed by serious critics.

I took ROTC. This was not because I felt there was something about a soldier that was fine fine fine, but because putting on the uniform a couple of times a week was better than the alternative: *gym.*

There must have been lots of kids who liked gym, even looked forward to it, but I was not one of them. A certain amount of hopping, jumping, running, bending and turning was okay. But attempting spread-eagle leaps over gym horses, with the ever-present possibility of not leaping quite high enough to avoid injury to the groin, was not anything I looked forward to. When the gym horses appeared, I wanted to disappear.

I also viewed unhappily the dropping of the rings. They were brought down to be grasped for hoisting and doing all kinds of gymnastic performances, which I regarded as potential arm breakers. Still another depressing piece of equipment was the poles. When it was announced that they were to be lowered, I knew what came next. We were to climb them as rapidly as possible and descend as rapidly as possible. We had kids in gym who must have lived for the moment when they could scoot up the poles, touching the top horizontal bar and descending (Ta-daaa!) in record time. When they came down, I was still going through the motions of pulling myself a few feet off the floor.

Later, in Army training, the same thing was done with ropes instead of poles. My objection to poles and ropes was the same as to mountain climbing. After you got up, there was still the matter of getting down. To what purpose should a guy strain himself to reach the tippy top of a pole or rope only to be pooped and drop maybe 20 feet to the ground.

My feelings about ropes, poles and heights in general (come over here to the edge, you can see all the way straight down) were summed up by comedian Bert Lahr, who did a skit in which thousands cheered as Lahr, a round-the-world flier, emerged from his plane. Falling on his knees and kissing the ground, he cried, "Good old terra cotta."

ROTC required little enough—a couple of hours a week marching or being instructed by a Sgt. Russell. He was a small, thin birdlike man and a World War I veteran, whose frequently repeated slogan was "Results counts." Mere attendance, in uniform (with cloth puttees), was sufficient. Of course, some classmates went onward and upward even in ROTC, until they wore leather puttees, won commanding positions and became insufferable. It was easier to tolerate them when I thought about the gym class, the rings and the poles, and (careful) the gym horses.

Athletic participation was not my bag, unless you count a golf bag. And my use of the clubs would not qualify me for any kind of team. It was a game I could play with others, if they were not appalled by some of my shots, and could even practice alone. While my game was not as good as my brothers', I could enjoy it. And like most duffers, I was constantly in search of a magic club or gimmick that would convert my erratic play into a low-handicap score. To that end, this boy golfer even oiled the handles of his cheap, ill-assorted clubs, no doubt feeling that they would somehow respond to this extra care.

On the first hole at Lincoln Park, where the crowd of golf regulars let me tee off as a single, I got off a shot that lacked the hoped-for distance but was in the fairway within sight of all the players waiting at the first tee. I quickly took off after the ball and found it. Unfortunately, the ball—and the clubs I set down on the ground—were within range of grass sprinklers, which I suppose most players had no trouble clearing. I stepped up to the ball, clutched the well-oiled handle of my club and took a full swing.

Here the old saying about oil and water was verified. They do not mix. At the conclusion of my swing, the club took off from my hands, traveling a greater distance upward than the ball traveled forward—all this still visible from the first tee and the players waiting to follow. I grabbed my wet canvas bag of clubs, picked up the ball and hastily made my damp way to the next tee, hidden by protective bushes.

In one form or another, I continued playing golf for most of my life, getting off just enough occasional good shots to keep me coming back. In Washington, D.C., I often played with Fred Blumenthal, correspondent of *Parade* magazine, who generally hit a longer ball than I did, but whose overall score was at least within my range. We played a kind of psychological game in which the belittling of each other's efforts was about as important as the scores themselves. On one occasion, when I was completely off my game—even for *my* game—he beat me decisively. It was as we stepped off the last green and headed toward the clubhouse that he delivered the ultimate crusher. "It's all right, Herb," he said, "you played your very best."

5

The Column

One of the popular daily newspaper features of the time was the contributors' column. It generally ran straight down the middle or side of the editorial page. Along with paragraphs and poems by the "column conductor" were reader-contributed verses and quips. This type of feature was probably on its way out when syndicated personality and political columns were coming in. It was part of a post–Gilbert-and-Sullivan era of "innocent merriment."

Among the best-known columnists, identified by their initials, were F.P.A. (Franklin P. Adams) in New York and R.H.L. (Richard Henry Little) in the *Chicago Tribune*. With the possible exception of the comic strips—which at that time ran about 12 inches wide—Dick Little's column, "A Line O' Type Or Two," was the most widely read feature in town and certainly brought in the most mail.

Having a contribution published in that column was called "making the Line." For reasons probably having to do with romantic notions about writing, most contributors used a nom de plume. Some spelled their names backward. My brother Rich, whose initials were R.M.B, signed himself Rumba. Among poetry contributors were "The Dark Lady Of The Camellias" and "Le Mousquetaire," as well as some straight-out names like MacKinley Kantor. Regular paragraph contributors used such signatures as Snowshoe Al and Jazbo Of Old Dubuque.

So when I started submitting paragraphs, I thought about a *name*. My father suggested the combination of first and last names into one, which provided a pen name and was still reasonably recognizable. This was the origin of a signature that continued into the cartoons and has caused needless confusion to some letter writers.

I sent in paragraphs daily. Many of them appeared and Little frequently ran two in one day. He started a running gag about this two-a-day fellow, which brought in more mail from other contributors.

With my father's encouragement, I went to see R.H.L. who occupied a space in the newsroom of the Tribune Tower. He gave me a warm and friendly reception, and I began dropping in from time to time. He was a tall, shambling man, somewhat stoop-shouldered, probably older than my dad, and he chain-smoked. He told of how, as a young man, he was smoking while scrunched down in the depths of a hotel lobby chair when a woman approached him. She asked, "Young man, do you know what smoking does to you?" He unwound himself from the chair, rose to his full height of six and a half feet or so and said, "Yes, ma'am. It stunts your growth."

A former war correspondent, Little had a keen interest in veterans and visited their hospitals. My father came up with ingratiating gifts and games for me to give Little to take to the veterans, and the columnist was undoubtedly impressed by the thoughtfulness of this high school kid.

But for all my father did to advance me, he was poorly repaid. He gave me a summer job answering the phone in his office, where I was often alone because he was off working in his laboratory or on some project. There I read the newspapers and typed out my paragraphs for the column. Feeling they were hot copy too current to waste time in the mail, I would run the block or so from my dad's office up Michigan Avenue to hand them to Dick Little. He was usually typing his own paragraphs and would greet me with a friendly roar, "SIT YE DOWN HERBERT!," followed by, "while I get this here now column writ." I was too awed and too dumb in every sense to say that I had something else to do, such as getting back to my father's office, which I had left unattended.

When my dad discovered these absences that may have cost him god-knows-what in calls and clients, he was more pained than angry. His forbearance was more awesome than his anger would have been, and I was ashamed. He made other office arrangements but said nothing to discourage my *Tribune* visits.

Little married one of his more literary contributors, Shelby Melton, and they got to taking me to lunches or dinners at their Near North Side apartment. I did some preliminary culling of the large volume of column contributions, ran errands and sometimes stayed overnight with them.

The height of glory came when Dick and Shelby went out of town for a day or so and left me to make up the column from a large bank of typeset material. Since my paragraphs often ran two or three times a day, by now under assorted names, I hesitated only briefly before including one of my own contributions. However bashful or backward I was in other respects, I was not too shy to do that.

I was, in a way, living in two pleasant worlds—the world of home, family and school, and the world of Dick Little, newspaper celebrity, who was sometimes pointed out on the street as we walked along while he told me stirring war stories and anecdotes. At times, if he wanted to look in on a matinee or a rehearsal, we would be ushered into a theater where Beatrice Lillie or some other star was onstage, and then ushered out when he was ready to leave. In that city, his name was magic, or so it seemed to a boy of 14-15-16.

The Littles had parties that included many contributors, all of them older and more talkative than I, and some of them pretty good drinkers. The Roaring Twenties were my not-very-vocal teens.

I was not part of the Chicago "toddling town" scene. Among the older or more sophisticated schoolmates, there may have been some high school Casanovas. But the closest I came to approximating a great lover, or any kind of lover, was to try looking like Rudolph Valentino by slicking down my hair with so much Stacomb that sometimes traces of the pink cream were visible in the comb tracks. My idea of being rakish was to wear a hard straw hat tilted at such an acute angle that Dick Little once warned me with a straight face that I had better be careful it didn't fall off. And it was not till I went to work at the end of the decade that I saw the inside of a speakeasy.

But Chicago politics and newspapering were colorful and exciting in those days of *The Front Page,* Al Capone and "newspaper wars," in which trucks and newsstands were part of physical battles. Mayor William Hale Thompson's signature appeared on large billboards under the slogan: "Throw away your hammer and get a horn. *Boost Chicago.*" It was this mayor who, when the King of England visited America, said that if King George came to Chicago, he would bust him on the snoot. I recall looking in on a political meeting where the "debate" was with opponents who were represented by a couple of mice in cages.

The publisher of the *Chicago Tribune* was the imperious and eccentric Col. Robert R. McCormick. And in the lobby of the Tribune Tower hung a huge American flag. On one occasion when McCormick became dissatisfied with an action taken by some state of the union, he commanded that the star of that state be removed from the flag.

My brother Bill, a top reporter for the *Chicago Tribune*—and later for the *Chicago Sun* when it began publishing—was closer to the action of those days. He knew Jake Lingle, another *Tribune* reporter, who was gunned down in a subway entrance to an interurban train station. I saw all the exciting headlines and stories, including some of Bill's firsthand accounts. But I was no closer to the gangland-era action than recognizing that the movie house where Dillinger was shot (the Biograph) was a neighborhood theater we used to visit. Crime was something you read about, not something that kept you from walking down the street at night.

My newspaper experience was only with the column and the Littles. They came up with ideas they thought would be beneficial to me, including reading matter, of which there was no shortage. My father had shared his enthusiasm for Mark Twain, Robert Louis Stevenson, O. Henry, Jules Verne and such earlier favorites as Jerome K. Jerome and humorist Bill Nye. Shelby fostered an interest in writers like George Jean Nathan, Chesterton, Belloc, Anatole France, Saki; the verbal thrusts of Whistler and Wilde; and the literary soufflés of Max Beerbohm. But Dick Little gave me *Two Years Before the Mast,* the writings of Richard Harding Davis, stories of the French Foreign Legion and other books of adventure and war.

He didn't think I ought to sail away or march off to fight somewhere, but he thought a little Army routine would do me no harm. *"Mens sana in corpore sano!"* he would declaim, striking his cane on the floor for emphasis. "A sound mind in a sound body!" And with my parents' full approval, I signed up for a brief course at a Civilian Military Training Camp that he had cased. It was located at nearby Fort Sheridan, not far from the North Shore suburb that was now home.

The training ran for about a month. But for a city boy it was an experience to sleep in tents, leap up at the sound of a bugle, do some routine drillings and horse around with other kids who also had no previous military or camp experience.

On graduation from high school I wanted to emulate Dick Little as well as my own brother Bill, who had begun his reporting career on the Chicago City News Bureau when he graduated from high school some five or six years earlier. With their recommendations I got a job at the Bureau, a citywide wire service, as a police reporter at the salary of $12 or $15 a week. This was before the Depression. What I got was the prevailing wage for beginners at the Bureau at that time. I wasn't primarily interested in the money but in being a *reporter*. I even told Bill that maybe I wouldn't put in for expenses (probably a few streetcar rides and nickel phone calls), but he advised me that I'd darn well better claim my expenses or I'd make the other guys look bad.

The job included covering several police stations, mostly by phone, sometimes making the rounds of the stations and courts, chasing fires and whatever else. I stayed downtown at the Littles' apartment and woke up nights thinking I heard fire engines that needed to be followed. A couple of weeks later I received my last paycheck, with no explanation for the termination. I was crushed—*A Failure At 16.*

Following this, I did some freelance poster work and some cartoons for local papers. I even tried an apprentice art department job at the *Chicago Herald Examiner,* which involved nothing useful. It was not encouraging to meet men there who had been retouching photos for 10 or 15 years after they had come in with drawings and cartoons under *their* arms for brief terms as apprentices.

I also spent more time at the *Tribune,* where the Littles now had another project. In his column, Dick ran a word-change game that produced a lot of mail. The idea was for one word to become another by changing one letter to form a new word each time, with the fewest number of substitutions. In its simplest form, "this" to "that" would be "this," "thin," "than," "that." As the word game continued and picked up more and more interest, Dick came up with the idea that Shelby and I should collaborate on a book. We would get up appropriate words for well-known people, who would approve and autograph the words we had prepared for them. (The actual word games would be played by the readers, with the celebrities' solutions in the back of the book.) Part of my job was to go see the people we wanted to sign up. Many cooperated easily, but I remember particularly a couple of the cases where again I felt I faced Failure.

For Clarence Darrow, Shelby came up with "jail" to "free." I went to his office, met him and explained what was wanted, but he demurred. He didn't like the words and was sorry. As a kid who usually maintained a respectful silence toward any adult, I was hardly qualified to argue a case with Clarence Darrow, but I didn't want to go back empty-handed. After I had done my halting best and he returned to work, I remained in what served as a kind of waiting room, looking dejected. As Darrow shuttled between offices, he noticed me and finally came over and explained gently that I should tell Dick Little he'd be glad to do something but didn't like the "jail-free" combination.

Then there was Babe Ruth. I saw him in his hotel room before a baseball game. As a National League Cubs fan, I had never seen him and didn't realize that the nickname Babe had nothing to do with his size. Big man. He was wearing a bathrobe, an appropriate outfit for those non-air-conditioned summer afternoons. He probably didn't know Dick Little, as most of my interviewees did, but he knew what was wanted and explained that he couldn't do this thing for a book without first getting an okay for it. He too was very nice—and patient.

Again, I felt that I would have Failed if I went back without his signature and approval (a simple autograph probably would have been easy), so I tried to change his mind. He said in a rather kindly, gravelly way, "Look, kid, I'd be glad to do it, but my agent [or manager-whatever] would have to see it." We continued to sit across the little hotel room from each other, with his eyes looking like those of a St. Bernard dog, and with me feeling like a St. Bernard dog looks. He waited like a good batter who knows a pitcher can't keep serving up foul tips indefinitely, and I finally thanked him and left. He saw me to the door still explaining that he'd be glad to do it, kid, if he could get an okay. He was all right.

After phone calls or letters from Dick Little to Darrow and perhaps to the New York Yankees manager, both men did go along with the word-game book. But I felt that they were not, as they used to say on the cop shows, "my collars."

Some years later I got to see Ruth play when my dad, brothers and I got seats high up at the far end of the field for the first All-Star Game. The big guy did not disappoint. He banged out a home run that we thought was going to land in our laps.

After the City News Bureau job didn't pan out, Dick had another idea for me—college. Again he cased the situation and came up with what seemed to be the best place for me—Lake Forest College, only a little farther from town than Winnetka, where my parents now lived. The tuition was modest enough that I could make it as a day student. Again my parents were in hearty agreement. I applied for admission and was accepted.

Shortly after that I got a phone call from the City News Bureau explaining that I had been on a tryout while one of their men was on vacation. They now had a vacancy for a regular job. This boosted my spirits but it required a decision. I consulted with my folks and the Littles and, of course, Bill. By now I had been looking forward to going to college, and reluctantly gave up the chance to start as a real reporter.

In September, I showed up at Lake Forest, registered, was given a little green freshman cap and joined a fraternity.

6

Lake Forest

In a time of boom prosperity, peace and low tuition costs, life at small, co-ed Lake Forest College was idyllic. Some 400 students moved about a comfortable campus where most of us knew each other and where the ratio of faculty to students allowed not only for small classes but for one-on-one meetings with professors. It also provided a chance for a student to take part in just about any school activity that might interest him.

Morning chapel involved some hymn singing and general announcements by faculty and students. Once a student stood up to say that he was starting a press club if anyone was interested. I rose to say that I was interested in journalism. He then explained that he meant he was willing to press trousers and jackets.

As a pretty good runner, I was encouraged to try out for track, but after a couple of laps around the gym I continued right on to the showers. The prospect of devoting a lot of time to this activity did not appeal. However, there were school publications that did and where anyone who could write or draw a few lines was welcome.

There was no art course, and as the only person who could do any drawing at all, my efforts were as highly regarded as if I had been a real pro.

The political science professor was David Maynard, a man who had spent some time working in the secretariat of the League of Nations—the kind of internationalist who I'm sure would have given fits to the *Tribune*'s Col. McCormick.

Maynard did some horizon stretching for a student who had been brought up in "Tribuneland" where the "World's Greatest Newspaper" relentlessly preached isolationism and distrust of foreign governments, which were trying to lure us into entanglements and play us for suckers.

When I left school, Maynard sold me his membership in the City Club of Chicago, and I took his place there in its foreign affairs group. This made me feel pretty worldly, even though my knowledge of the world and its ways was just about zilch in every respect.

A history professor who had served in the Great War made us feel a little better about exams by telling us of a philosophy that an officer had passed along to the troops: If you go into the service, the chances are you won't see action, so there's nothing to worry about. If you see action, the chances are you won't be hit, so there's nothing to worry about. If you should be hit, the chances are you'll survive, so there's nothing to worry about. And if you don't survive, you're dead and are beyond worrying about anything.

In this happy environment I was beyond worry anyhow. With the exception of overnight stays at the fraternity house, I commuted daily between suburban home and suburban Lake Forest. This did not preclude school activities beyond classes. And one of these was a tryout for the freshman class play consisting of a reading that was done in the office of the drama teacher while sitting next to his desk. On the basis of that reading he gave me the lead part.

Because some members of the cast—notably the lead—never succeeded in mastering the lines for the entire play, it was eventually decided that we should put on just the first act. This one-time exercise was attended by a number of students, who came to kill some time in the afternoon. Such an abbreviated show did not rate scenery, so it was performed against a splotchy, faded curtain that went around the rear and sides of the stage. This did not help my opening line, which was, as I looked around, "So this is where she lives!"

The laughter from the audience set the tone for the remainder of the performance. I had decided that my part called for a rather sophisticated fellow and that I could play it best, while at the same time doing something with my hands, by smoking a cigarette. The voices from the audience seemed to me to project as well as anything said on the stage. And as I continued, there were more than audible whispers of "He's got some cigarettes! He's going to light a cigarette! He doesn't smoke. . . . Look, he's smoking. . . ." Considering that I did not go into a coughing spell, I thought I was doing pretty well, but the audience could not have felt it was a better show if I had burst into flames.

When it came time to meet the girl who lived there, I had to dispose of the cigarette, but found no ashtray. I guess I had neglected to tell anyone about my ingenious piece of stage business. In any case, behind a couch was a water glass, and I tried to snuff out the cigarette in it. Of course, this attempted sleight of hand did not escape the audience, which continued to enjoy itself enormously. And as I proceeded with my lines, the whispers kept coming back: "He tried to put it out. . . . Look, it's still smoking. . . . It's still smoking . . ." (more laughter).

After the performance the drama coach (who, I think, had a glass eye) came to the dressing room and told the supporting actor that he had done very well. He then stared at me (it *was* a glass eye) and left. He and I had both discovered that an ability to read and to speak distinctly did not necessarily mean an ability to act.

However, the drama-and-speech course was not a total loss. I tried out for debating and the speech instructor made me captain of the team. Of course, on the debating platform I did not light up and try to act nonchalant.

In addition to the various English classes, there was an economics course. Over a period of many years, through depressions and booms, economic theories may have changed, and they vary widely today. But one thing seemed to me to represent an enduring and unchanging truth—The Law Of Diminishing Returns. It applies to everything, whether trying to patch up a drawing, pouring money into a venture, pursuing a reluctant love or whatever. There comes a point where the increased effort, money or time does not produce relatively increased results. It's an immutable law and it made the whole course worthwhile.

Even before going to college I had begun drawing some cartoons for a suburban paper, the *Evanston News-Index,* mainly for the pleasure of being published. I also drew, and was paid for, some cartoons for Republican Party organizations. This made me feel I had arrived—a political cartoonist. Drawing for the Republicans involved no sacrifice of principle because in this best of all possible worlds, everything, including the party in office, was fine. The Republican Party had even been the party of Thomas Nast, whose profusely illustrated biography had early made a great impression on me. The GOP also got a lot of support from contemporary cartoonist "Ding" Darling, an idol whose work I followed closely.

Toward the end of my second year at Lake Forest, I took some of these published cartoons from the Evanston paper and others downtown to the *Chicago Daily News* in the hope of getting a summer job. The editor who looked at them said they'd get in touch with me if they had anything. I had earlier tried the *Journal* and the *Post,* and had little expectation anything would come of this visit.

But a few days later they phoned and asked me to come in. An editorial page cartoonist was leaving the city and they could give me a tryout; could I start Monday? Yes. Yes, I could. Yes, I'd certainly be there. Apparently one of the determining factors was that they had seen my column contributions in the *Tribune.* The editor said, "Well, you don't seem to have any trouble coming up with ideas." Calling at the *News* just when I did was at least the luckiest idea I could have had. I started Monday and never went back to school.

Many years later my economics professor, who had become president of Lake Forest, helped me finish school by making me an honorary doctor of laws. Chatting with him after the commencement ceremonies, I mentioned a line in the conferring of the degree that referred to the "rights and privileges appertaining thereto"—and said I supposed this meant I could now hang out a shingle and file lawsuits. He replied with a story told by Stephen Leacock, the Canadian humorist, who had received an honorary degree just before boarding a ship for Europe. He signed himself on the ship's register as *Dr.* Stephen Leacock. That evening there was a knock on his cabin door and he was told that a *Follies* girl on the deck below might have sprained her hip, and would Dr. Leacock be good enough to examine her? Leacock said, ''I was down there like a shot, but not soon enough—two doctors of divinity had got there before me.''

7

The News

When I began work at the *Chicago Daily News* it was located on Wells Street in the "old building," a rattletrap structure that fully justified the term. It had a caged elevator that an operator started by pulling on a rope and that jerked to a shaking halt at or near the couple of floor levels. Besides the wooden stairways, there were sets of three or four steps leading from one part of the same floor to another.

Not long after I started working there, the *News* moved to a magnificent new building on the Chicago River. There was an affectionate wake for the rickety old firetrap that dated back to the paper's earliest days, and all hands gathered for farewell talks amid the clutter of old furniture and paper.

Staff writer Robert J. Casey closed the proceedings with a few words, and then, slapping a metal rule on a table, he declared that all of us who had worked in this building could be officially declared old-timers. The thought of being a newspaper old-timer sent a surge of pride through a new staff member just winding up his teens who could hardly wait for the aging process. To further the old-boy effect, I later tried growing a mustache, which was so pale and scraggly that its coming and going were scarcely noticed even after I had tried to augment the effect with a black drawing pencil.

Cartoonist Clare Briggs used to draw a panel called "The Thrill That Comes Once in a Lifetime." Such a moment came in one of those early days on the *News* when I was riding a bus, seated behind two men who were reading the papers. One of them nudged the other and handed across his folded paper, pointing to something in it. And looking between their shoulders I could see what he was pointing at—my cartoon! Not family or classmates or colleagues, but a couple of people I didn't even know!

The new building was connected by an enclosed walkway to the Chicago and Northwestern Railroad Station. This linkage not only made it possible for me to take the suburban train from home right into the building concourse, but the station also provided a great expanse of space for pacing around unnoticed while thinking up cartoon hunches. Some people sit and look out a window or stare at a blank sheet of paper. I've always liked to walk around.

The actual working space was a desk in a large art department that had a photo darkroom in one corner. In the rest of the room were photo retouchers, caricaturists, advertising artists, layout people, a fashion artist—all together except for the front-page cartoonist, Vaughn Shoemaker, who had a little office of his own across the hall. My cartoons occupied a two-column box on the editorial page, and like the cartoons of my predecessors in that space, they were sent out to a newspaper syndicate. This was probably because they were generally in a light vein and involved no local issues, as did the front-page cartoon.

One of the commercial art toilers at a nearby desk was Chester Gould. Before this stint at the *News*, he had done a comic strip for another Chicago paper, and he was determined to get back into that field. He must have spent all his evenings and weekends getting up new strips and sending them around. Meanwhile, he was constantly in motion at the office. Once when the papers carried news of foreign fliers visiting Chicago, he occupied himself by drawing a formation of tiny little airplanes on one of the windows. He then called everyone over to see the air armada. His persistence at creating strips finally paid off. The *Chicago News* bought a girl strip he had submitted. But it was short-lived because at almost the same time the *Chicago Tribune* accepted a different kind of strip from him—''Dick Tracy.'' He didn't forget his old friends in the art department and named a couple of good-guy characters after them.

A list of some of the outstanding staff members then at the *Chicago News* sounds like an Irish mafia, which it was not. Hal O'Flaherty, correspondent and later foreign editor, played an important role on the *News* foreign service, which was rivaled only by the *New York Times*. Howard Vincent O'Brien, columnist, was one of the most sensitive and graceful writers around. Henry Justin Smith was a great and justly celebrated managing editor. On the city desk were Clem Lane and later reporter Ed Lahey.

Drama critic Lloyd Lewis wrote a biography of General Sherman and became so immersed in that historical period that his wife used to say she lost her husband in the Civil War.

Among the reporters was Mary Walsh. Long afterward, when I met Ernest Hemingway's widow at a party and she talked about our old days at the *News,* I realized she was the same Miss Walsh I used to see in the newsroom.

Charles H. Dennis was editor. Bob Casey was roving correspondent, author of books and writer of humorous feature stories, which generally began on page one. All of these staff members were friendly and encouraging to a young cartoonist. Casey amended the current cliché ''Being a newspaperman you must meet such interesting people'' with the words ''other newspaper people.'' His humor bubbled up in many ways. At a time when expense accounts were under close scrutiny, he returned from a downstate trip that involved tracking a wolf and included in his itemized expenses wolf bane: 25 cents.

On a western trip, when he learned that some explorers were about to climb a mesa to see what secrets the top of it might reveal, he hired a plane to fly over the mesa the evening before. From the fully loaded little plane, he dropped spark plugs, rusty automobile mufflers and whatever other junkyard items he could take aboard. He told me that after the explorers made their descent, they said nothing about their findings.

It was to Dennis, the editor, that Shoemaker and I submitted our sketches. There was no set schedule, and sometimes we would arrive in the outer office at the same time and chat while we waited our turns.

Dennis was an erect, white-haired man, generally seen arriving at his office or departing from it taking fairly short, rapid steps, so that he seemed to be almost gliding, with head high, a folder of papers under his arm. He was a kind man and not as starchy as his collar might indicate. A onetime colleague of Eugene Field, he seemed to have a sympathetic feeling for humorists, versifiers and cartoonists.

When I first brought sketches to him, he smiled, selected one and expressed approval of the others. When I took in a new batch the next day, he asked what happened to the others from the day before. So I took to bringing in some previous ones, along with new sketches each day.

When his secretary indicated it was all right to go in, I'd usually find him busy with some papers, but he would soon give a greeting and have a look at the offerings. I recall his saying to someone who was engaging him in important conversation or waiting to see him on business, "Just a minute while I make this young man happy." He did. I liked him.

When Dennis was not there, I submitted my sketches to the associate editor, Mr. Macmillan—a stocky, balding, taciturn man who wore glasses with thin metal rims. I don't know now what his first name was—he was and will always be Mr. Macmillan to me.

I'd kind of slide into his office and let myself down into the chair next to his desk, and finally he'd look up over his glasses and say, "Oh." Then I'd give a little smile and hand him my sheaf of sketches. He'd look at each of them *without* smiling—he'd *study* each of them. Then he'd carefully lay them all out on his desk and study them some more. And then he'd slowly swivel around in his chair and look out the window. Also silently. He'd be looking out the window, and I'd be looking at his back, and we'd sit like that for an eon or two.

The pages would drop from the calendar on the wall. Outside, the leaves would fall from the trees. Then the snow would come down and cover the branches. Later the snow would melt and the buds would begin to come out, and we'd still be sitting there, kind of frozen in time, like one of those stop-action frames at the end of a movie. When the silence became unbearable, I would try to clear my throat and say,

"MMMMmmmm. . . . Uh, Mr. Macmillan, I'll go back and get up some more sketches." At this, he would slowly swivel back to his desk and say, "No, these are all right. I was just thinking." Then he would study the sketches some more, usually come back to the first one I had shown him, linger over it awhile longer and say, "Yes, I think this will be all right." When I got back to my desk, I'd be a little too shaky to start drawing right away.

But unnerving as our meetings were, I did manage to stand up to his editing. The least aggressive animal, when pushed far enough, will act in defense, especially of its cubs. I had done a pre-election sketch that, in the days before scientific polling, voter analyses and depth-of-feeling studies, expressed what seemed like a fresh idea. I had one man asking another, "Who do you think you'll vote against?" Mr. Macmillan thought the point was all right but not the wording. He said it should be "Against whom do you think you will vote?" or (throwing caution to the winds) "Whom do you think you will vote against?" This was technically correct, but I knew it was not the way people talked—at least not in my cartoons. I stuck with "Who" and it was printed that way, with no objection. Incidentally, I have never liked using the word "whom" and have been heartened by language experts who feel the same way. That opinion is simply addressed to whom it may concern.

Under special circumstances I occasionally submitted cartoons to one other person—Col. Frank Knox, the publisher who took over the *Chicago Daily News* a couple of years after I began there. He was a bright-eyed man who wore pince-nez glasses and had a wide smile. Col. Knox had served in Cuba with Theodore Roosevelt, and before acquiring the *Chicago News* he had been publisher of papers in Manchester, New Hampshire. He was a Republican who later tried for his party's nomination for president—and still later became secretary of the Navy under Franklin Roosevelt, when FDR raided the Republican Party.

He had become his party's nominee for vice president to run with Alf Landon, in 1936. As I heard the story, the convention powers were all set to choose as running mate Sen. Styles Bridges of New Hampshire when somebody said, "Landon-Bridges! For God's sake!" The prospect of a ticket ready to fall down before it started running supposedly gave the nomination to Knox—who, the story went, got the news as he was relieving himself at a stop on the way back to Chicago.

At the time I knew him in 1931 and '32, Knox was simply "the publisher." He held daily conferences that included editors, editorial writers and political cartoonist Shoemaker.

When Shoemaker was on vacation, I filled his space in the paper and at the editorial conference, where I don't think I ever said peep unless spoken to. I was sometimes happily embarrassed to hear Mr. Dennis make some nice remark to Knox and the staff about my cartoon of that day, or the fact that I had introduced pencil and crayon cartoons to the *News*.

During one of these filling-in periods when I submitted sketches to the Colonel, we had a problem. He looked over my cartoon roughs, smiled, chuckled and nodded approvingly, but he had a suggestion. How about a cartoon showing William Randolph Hearst as Horatius at the Bridge, holding back I-forget-what, probably international cooperation. I listened with what must have been a sickly smile, and said I would go back and do some more sketches.

I drew up several more, went down the hall, was admitted to the Colonel's office again, walked to his desk and offered him my new roughs. He looked them over, smiled appreciatively, commented on how prolific I was and found them all good and worth using. But he mentioned that he still thought the Hearst idea would be a good one. I don't know how many times I went back and forth with sketches. Each time he smiled and complimented my work, but he still thought the Hearst idea would be best for that day.

That day was eventually so far gone that there was only enough time left to draw a cartoon and turn it in. I decided to do the cartoon of Hearst at the bridge, and maybe jump off the next bridge the publisher suggested.

It wasn't that I disagreed with the idea. I didn't. The trouble was that it wasn't *my* idea, and I didn't like drawing up something at the publisher's request.

While I was doing the cartoon, the Colonel came back to the art department to peer over my shoulder and express his delight at what I was doing—undoubtedly also to make sure I was actually drawing it. I finished the cartoon and turned it in, but without signing it. I hoped the white space in the corner where the signature would have gone would be noticed. I went home wondering whether I should offer my resignation then or with the next idea from the chief.

The next morning the Colonel was all bright, bouncy and happy with still more of my sketches, which he approved readily. For whatever reason and to my great relief, that was the only time he had a suggestion for me.

One day I came back from lunch to find on my desk a piece of copy paper. The distinctive handwriting on it written boldly with black copy pencil said:

> Dear Herblock—Your "Corn-Husking Champ At Home" is the funniest cartoon I ever saw.　　Carl Sandburg

I had read Sandburg and seen his poems in anthologies at school not long before—and "living legend" is the term that comes to mind. I raced down the hall to his cubicle, where he wrote his once-a-week-or-so columns for the *News,* to introduce myself and thank him. That evening I took the treasured sheet of copy paper home to show my folks, and it was promptly framed.

The meeting at the *News* was the beginning of a long acquaintance. Later when I was working in Cleveland and returning to the office after a long lunch with the visiting Sandburg, the editor announced to the entire staff, "Herb's coming in on little cat feet."

His daughter Helga has written about our having dinner with him in Washington. Midway through the meal, news came that Ernest Hemingway had won the Nobel Prize and had said that it should have gone to Sandburg. Helga got on a phone and did a fast rundown of Hemingway's current location, and Sandburg wired a warm message to his fellow author.

On Washington visits he would occasionally spend an evening with a few friends, playing his guitar, singing and swapping stories. A Sandburg blessing, sometimes given in letters and sometimes verbally with his smile and twinkling eye, was: "You ain't what's wrong with this country."

Before he became a famous writer, Sandburg had been secretary to the first socialist mayor of a U.S. city. He told of how, on the first day in office, he and the new mayor talked excitedly of bright tomorrows—

socialist mayors in other cities, socialist governors and eventually socialist presidents in the United States and abroad in a new and peaceful, happy day for everyone. While they were projecting this great future the phone rang. It was a call from a man who said, "There's a dead dog out here in front of my house. What are you going to do about it?" Suddenly the two men realized that, as Sandburg put it, before you can remake the world, you have to get that dead dog off the street.

After working on the *News* awhile, I got an apartment in town. It was, as I explained to my parents, closer to the office, where I could work late without regard to train schedules and often did. Of course, it also made dating easier. But I could still see my parents weekends, go to shows with them, whatever.

There was also time to make contributions aside from the daily cartoon, and the *News* was receptive to these offerings. Occasional book reviews were welcomed. And more often the extra drawings were of show people. In 1932 the *News* ran my sketches of the biggest shows in town—the Democratic and Republican conventions, both held in Chicago. It was here, incidentally, that Roosevelt broke the tradition, begun in horse-and-carriage days, of waiting for a delegation at some future time to notify a candidate of his nomination. And a nominee being completely surprised by the news was a natural for a cartoon. FDR ended all this by going directly to the Chicago convention—and not by train but by airplane—to deliver his acceptance speech.

Most of my extra drawings were on less exciting subjects. Roy Nelson, a brilliant caricaturist and feature artist, handled the entertainment beat, and some of my "showtime" drawings reflected the influence of his style. But he didn't mind my getting into the act, and we sometimes went to entertainer affairs together.

It was after he had suggested I go along on what promised to be a good party that I rolled home late one night and dropped into bed. It *had* been a good party, but for some reason sleep wouldn't come, even at 2 or 3 A.M. Something was wrong. I finally sat upright with the realization of what it was—I had not turned in a cartoon for the next day's paper. I had left the office early for a pleasant interlude with the full intention of returning to work later, which I now did at about 4

A.M. Fortunately, the early edition of the *News* did not come out till about 9 or 10 A.M., and I could do the drawing and the engraving crew could still make it into print in time. I've often cut the deadlines pretty close, but this was the only time I almost forgot one.

One evening I helped a colleague make his deadline. The movie critic walked unsteadily into a nearly empty city room, saw me and asked if I could use a typewriter. I said I could do some pecking, and he stood beside me, swaying slightly, as he dictated what his fingers were too uncertain to type.

Despite the era of prohibition, when newsmen supposedly worked with a pint of liquor in the pocket, I didn't see evidence of much drinking around the *News* and didn't do much of it myself, even outside the office. During hard times I think most of the thirstier ones felt jobs were too precious to risk.

Happy at work and with youthful confidence, I not only didn't feel the Depression but wrote to Mr. Dennis asking for a raise. The letter said that I didn't mind for myself, but I had this dog, Ben—a good dog, a faithful dog, an uncomplaining dog, and I hated to see him looking wistfully at scraps—something like that. Since this was some time before Fala and Checkers, Mr. Dennis found it novel and amusing and gave me the raise—I think from $40 to $50 a week.

Under Col. Knox I got into high finance again. I was delighted to see my cartoons appear in newspapers in Detroit, New York and elsewhere, usually larger than they appeared in the *News*. But one day the man who handled the mailing of the syndicated features confided to me that my cartoons brought into the paper m-o-n-e-y. He gave me the figure—not huge, but certainly more than my salary, maybe $70 or $80 a week. I took my case to the Colonel. A man sometimes given to chichés, he told me that these days a fellow was lucky to have a job. Nevertheless, after some discussion he came up with a solution. He said he'd split the return with me. My salary then got up toward what humorist Calvin Trillin might call the higher two-figure range.

On the non-pay side, I also tried some lighter-vein talks and chalk talks, including one at the City Club of Chicago. It was—okay—well received, and a *Daily News* editor who was there asked if I would do one for the Women's City Club, which his wife belonged to. I gave that one too and it went all right. But the editor said afterward that he had hoped I'd have given the one I did at the City Club. Ironically, one of the reasons I had prepared an entirely new talk was because I knew he would be there. I thought each one should be different, like the daily work, and never really got over the idea that it would be an embarrassment if anyone heard me give the same speech twice. It's lucky I never got into politics.

With the Depression on, plenty of places welcomed a free talk, especially something fairly humorous, and a kind of informal agency was set up that scheduled speakers for schools, churches, YMCAs and community auditoriums. These efforts were not all that altruistic. I enjoyed the recognition and applause.

At one of these talks I had a small dental problem. I was not chewing my words. To replace a front tooth that had been missing since some early horseplay with my brothers, a dentist had rigged up a bridge, cementing in a new tooth with a band that clipped around an adjoining one. It was not the most cosmetic job, but the new tooth stayed put. However, toward the conclusion of my talk, it somehow snapped out, flying into the air. With a sweeping gesture, I caught it in my hand and brought the talk to a quick conclusion, literally keeping a stiff upper lip.

With some recementing, it held firm again, lying in wait for years to find an even more inopportune time after I got to Washington.

After a couple of years on the *News,* and with cartoons reprinted in other papers and *The Literary Digest,* I took a vacation tour to New York, Boston and Washington. I soon learned something I never forgot—that except for cartoonists and some other journalists, few people knew or cared about signatures on political cartoons, and it is best never to suppose the people you meet casually know who you are or what you do. But the cartoonists were interested in getting together and we had some good visits.

In Washington, the *Chicago News* correspondent Leroy T. Vernon took me to a White House press conference where Herbert Hoover read prepared answers to prepared questions. Vernon asked me to come back the next morning, but I overslept and got to his office late. He had intended taking me to meet the president. With or without meeting a president, I liked Washington and wanted to return there.

Toward the end of that administration I heard from the Newspaper

Enterprise Association (NEA), a package feature service put out by Scripps-Howard, suggesting that I draw some cartoons for them. What they wanted was to try out different ones for client and reader response. I asked Knox if I could do this, and he readily agreed. After a while NEA offered me the editorial cartoon job at Cleveland, where their main office was located.

I told Knox about it and again he was warmly approving. "You want your place in the sun," he said. But it was a wrench for the family—this time not just moving to an apartment but leaving home for another city. My dad and mother were wet-eyed seeing me off, but still happy for me to make progress. I would write often, I would phone, I would come home regularly. Friends at the paper were glad for me, and one of the nicest things I heard was from Mr. Dennis. He wished me well. And then, in the midst of the Great Depression, he mentioned that if I decided I wanted to, I could come back to the *Chicago Daily News.*

"THIS IS THE FOREST PRIMEVAL——"

First daily cartoon
Chicago Daily News
April 24, 1929

AT THE NEXT INVESTIGATION

Oct. 1932

ALL IN A LIFETIME

March 1932

THE RISE OF AMBROSE J. CIGARETTE

1931

GROWTH OF A CITY

1931

EVOLUTION IN GERMANY

Oct. 1932

HINDENBURG LINES

Jan. 1932

MAYBE WE'VE BEEN WATCHING THE WRONG DOOR

Aug. 1932

8

Cleveland

The Cleveland job was a whole new ball game—new city, new year, new place to work, new friends, new papers to read. And, at the beginning of 1933, there was a new president ready to take office in a couple of months with promises of a New Deal.

Cleveland's weather made me feel at home. The January winds that whipped down Lake Erie came direct from the same North Pole as the ones that came down Lake Michigan. The NEA office stood squarely at the corner of West Third and Lakeside (as in right-by-the-side-of-the-lake). This meant that after a streetcar ride to the public square, the walk toward Lakeside required ducking into doorways along the way to keep from arriving at the office in a condition that required handling with ice tongs.

The two-story NEA quarters in Cleveland were definitely not new. The first floor housed, mostly in one large area, editorial, sports, writers, artists, some cartoonists and illustrators. There were also photo and engraving rooms and a mail room. Most of the second floor was occupied by the business staff. But, unaccountably, at the far end of that floor was a caged-off section where dressmakers were at work. I don't know what the arrangements were between NEA and the dressmaking company. The women dressmakers seemed to have their own entrance, but there they were.

In a corner farthest removed from them was another and smaller wire-caged area. This was a cartoonists' hutch, where I worked alongside some comic strip artists. Each of us had a drawing board and a little inkstand with a couple of drawers in it. I sat next to Roy Crane, an excellent artist and creator of "Wash Tubbs and Captain Easy," probably the first adventure strip.

I worked on a day-to-day schedule and Crane had to do his strips weeks ahead, but we were both inveterate deadline pushers. Later he moved across the country and mailed in his strips. Crane started by simply dropping them in a mailbox. Soon he began looking for the last mail pickup. Then he found he could work still later by going directly to the post office—then to the train station itself. He finally found himself driving across roads at night to catch a later train in the next town. And he then discovered a later train stop at a town a little farther away. He was now dividing his days between drawing to the very last minute and driving to catch the very last train in the area.

With similar work habits, I understood how this could happen. And like Roy, I also got away from the cartoonists' cage. I leased a room in a building across the street from NEA, where I could enjoy the luxury of an office of my own—complete with desk, easy chair, cabinets and plenty of room for constantly accumulated clutter. I then made my way back and forth with sketches and drawings.

The attraction of NEA, aside from some increase in salary, was that I was *the* editorial cartoonist there, with full-size space; and, NEA claimed, the work went out to some 700 papers in addition to the Scripps-Howard chain. Many small subscribing papers merely added some local news and views to a service that included editorials, comics, photos, Hollywood notes, sports, fiction and other features.

The large number of papers was not entirely a plus. A common observation was that the papers receiving the whole package for about $5 a week did the most complaining. One of them wrote that he had discovered what NEA meant: Never Expect Anything. Another, complaining about a cartoon I had done, said, "If I'd looked at it first, I wouldn't have run it."

Holiday and election preparedness pictures, cartoons, poems and articles were mailed out well in advance with notations that these would be appropriate if held for such-and-such occasion or on a certain date—or for the election of Candidate A or Candidate B. This did not keep some of the papers from running everything as soon as it arrived, again without looking, including the notes to editors to hold for future use. Some of the papers changed the typeset captions on my cartoons—not to alter the meaning, but to make sure everything was spelled out for the lowest-denominator reader, or just to show they were "editing."

Because so many clients used just about everything sent to them, NEA had a fear of running anything that might offend anyone. I heard that at an earlier time pictures of radio sets had been ruled out of comic strips because some newspapers did not wish to recognize this upstart competing medium. And "Abe" Martin, who did a girl strip, "Boots and Her Buddies," told me that once when NEA was concerned that some editors might find his drawings of highlighted dresses too sexy, they asked him to "anyhow try to not polish up the asses so much."

I also learned about the fallibility and herd instincts not only of certain client editors but of some at NEA and elsewhere. Having started out as an under-age kid submitting work to a great old editor on the *Chicago News,* I began with the feeling that all editors must be pretty wise. One day I showed some sketches to an associate editor at NEA who gave me a hard time about the cartoon I wanted to draw that day. Several days later he said, "I guess I owe you an apology. I noticed that cartoon I objected to was reprinted in Sunday's *New York Times.*" At this I couldn't help but point out that he was supposed to be an editor with judgment of his own, and that it shouldn't make any difference what somebody on another paper—possibly with no more smarts than he—chose to throw into a weekly review section.

One of NEA's biggest coups was its successful bidding for the exclusive pictures of the Dionne quintuplets for a period of many years. This triumph may have been due to general manager Herbert Walker's decision to offer not only umpty thousands of dollars but also to add to the big round numbers a small odd figure—say $565. The theory was that in this added number of dollars Papa Dionne could visualize something specific like a new car or home improvement.

Unconnected to the Dionnes was a Canadian "baby derby," in

which someone had offered a prize for the largest family by a certain date. A correspondent told me of interviewing the runner-up, a woman with a house full of kids, who said that not winning was all right—it had been a lot of fun anyhow.

NEA had its own production ideas. Each cartoonist was expected to do some kind of extra feature. Strip artists did an added smaller Sunday strip or special panel. I did a daily one-column-wide Almanac, based on dates of past events, usually with some kind of gag at the end. And each December I did, in strip form, a review of the year's events.

After those first political conventions in Chicago in 1932, I went on to attend others as they came along. Since they ran for an indefinite number of days, sketches airmailed back could still make the papers without seeming too dated.

The traveling technique was to take along some drawing paper and ink, and to turn a hotel bureau drawer upside down to serve as a drawing board. Eventually, shorter conventions and wide television broadcasts made these sketches seem less worthwhile. However, with recent television coverage consisting more and more of TV people talking to other TV people, I'm tempted to attend conventions again just to see and hear what's happening on the platform.

At these political circuses, it was interesting not only to see candidates but also to see the presidential bug working on them. At one convention, a colleague and I went to talk with newspaper founder and presidential candidate Frank Gannett. We walked through an entire largely empty floor in a hotel, where signs on the doors of rooms along the corridors bore names of Cabinet departments and agencies, as if a government-in-waiting was ready to assume control. In Gannett's suite, we asked him when he was planning to go downstairs or to the convention hall. This was out of the question because he seemed to feel he would be mobbed by waiting throngs. There were no waiting throngs. Somebody had apparently woven this wealthy publisher a set of invisible robes with the presidential seal on them and kept him confined to his hotel suite and out of touch with political reality.

Sometime during the '30s, a couple of us went to see Gov. Philip La Follette of Wisconsin. He had with him a flag containing a large black voter's X in a white circle that stood out against a bright background. It was apparently his idea that if Germans would unite behind a swastika flag, Americans might rally to a political flag like this. A real non-starter.

Apart from the conventions and political interviews, I made other trips—one to Rapid City, South Dakota, where a record balloon ascension by Auguste Piccard was to take place. Visiting Mount Rushmore, I met sculptor Gutzon Borglum and was impressed by his informality as he came strolling out to a lawn chair in what appeared to be purple pajamas. He said that he expected Rushmore to be a lifetime work. It was, and the remaining job was carried on by his son.

Years later I happened to mention his name in a conversation with a young woman who drew a complete blank on it. I said, "You know—Gutzon Borglum, the sculptor who did Mount Rushmore." In a truly great attempt at a recovery, she quickly said, "Oh, *that* Gutzon Borglum."

On a couple of visits to Washington, the correspondent there took me to Roosevelt press conferences, cautioning me to move in quickly if I wanted to see FDR. He was right. At the opening of the door, the reporters rushed in like a thundering herd. I didn't get up real close, but managed to avoid being trampled to death, and by standing on tiptoe could see the seated FDR as he had his fun with the correspondents.

The cast of characters at NEA was as good as any strip. There were a couple of artists who almost single-handedly supported a nearby bootleg booze joint called the Silver Moon, because it operated in a small basement room where the few occupants shared space with a boiler painted silver. One of them, a sports cartoonist, continued drawing even when he was in the last stages of being done in by cheap alcohol. And when visitors who came by watched him work, he would turn up his big bloodshot eyes and say, deadpan, "It takes a steady hand to do this." In the sports cartoon style then current, his drawings featured a large head, drawn from a photo with the aid of a copying device called a pantograph. He once criticized something written by a sportswriter who delivered the devastating answer, "Well, they haven't yet figured how to hitch up a pantograph to a typewriter."

Practical jokes and pranks were a top priority with some of the artists. A couple of them told me proudly of how they had tacked a fish under the seat of a chair where an earnest no-nonsense artist sat; they said he left his drawing board twice to go out and wash his hair.

By far the most colorful character at NEA was Harry Grayson, a sportswriter transferred to our office from New York. He longed to return there and regarded the Cleveland post as a form of exile, if not cruel and unusual punishment. Once, when a car pulled up to the curb and a tourist asked what was the quickest way out of town, Harry instantly replied, "If I knew, fella, I'd take it myself."

Harry was probably born with a cigar stub in his hand. And I'm sure it must have been soon after that he became a rapid-fire talker.

When he first came to Cleveland, we had dinner at a downtown restaurant, from which he emerged to say, "Where's the downtown section?" His quick summation of Cleveland then, with a shake of the head: "Jeez Christ, they got a lake you can't swim in, a ballpark you can't play ball in and you can't get shaved after 7 o'clock."

At NEA there was an "exchange table"—a stretch of boards on which were kept some of the client papers that came in—enough of them to be several papers deep for several feet. And some mornings when I got in early, I'd find Harry asleep on this bed of newsprint.

When an artist offered to give Harry a ride home one Saturday afternoon, he followed Harry's directions to turn here and turn there and turn here, until finally he realized they were going in circles, and said, "Harry, exactly which is your house?" Harry, with his head out the window looking left and right as they drove along, said, "Jeez, I don't know. I never saw it in the daytime before."

At the office one day I saw Harry looking up the spelling of a word. He stood at the table, cigar clenched in his mouth, flipping page after page and finally slammed the book shut, saying "Goddam-fucking-dictionary-you-can't-find-anything-in-it." I looked to see what was wrong with this dictionary. It was the phone book.

Among the stories about this legendary figure, one concerned his arrival at a Florida hotel, where he had insisted on an oceanfront room. He soon called the manager, who came up to hear Harry's complaint about all that noise out there. The manager listened and said, "That's the surf, Mr. Grayson."

At another hotel, Harry reportedly called room service to order a dinner including a well-done steak. Dissatisfied when he started to eat it, he hurled it out the window, nearly beaning a passerby with the platter, meat and metal lid. When the missiles were picked up and identified as having come from his room, he was asked, ''Did you throw this out the window?'' His immediate response was ''Yes, and do you call that steak well done?''

A correspondent also reported back on a Grayson trip to Japan where Harry was introduced to a high official who kept bowing and repeating some sibilant Japanese phrase of welcome. Harry waved a hand in the direction of the dignitary and said to the interpreter, ''This guy's in a rut.''

The last time I ran into Harry was after having been away a long time. I was walking along a ballpark deck at a World Series game in another city. I saw Harry approaching from the other direction and was all ready for an exchange of greetings and a fill-in on what we'd been doing. When we got within hearing range, he called, ''Hey, Herb, where's the john?'' Right to the point.

If we followed the Chinese practice of designating years by animals, the period at NEA would have been the years of the horse. Several of us liked to ride and we also enjoyed going to the races. We would all get caught up in the excitement of betting on an event like the Kentucky Derby, which had everyone crowded around the office radios. After some losing bets, one of the artists and I decided that we were on the wrong end of the betting—the way to win was to book the races. So we let it be known that we would take all bets on the next big event, the Preakness. This was fine with the rest of the people at NEA, most of whom bet on the Derby winner to repeat. Unfortunately for us, the winner that year was Omaha, one of the greatest of all racehorses, who went on to win the Triple Crown. Bad timing. We lost our enthusiasm for betting and booking, and left the races to the sportswriters.

Among the most talented people on the editorial side was Bruce Catton, who was so versatile that he served at various times as editorial writer, poet, fiction serial writer and magazine section editor. A Civil War buff, he relaxed at home with mockups of battlefields and soldiers. Later, when he wrote his award-winning books on the Civil War, he said he felt like the girl who found she could get paid for what she had been doing just for fun.

Another friend at NEA was Willis Thornton, also an editorial writer, whose father had owned a newspaper in Akron and who was understood to be wealthy. Whatever his possessions, they did not interfere with his empathy for the little guy. I spent many evenings with Thornton and his wife, often at a small café they discovered that featured some popular local singers. It also had, off in a corner, a piano player we liked named Art Tatum. This blind musician sat with his back to the room as he played on an upright piano that stood against a wall and obliged patrons who came over to make requests. I once asked if he minded these and he replied No, only when everyone who came into the place during an evening asked for "Stormy Weather."

The editor of NEA Service was Pete Edson, who sometimes took a hand in selecting photos for the picture pages. At one such conference, he made the memorable observation that "any photo looks important if you run it big enough."

The Thorntons and I spent an evening at a local carnival in some kind of bowling game where we succeeded in scoring enough points to win a prize we had picked out for Edson and his rather staid wife. It was a lamp, in which the shade was supported by a plaster police dog, colored purple and gold with rhinestone eyes. We found some occasion to present this to the Edsons, and when we visited them for dinner it sat atop their grand piano. We were never sure who was kidding who about this gift.

In answering letters from people with secretaries, Thornton would type his reply, with the initials in the lower left-hand corner WT/bh. This meant Willis Thornton/by himself.

Conversations with colleagues like Catton and Thornton and exposure to such bright columnists as Heywood Broun, the early Westbrook Pegler and *Cleveland Press* writer Jack Raper presented new viewpoints and stirred up a few brain waves. And the New Deal itself brought home to me what government was capable of doing to serve its people.

One evening Broun came to town to give a talk, and many of us turned out to hear him. After the speech I found myself with a group of more senior press people sitting around a table in a restaurant-bar having a beer with the famous man.

In Broun's newspaper column he sometimes used the expression "shoot the works," a sentiment he lived up to in his Cleveland speech calling for the creation of an organization of working newspaper people. He concluded it with the story of a Spaniard, tired of spending his life in a backwater area, who determined to try for the big city. He told his wife, "Pack up, we're going to Seville." "*Deo volente,*" she reminded him, "God willing." "Never mind that," he said, "pack up." At this, he was suddenly transformed into a frog and spent several months going "Ribbit ribbit." When he was at last changed back to himself, he ran to the house and resumed packing. "What are you doing?" asked the wife. "I'm packing," he said. "We're going to Seville." "*Deo volente!*" she cried. "*Deo volente!*" To which he replied, "To hell with it—on to Seville or back to the frog pond!"

Spurred by Broun, a few local newspeople risked publishing-industry consignment to frog ponds by forming the Cleveland Newspaper Guild. I heard that they practically met in dark alleys to plan and organize this single-unit organization that later became the first chapter of the Newspaper Guild. I was not one of those pioneering founders, but did join that first unit, and am still a member of the Newspaper Guild.

Meanwhile, along with the fun and games and meetings with colleagues, there were still the daily cartoons. The drawing style had changed some since the *Chicago News* days when many of the figures were squashed into a small space. More than that, my artwork went through various phases as I became fascinated with one technique or another, often at the expense of the basic drawing, which was sometimes absolutely awful. Nevertheless, the cartoons were widely printed and reprinted. What also underwent some change was the viewpoint; and this led to some problems with management.

"HAIL HITLER!"

One of the first NEA Cartoons
Jan. 1933

HIS MARK

Jan. 1933

THE WORLD AS IT LOOKS RIGHT NOW

March 1934

"NO FOREIGN ENTANGLEMENTS"

Jan. 1935

"SUFFER THE LITTLE CHILDREN TO COME UNTO ME"

Sept. 1934

9

Trouble

L ife is real, life is earnest,'' wrote the poet. The reality and ear-
nestness of the national situation finally intruded on my relationship with NEA. As the New Deal took shape, I became, for want of a
better term, more ''liberal,'' which put me close to where the Scripps-
Howard policies were. But we were moving in opposite directions.

While the early cartoons were not exactly on the cutting edge of
national policies, they gradually represented more and sharper opinion
than NEA had been accustomed to.

There was no disagreement about cartoons against such things as
war and crime. Some of the early '30s cartoons attacked munitions
makers, who were then under investigation and unpopular enough to
figure in Robert Sherwood's play *Idiot's Delight*. With brutal dictatorships, wars and threats of war, I did a cartoon of one kid asking
another, ''What are you going to be if you grow up?'' Much later, it
might apply even better to life expectancy in our inner cities.

Cartoons supporting the FBI in fighting gangsters and racketeers
brought letters from J. Edgar Hoover (which probably went to all who

60

drew similar cartoons), and sometimes an actual G-man came to pick up some promised drawing for the head man. Later, when Hoover went from pursuing criminals to pursuing "subversives," such as civil rights leaders, the cartoons about him and his agency were less complimentary and he returned the less-compliment.

Another frequent drawing-requester was labor leader John L. Lewis, who wrote letters couched in quite modest language that ended with a heavy signature about two inches high. As situations and the cartoons changed, I also lost this pro forma pen pal.

There were lots of drawings about the new "alphabet agencies." Among the most prominent were the AAA (Agricultural Adjustment Administration) and the NRA (National Recovery Administration). Both of them ran afoul of Supreme Court decisions, which were among those that prompted Roosevelt to try expanding, or "packing," the Court.

The AAA was best known for its connection with efforts to raise farm prices through the "plowing under" of crops and the "slaughter of little pigs"—which had been raised for slaughter anyhow.

The NRA had its own insignia, the blue eagle, and slogan, "We Do Our Part," for businesses that complied with its rules. The blue eagle insignia was featured by businesses all over the country in signs and on products. Garment manufacturers sewed it into clothing, along with their own labels.

One of the most successful and permanent agencies was the TVA (Tennessee Valley Authority), which brought power and electric lights to rural areas that never had them before.

Sometime in the 1950s, on a speechmaking trip to Tennessee, I toured TVA and picked up an interesting sidelight. I was told that visitors from all over the world had come to see this mighty project. But the administrators discovered to their dismay that many of the visitors' cameras were pointed not at the great dams and power lines but at lesser facilities that bore signs reading "White" and "Colored." Without waiting for formal approval, court decisions or a civil rights movement, the TVA directors quietly removed the signs, bringing to an end another kind of darkness.

The cartoons on foreign dictatorships were consistently tough—as were those on petty dictators at home. Among the more controversial cartoons—in addition to those on civil liberties—were the ones on political bosses and demagogues. Huey Long, governor, senator and actual ruler of Louisiana, and Father Charles Coughlin (the "radio priest" of Royal Oak, Michigan) were among the most prominent. Their voices on the airwaves attracted large followings. Coughlin, who seemed to preach a kind of home-grown fascism laced with antisemitism, was virulent in his attacks on the Roosevelt administration. Long was more cunning. He would begin a broadcast by saying something like "This is Huey Long here. Now I'm just going to talk along for a couple of minutes while you call five of your friends and tell them to tune in."

Almost from the beginning I did cartoons critical of the congressional Committee on Un-American Activities, when it was known as the Dies Committee, after Martin Dies of Texas. Congressmen who set themselves up to decide what was un-American did not strike me as being bona fide Uncle Sams.

In Roosevelt's second term Scripps-Howard and I had pretty much switched places.

Fred Ferguson, president of NEA, had his offices in New York, but on his occasional visits to Cleveland he would take a few of us on the editorial staff to lunch. While nobody told me what to put into the cartoons, I discovered that it was more difficult to express an opinion when it seemed to fly in the face of one put forth by the management. This, incidentally, is one reason I've never cared for taking part in editorial conferences.

Ferguson, often referred to by the Cleveland staffers as Little Napoleon, was quite vocal in stating his likes and dislikes. At luncheons during that period, he might say, for openers, "Well, have you seen what Roosevelt has done *now?*" This was followed shortly by his strong and highly unfavorable view of what FDR was doing. To avoid the problem of seeming to oppose his views directly, I learned to jump in early with my own. Thus, in answer to "Have you seen what Roosevelt has done *now?*" I would say quickly, "Yes, isn't it great?" While this did not exactly stop him, it slowed him down. And at least I did not surprise him later with a cartoon that seemed to be an act of defiance. Our differences on foreign policy were hard to reconcile.

While I never got through the important-looking copies of *Foreign*

Affairs that kept piling up on a table, I felt I ought to learn more about the world beyond our borders. So in Cleveland I took part in some Foreign Policy Council meetings and attended a class at Cleveland College where foreign affairs expert Brooks Emeny lectured.

One day I saw a notice that Ohio's Senator Robert Bulkley was to speak and dropped in that evening to hear him. I thought he was great and went up afterward to meet him. But whatever the mistake or change in schedule, it was not Bulkley who spoke; it was a college professor and radio broadcaster named Henry M. Busch. I enrolled in his lecture course.

I had heard some of the foreign policy people speak in pear-shaped tones about diplomatic nay-go-see-ay-sions and make cool historical observations about pogroms being an old story. I attended a couple of cocktail parties where former State Department officials held forth. These actual diplomats, who were dignified and obviously sophisticated, viewed events with professional detachment. They were impressive, yet there was something unsatisfying about them and what they had to say.

Busch was for the New Deal and was also knowledgeable about foreign affairs. But he talked differently than those other experts. He spoke about the threat of Nazism and the Axis powers. He saw early and said plainly that Hitler must be stopped. And he could back up his views with facts.

I liked what Busch had to say and we became good friends. I heard him debate Sen. Robert Taft at the Cleveland City Club, when Taft described lend-lease aid to an ally as being like lending somebody your chewing gum.

For my money, Busch was the clear winner. Long afterward, he was, literally for my modest money, a worthy candidate for office. Sometime after I came to work at *The Washington Post,* Busch ran for the Democratic senatorial nomination in Ohio. When the American Newspaper Guild gave me its annual Heywood Broun Journalism Award, I thought a gift of the award money and the attendant publicity might help my old friend in his uphill campaign. I inquired if the Guild officers had any objection to this public use of their award and they did not. They liked the idea.

But the *Washington Times-Herald,* sister paper of the *Chicago*

Tribune and bitter opponent of *The Post,* pounced on the story. Skipping my friend Busch, they characterized my contribution as illustrating a deep hatred for Robert Taft, Republican senator. Since this spin on the story was also taken up by similar publications, they succeeded in making my once-in-a-lifetime campaign contribution backfire against me without helping Henry as much as I hoped. He didn't get the nomination, but he ran a very good race.

Back in pre-war Cleveland both of us supported the William Allen White Committee (Committee To Defend America By Aiding The Allies). And in 1941, when Busch and some newspaper friends put out a pocket-size magazine called *Vital Issues,* I drew cartoons for it.

Most of us probably feel that history doesn't really count until we are born. The fashions, phrases and language of previous generations are quaint or laughable; the things that went wrong in the past were because people were stupid, and the things that came out right were obvious and inevitable.

But inevitability is something combatants don't know about while they're engaged in these battles; and as we finally discovered in Vietnam, victory is not always assured, even to the United States. In World War II it was hardly a sure thing. There was, first of all, the chilling possibility that the wrong side could have developed The Bomb before we did. The survival of England was anything but certain, even though Hitler missed the opportunity to invade it. And with a little different timing, a little different scenario, the Soviet Union's resistance might not have been enough. Before Pearl Harbor there was no unity of opinion in the United States, where, in 1941, renewal of the military draft act passed Congress by only one vote.

We were officially neutral and we wanted to stay out of the war. The big issue was on helping the Allies. The fall of France in May 1940 and the widespread belief that Britain would go down next sharpened the issue. Against aid to Britain were the America First Committee, the Liberty Lobby and many leading senators. Charles Lindbergh was a strong voice on that side. And the Scripps-Howard newspapers' management, parent of NEA Service, also held that view.

When the draft went into effect, I registered as required. Later I got a message to see the man who headed the local draft review board, a lawyer named J. M. Ulmer. He noted that I had indicated I was all ready for service but also saw that I had a dependent, my mother.

"What about her?" he asked. Partly because of childhood recollections of World War I, when "slacker" was the term for men who didn't want to go, I felt that a readiness to march off was the patriotic thing. More than that, I supported the preparedness measures.

Ulmer explained to me that the government was not bashful about telling men to go. Later on they would probably get around to me, but that in the meantime they were not ready to have me kiss my ma goodbye. He marked me deferred—for the time being. I don't know now whether he was familiar with my work or whether he screened the papers of all potential draftees. Eventually we became acquainted and he was interested in what I drew. I think he felt I could be more useful continuing my work at this time than I could be in the service. In fact, I felt that way too. So I was glad for the reprieve and the chance to continue coping with isolationism.

As the Nazi war machine rolled on, Ferguson's dissatisfaction with my anti-isolationist cartoons increased. He told the editors in Cleveland to be more careful about which sketches they approved. And as the cartoons continued going in an unwanted direction, he pressed the editors to be still more vigilant. When that wasn't enough, he had me submit my sketches to the general manager of NEA, who tried to select those he thought would be acceptable to the chief in New York. But even this did not satisfy Ferguson, who then required that I mail my sketches to him in New York every day for his personal approval.

About midnight each night I would go down to the main post office with an envelope full of sketches and get them off airmail special (which meant next-morning delivery). I would then go home to fold up, and the next day wait for word from New York. Sometime that day he might wire back, "Number seven okay." Occasionally I would even hear that the sketches had not been received at all—and send on another batch. This was a wearing business. The conflict in views was grinding. The loss of time numbering and copying sketches (no copying machines then) and waiting for a wire of approval didn't help. Whether the policies were Ferguson's or Roy Howard's, it was a miserable way to work.

Early on, when Ferguson found my cartoons not to his liking—or not in accord with Scripps-Howard policy—he asked me to come to New York to see him.

I went, at NEA's expense, and met with him. He gave me a little lecture on how things should go and told me that I should not be an "interventionist"—while I told him I was simply "anti-isolationist." With both of us trying to be agreeable, he concluded our talk by telling me to go out and see a good show and forget about all that stuff in Europe. He said, "Let them have their war," which he seemed to feel every generation was entitled to, but which was none of our business.

After I returned to Cleveland and the work situation continued to deteriorate, he finally demanded that I come to New York to see him again. I inquired if NEA was paying my expenses. And since it was not, I said I would see him when I next came to New York on my own, which would be in May 1942, when I wanted to come east for a springtime visit to Washington.

The difficulties at NEA did not improve substantially even after Pearl Harbor. In fact, things took what seemed like another nasty turn. The NEA management decided that since Roosevelt wanted everyone to save paper, they were going to shrink my cartoon, making it a horizontal size with the same width. The government did indeed encourage the saving of newsprint, but there was something gratuitous about starting with the cartoon and commenting that since I approved of FDR's policies I shouldn't mind this way of saving paper.

By the spring of 1942 and the New York date we had agreed on, I was at pretty much of a low point.

In 1939 my dad had died after a three-year bout with cancer—a few months before the war in Europe and the tougher situation at NEA.

The girl I was going with during the last of my stay in Cleveland told me that if I didn't want to marry her—which I didn't—she would go to work on a paper in another city—which she later did.

My current contract with NEA was running out, but this time there was no talk of renewing it, as there had always been before. And the probability of changing jobs now didn't seem likely since I was a pretty sure bet to be drafted.

I hadn't quite got down to visualizing a Tomb Of The Unknown Cartoonist, but I was feeling tired and depressed. And I gloomily saw the possibility of a useful career that had been getting up a pretty good head of steam coming to an end.

I might have imagined it, or perhaps I arrived at the New York office at a busy time, but when I got there it seemed that there was less of the glad-to-see-you and chitchat than on previous visits—more of what Damon Runyon would call the small hello.

As for Ferguson, I was told that he could not see me yet and would let me know when he was ready. While I was, as the phrase goes, cooling my heels, I went to the office of Don Sutton, the New York NEA editor. He asked what my immediate plans were, and I told him that after seeing the head man, I planned to take the train to Washington and return to Cleveland from there. He asked if I had a hotel reservation in Washington. I did not, and he pointed out that with the war on, things were pretty tight there. So he put in a phone call to the Washington office to inquire about a reservation for me.

Time passed with still no word from Ferguson, and while Sutton went back to the paperwork on his desk, I sat in his office and waited. In time the phone rang and he answered it. After a brief conversation, he hung up and said, "Congratulations." "I've got a hotel room in Washington?" I asked. He smiled and held out his hand. "You've won the Pulitzer Prize."

After we shook hands, he took me directly to Ferguson's office and rapped on the door. When Ferguson opened it, Sutton said, "I think we should take this young man out and buy him a drink." *"What for?"* Ferguson looked at Sutton as if this trusted editor had suddenly lost his mind. "He's won the Pulitzer Prize," said Sutton.

The expression "mixed feelings" never showed so clearly on a man's face. Ferguson gave a sort of anguished smile. It was the only time anyone at NEA had won such a prize, but it was the wrong person at the wrong time.

He congratulated me, begged off on having a drink as he wasn't feeling well and said we could see each other some other time. Staff members joined Sutton and me for drinks at a nearby bar instead.

The trip to Washington, which I had thought of as a kind of half-step march with muffled drums, became something of a joy ride. The people at the *Washington Daily News* (Scripps-Howard) gave me a rousing welcome, and there was no problem about getting a hotel room. They thought the way I got the news was funny enough for an article by itself.

During my stay, while doing the old traveling routine of turning out a cartoon on the bottom of a dresser drawer, I received a wire from the office: RESUME DRAWING CARTOONS FULL SIZE.   BEST WISHES.

Back in Cleveland everyone was excited and happy. And in the words of the Hammerstein song, ''We all had a real good time.''

The Pulitzer had been for the year's work during that period of divisiveness before we were in the war. The issues of that time were now settled.

And when I was called into the Army early in 1943, I could feel that whatever life in uniform held for me—which turned out to be inconsequential enough—I was more or less going in style.

THE CROWN JEWELS

April 1935

69

"When the time comes in 1940 when there is only one party and a dictatorship, I shall be the one to ask you to put aside your ballots and use bullets."

"God's philosophy was to increase and multiply. Roosevelt's is decrease and destroy. Therefore I call him anti-God and a radical."

Oct. 1936

—Excerpts from Father Coughlin's Cincinnati speech.

70

One of the year-end reviews
1936

HISTORICAL FIGURES

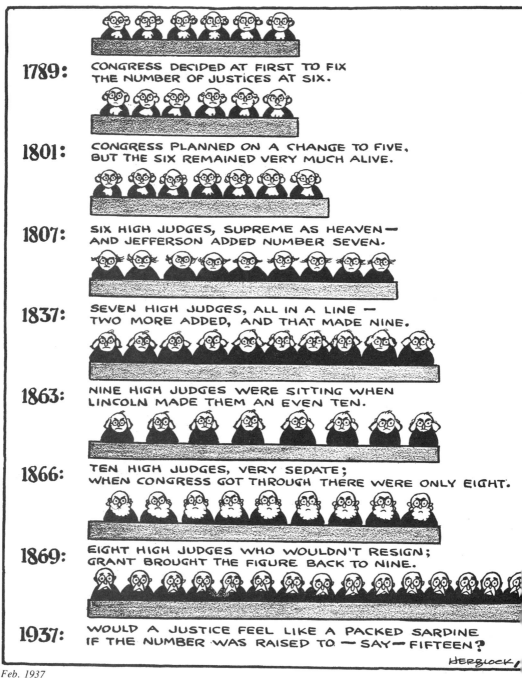

1789: CONGRESS DECIDED AT FIRST TO FIX THE NUMBER OF JUSTICES AT SIX.

1801: CONGRESS PLANNED ON A CHANGE TO FIVE, BUT THE SIX REMAINED VERY MUCH ALIVE.

1807: SIX HIGH JUDGES, SUPREME AS HEAVEN — AND JEFFERSON ADDED NUMBER SEVEN.

1837: SEVEN HIGH JUDGES, ALL IN A LINE — TWO MORE ADDED, AND THAT MADE NINE.

1863: NINE HIGH JUDGES WERE SITTING WHEN LINCOLN MADE THEM AN EVEN TEN.

1866: TEN HIGH JUDGES, VERY SEDATE; WHEN CONGRESS GOT THROUGH THERE WERE ONLY EIGHT.

1869: EIGHT HIGH JUDGES WHO WOULDN'T RESIGN; GRANT BROUGHT THE FIGURE BACK TO NINE.

1937: WOULD A JUSTICE FEEL LIKE A PACKED SARDINE IF THE NUMBER WAS RAISED TO — SAY — FIFTEEN?

HERBLOCK

Feb. 1937

THE WAR TO BEGIN WAR

Jan. 1937

OVERLAPPING DREAMS

IN WORLD AFFAIRS

Aug. 1936

SOUTH FOR THE WINTER

Nov. 1938

WAIT TILL THE DIES COMMITTEE HEARS ABOUT THIS!

AN INTERNATIONAL AGENT WITH HEADQUARTERS CLOSE TO SOVIET RUSSIA —

HEAD OF A GIGANTIC ESPIONAGE RING, WITH FILES ON MILLIONS OF AMERICANS —

OPENLY OPPOSED TO THE PROFIT MOTIVE, AND FLOODING THE COUNTRY WITH PROPAGANDA—

LARGELY FINANCED AND AIDED BY MEMBERS OF CLUBS IN EVERY STATE OF THE UNION —

RESPONSIBLE FOR THE FOMENTING OF PLOTS AND SECRET ACTIONS IN COUNTLESS AMERICAN HOMES—

PLANNING TO ENTER THE U.S. ILLEGALLY AND UNDER COVER OF DARKNESS—THE NIGHT OF DEC. 24TH!

Dec. 1938

UNDER THE HAMMER AND SICKLE

June 1937

"LIGHT! MORE LIGHT!"
——Goethe's Last Words

Jan. 1938

THE ARRIVAL OF SPRING

March 1938

"I SHOT AN ARROW INTO THE AIR IT FELL TO EARTH I KNEW NOT WHERE"

Jan. 1937

THE REPRIEVE

1934

NOW PLAYING IN THE FEDERAL THEATER

June 1939

"PLEASE, LITTLE GIRL GO AWAY"

1938

"GRANDMA—WHAT BIG EYES YOU HAVE!"

Copyright, 1938, NEA

"WHEW! THAT WAS A CLOSE CALL!"

Sept. 1938

78

VICTORY IS IN SIGHT

March 1938

"BETWEEN THE CROSSES,
ROW ON ROW"

May 1940

BRINGING THE LITTLE NATIONS INTO A
COMMON FRONT

Dec. 1939

NORWAY

May 1940

TRAGEDY AT SEA

FAILURE OF MACHINERY

FAILURE OF MAN

June 1939

STORY OF THE LAST SEVEN YEARS

May 1940

NEA Service, Inc.

LET JOY BE UNCONFINED

SKY PATTERN

Oct. 1940

VETERANS

Oct. 1940

LINDBERGH, 1941

1941

COMÉDIE FRANÇAISE

1941

TRAVELOGUE

AND SO WE SAY GOOD-BY TO ——

NORTH CHINA

ETHIOPIA

AUSTRIA

CZECHOSLOVAKIA

ALBANIA

POLAND

KARELIAN FINLAND

DENMARK

NORWAY

LUXEMBOURG

HOLLAND

BELGIUM

HERBLOCK,

NEA Service,

June 1940

84

PARDON US IF WE MAKE A FEW CHANGES TOO

Sept. 1940

HANDS ACROSS THE SEAS

Sept. 1940

"THINK WE SHOULD SLOW DOWN?"

Sept. 1941

THE ROAD TO THE EAST

1941

85

WELL, MUSSOLINI MADE THE TRAINS RUN ON TIME

March 1941

JUST DON'T BE SURPRISED, THAT'S ALL

Mrs. Roosevelt, whose syndicated column was titled "My Day," went to England in 1942.

1942

"THEY HAVE SOWN THE WIND——"

Dec. 1941

TOUGH GOING

Aug. 1942

GIVE THAT GENTLEMAN TWENTY SILVER DOLLA

Jan. 1942

10

The Khaki Suit

I am a natural-born civilian. And despite the high school ROTC and the post–high school weeks at Fort Sheridan, I never longed for the military life. It's not that I marched to a different drum. I've just never been eager to march at all.

My ideas of war were based on newsreels, photos and movies in which all the characters saw action. I did not realize that the fighting men were, as was later explained, only "the cutting edge" of the armed forces—backed at some distance by supply people, office personnel and other non-combat people in uniform.

The cartoons that Ferguson described as "interventionist" were done then with the expectation, however naive, that if the United States entered the war, I might end up a casualty. As things developed, many of the men I knew in the service did see action. But I was never on that "cutting edge." I was on the dull edge and sometimes the edge of dullness.

When Phil Casey, a bright feature writer for *The Washington Post,* was asked to fill out a biographical form, he came to the early 1940s and wrote: "Associated with the U.S. Army." It was that way with me.

My basic training at Camp Robinson, Arkansas, was probably about the same as that kind of training anywhere but with red clay mixed with the mud. The first order of business was an early morning lineup to hear a sergeant read "The Articles of War"—a series of paragraphs each of which ended with the punch line "Penalty: Death." We couldn't recall if these included "failure to square corners on bunks," but we got the idea that the Army's motto was not "Do your own thing."

Having spent practically all of my life being younger than most of my associates, it came as something of a surprise to find that now, at 33 or 34, I was regarded by the other trainees, age about 19 or 20, as a guy who was no longer in the bloom of youth. This realization came after a march that left me panting on my bunk while some of the 19- and 20-year-olds worked off surplus energy by wrestling with each other. I overheard one of them remark that "old Herb held up pretty well." Old Herb didn't feel any springier after an exercise that involved dashing across a field with full equipment—and learning that the officer who was critiquing our performances said of me, "There's a guy that tries like hell and just can't get his ass off the ground."

Toward the end of this training, I was sent to an Army Air Force base in Florida. The chief public relations officer there, who had been a newspaper editor in the civilians, had read that I was in the Army and had requisitioned me. The base, near Orlando, was called AAFTAC (Army Air Force Tactical Center). I did some cartoons there for the camp paper, and sometimes wrote a press release or made up a picture page. From the standpoint of an enlisted man, this was about as non-GI as a post could be. It was, in fact, a special base, with fancy war room—a place where officers from many countries came to study and train.

One incident illustrates the atmosphere of the base and our public relations office. A corporal on the camp paper staff, hurrying to meet a deadline and frustrated in making his way back to the PR office one afternoon, slapped his cap down on the desk in exasperation and said, "That hallway is lousy with generals again."

On one occasion I, a private, had to show some document to a high-ranking officer. As I approached his desk, he held out his hand,

and I smiled and shook his hand warmly. "No, no," he snorted, drawing his hand back, as if from a hot poker. "The paper—hand me the paper."

But even in this relaxed camp where there was so much brass that saluting was usually forgotten, the officers really got edgy when an appearance from the inspector general was scheduled. Before such a visitation, one of the camp's commanding officers would come around to make sure that everything was in perfect order. All desks were cleared for non-action. When the preliminary inspecting officer saw some crumpled pieces of paper in my wastebasket, he told me to get rid of them. It was no use explaining that this was what wastebaskets were for, any more than it would have helped to explain that you don't put out publications by making all the tops of desks visible. I stuffed the wads of paper in my pockets. If they had created too much of a bulge, I suppose I could have eaten them.

It's been said that one of the worst things in war is boredom. A sense of wasted time might at least be related to that. Even with all the informality of AAFTAC, barracks life in Florida in all seasons is not the same as winter vacationing at the beach.

On reading that Gregor Duncan, a former magazine artist drawing for *Stars and Stripes,* had died in a jeep accident in Africa, I thought the paper might have an opening for another sketch artist and applied. This was not a champing at the bit for action. It was simply a desire for change. Back came a wire from Col. Egbert White, who headed the publication, accepting me and saying he would see me in Algiers.

I packed my barracks bag, told everyone that I was off for Africa—and nothing happened. My travel orders never came through, and all attempts to track them down were fruitless. Eventually, I learned that *Stars and Stripes* was in transition to a strictly enlisted man's paper, and Col. White was no longer in charge. Having packed and said my farewells, I felt like a damn fool. Whether by coincidence or to help me out, the PR officer told me a man was wanted in New York to put out a clipsheet of material to be sent out to Army papers and would I like to go up there? I sure would.

Life in New York was even closer to civilian living. It *was* civilian living, but in uniform. It did not include barracks life or being rousted out before dawn to do exercises with the eyes only half open.

Most of us rented one-room apartments near the office on 42nd

Street. From my pad on 43rd Street, I could almost roll down the street and check in at the office without opening my eyes at all.

The place on 42nd Street was an Army publication headquarters. It housed *Yank* and Camp Newspaper Service, which featured Milt Caniff's "Male Call." It also produced the wall-size war maps and put out information-and-education material. One of the writers I got acquainted with in that I-and-E section was Alan Cranston, an internationalist and author of a book on the failure of the League of Nations.

The purpose of this Army clipsheet was to provide something interesting or humorous while plugging whatever minor messages the officials were trying to get out—like take-care-of-your-equipment-fellas, or buy-bonds-instead-of-losing-your-pay-in-clip-joints. In getting out this sheet that went to Army publications all over the world like a syndicated military feature, I wrote articles and drew cartoons. And as an editor, I was in command of a staff of one—a corporal I now outranked by one stripe.

Doing cartoons for the clipsheet had an effect on my style. Because some of the artwork had to go out to places where mimeograph machines comprised the only printing equipment, it was necessary to simplify the drawings. This was what an instructor had in mind long before when he looked at one containing an infinite number of lines and suggested that I "get the hay out."

To provide greater variety I solicited work from other cartoonists, generally asking them to do drawings for which I provided appropriate gags. They were all cooperative. Ripley drew a special Believe It or Not. And *The New Yorker* cartoonists were happy to help. Among these were Sam Cobean and Charles Addams, two of the very best.

What I remember most from visits to the Addams household was the extensive collection of crossbows adorning the apartment walls; a small black-and-white newspaper clipping of a couple of old comic strip characters like Mutt and Jeff set in an elaborate, heavy, rococo gold frame; and Addams's wife at the time, whose long dark hair parted in the middle made her look like the bewitching woman in his cartoons, or vice versa.

Al Capp contributed a cartoon in the form of a special Li'l Abner strip. But we didn't really get acquainted until later when he made visits to Washington. On one of these he told me of his unhappy experience with a hotel. He had been invited to take part in an early morning conference sponsored by President Eisenhower. To ensure that he was up in time for the meeting, he left triple-reinforced instructions with the hotel desk. They were to give him a wake-up call, followed later by another call—and a third. Then, to make absolutely certain he would be up, he ordered breakfast to be delivered to his room—if necessary with a passkey—a little after the phone calls.

When he awoke at a later hour, he was furious to find that he had missed his meeting, and quickly dressed to go downstairs and raise hell. In the hallway he met an almost equally unhappy red-eyed man in a Texas hat who had been out on the town very late the night before.

This man groaned as he described, step by step, how his sleep had been shattered by several calls, and finally—unbelievably—a waiter had opened the door to his room and rolled in a breakfast cart. Al had looked at the number on his bedroom door and given the desk what he thought was the number of the entrance to his suite. He missed his White House appointment, but at least had a better night's sleep than his tired neighbor.

In addition to cartoons and articles, a little cheesecake did no harm in a service publication, and I got an appointment to bring a photographer to do Mae West, who was in a New York play at the time. She posed for some shots in bed on the set. Some critic had observed that she did not at this point have a Mae West figure. When we were leaving, she said—almost asked—"Make me look good, boys." Of course. With the aid of an airbrush artist we helped to preserve a legend and provided the GIs with a good Mae West picture.

Evenings were free, and good Broadway show tickets generally could be purchased at the last minute when there were some returns. Night spots had such favorite entertainers as Lena Horne and Zero Mostel.

For a while I dated a girl whose folks lived at Gramercy Park. She had a key to the actual fenced-in park and made the entrance to it a little surprise. I didn't know such a private park existed—a tranquil island where we could sit alone at night in the middle of The Big City. Since the combat zones have moved from Europe and Asia to our urban areas, I don't know if anyone sits quietly in any big-city park at night anymore.

About the closest thing to Army life in the New York stint was a once- or twice-a-week march—or loping walk—in which the members of our group went in formation from our 42nd Street headquarters to a nearby YMCA to engage in gym exercises. Even these were not exactly under stern direction. The first time I went to the gym, I took part in an anyone-can-join volleyball game, where I soon realized that I was no help to the men on my side of the net.

I tried some exercise machines, which required no special playing skills, but gradually noticed during visits to the gym that the number of us marching over tended to diminish after we arrived. An investigation of the upstairs floor disclosed the reason. The gym mats were kept here, and on them in restful bliss lay the colleagues who had been roused before finishing their night's sleep. This was my kind of gym routine. From then on, the second floor was where I spent these sessions.

As we were marched back each time, I had a recurrent fear—well, anyhow, a thought. What if the end of the war should be announced during one of these returns from the gym? We would probably be showered with confetti and hailed as heroes—we who were making the long march of maybe four blocks back to office jobs after sack time on our YMCA mats.

Fortunately, it didn't work out that way, and on V-J day I went to the Times Square area for my second big-city end-of-war celebration.

The New York assignment required occasional trips to the Pentagon, then regarded as something of a labyrinth, to check in with an official on publication work.

It was not true, as the story went at the time, that a Western Union messenger had gone into the Pentagon and come out a few days later as a full colonel. But I learned the Army way of doing things even before boarding the train from New York to Washington. I was told that I was entitled to first-class travel, which meant Pullman sleeping car. I didn't *want* to take an overnight sleeping car for such a short trip. But, going by the book, the Army determined that this was what I was entitled to, and this was what I was going to get. I ended up buying a coach ticket and paying for it myself.

On one of these Washington trips in the autumn of 1945, a dinner date led to a meeting with Nelson Poynter. He was editor of the *St.*

Petersburg Times and was planning publication of *Congressional Quarterly*. Demobilization was imminent and Poynter asked what I planned to do when I got out of the service. I told him I hadn't made plans yet, but thought I'd like to get back to working on a newspaper.

My life has been full of lucky coincidences. About two days later Poynter ran into Wayne Coy, assistant to the publisher of *The Washington Post,* and asked where he'd been lately. Publisher Eugene Meyer wanted a cartoonist, said Coy, and Coy had been running around the country trying to find one Meyer would consider suitable. Poynter had a suggestion.

Shortly afterward Meyer asked me to meet him at the Yale Club in New York, which I did, still wearing the khaki suit. We had an exchange of correspondence. He asked to see more of my pre-war cartoons, adding, "and I'll send you a subscription to the paper, so you can see how *you* like *us.*" *The Post* at that time was probably the #4 or #5 paper in Washington, sustained only by Meyer's infusions of money, but it had a good editorial page.

Meyer obviously had no idea of suggesting cartoons. He said his policy was to get good people and let them do their work. He once joked that on those occasions when he made a suggestion to the news department that they accepted, the stories ended up on what he called "the bomber pages." "Bomber pages?" I asked. "You know," he said, "B-17, B-29." That was later. At the time the B section probably didn't boast that many pages.

There were other offers. I was most interested in one from Robert Hall, head of a fairly new syndicate. What I wanted to do was combine the newspaper cartoon with his syndication. Meyer insisted that he was in a better position than I to select a good arrangement, but in the end he went along with Hall. The one thing I wanted understood with Hall was that complaints from client editors to him would not be passed along to me, and that the syndicate would not tell me "they could sell more papers *if* I would only . . ." Hall agreed.

The Washington Post, Meyer pointed out, said on its masthead that it was published every day of the year, and he would like the cartoon to fit the same schedule. How far that newspaper has come since those days may be surmised by the fact that he also wanted me to print *The Washington Post* or © The Washington Post Co. under the signature to help publicize his paper around the country. I did that on all seven a week.

When I went to see Meyer in Washington, I met with him and his lawyer–general manager—just the three of us—and he had a contract ready for me to sign. When I said I'd like to take it along with me first, he reared back and asked, ''What's the matter—don't you trust me?'' This was apparently a tested ploy of his. He later told me of an appearance before a congressional committee during his service as governor of the Federal Reserve, where he went in planning at a definite point to take offense.

I'm sure an agent could have done much better for me, if I'd had one. But I liked the paper, had always liked Washington and soon joined up.

Living quarters at the end of 1945 were so tight that the current joke was about a fellow seeing a man fall from an apartment building window and running in to see if he could rent the apartment—only to find it had already been rented to the guy who had pushed the man out the window. The *New York Times* ran New York–Washington, D.C., apartment swap classifieds. Through one of these ads, I exchanged my one-room kitchenette place on 43rd Street for a similar one in the District of Columbia.

Despite the fact that my Army service had hardly been onerous, I felt that time had been lost, largely wasted, and was eager to get back to daily cartooning. I even made a mental resolve that, working again on a newspaper after the Army stint, I would make every day count. This was before starting work at the beginning of a new year, and like all New Year's resolutions, it was not fully lived up to. But, as in Cole Porter's ''Another opening, another show,'' it was a new beginning in another city—a captivating one that contained many of the people who populated the cartoons.

11

The View from E Street

The original *Post* building on E Street evoked memories of the *Chicago News* "old building." Its similarities included a single passenger elevator operated by an attendant, and patchwork additions requiring steps up and down from one part of a floor to another. Up a couple of steps on one floor was a small room that served as a studio, where broadcasters conducted interview programs for *The Post*'s radio station, WINX.

Phone calls went through a switchboard staffed by a few operators who knew everyone and who could even recognize voices of *Post* people who had been away for years. Less experienced operators filled in on weekends, and in those simpler times they occasionally woke me on Saturday mornings to say I had a phone call that was *long distance!* Such calls were usually from people I didn't know phoning from as far away as Baltimore.

Next door to *The Washington Post* building was the Munsey Trust Company—the bank most convenient for employees to cash paychecks or keep accounts. A lot of things of that period seem strange today, but an incident at this bank, where I had checking and savings accounts, remains one of the strangest. It had a policy that money deposited in savings accounts should not exceed a certain modest figure—maybe $100 or $200 at any one time—without approval of a bank official. Flush with some extra money, I wanted to deposit more than the limit, and a polite bank teller referred me to a vice president of the institution. This official asked rather sternly why I wanted to deposit this money—say $250—to my savings account, and I said I thought it might be a good idea to put aside something for taxes. To this he responded, as one who has cleverly seen through a despicable ruse: "Taxes—hah! What you want on that money is our *interest!*"

That bank, along with the old *Post* building, has long since gone. But after years of seeing banks offer gifts and better-than-other-banks interest rates to attract depositors, and thinking of how investments in a booming stock market would have paid far more handsomely than the modest bank rates then, I am still baffled. Well, at least the Munsey bank officials didn't ask me to give *them* a toaster.

Less than a block away from the *Post* was the *old* Willard Hotel, complete with the original marble sinks in the bathrooms. And even closer was an old-fashioned white-tiled Thompson's restaurant, one of a national chain. It was later to become famous in a Supreme Court decision on the "Thompson restaurant case," involving the seating of blacks in restaurants.

At Constitution Hall, the Daughters of the American Revolution banned blacks from the stage but allowed them in the audience. The National Theater, a few doors the other side of the *Post* building, allowed blacks to perform but not to sit in the audience.

I did cartoons on the DAR ladies when they held their annual conventions in Washington and passed resolutions expressing their fears about admitting refugees. I liked FDR's reminder, in addressing one of their conventions: "All of us are descended from immigrants."

In the early 1950s, the National Theater was being picketed for its segregation policies and *The Post* urged it to change. I had a cartoon ready to run on the subject when the editor asked me to hold it. The theater had agreed to end its policy if it could do so quietly without further confrontation or publicity. It made good on its promise, and theatergoers of whatever views never knew just when it happened.

But even after the early '50s, when segregation officially ended in the capital of the United States, the sentiment persisted among some members of Congress, who continued to make racial or ethnic slurs. Some from the South spoke of ''nigras'' in a way that made it difficult for listeners to know exactly how the word was spelled.

Not long ago a college student asked if I had ever drawn ''stereotype southern congressmen''—hoping that I had not. I explained that the ''Senator Claghorns'' of Congress were not stereotypes or made-up characters. There really were legislative bigots, and through safe seats and seniority quite a few held positions of power in Congress. It's a mark of progress that most of the southern congressmen of today are so different that a newer generation can hardly believe another kind ever existed.

Segregation in Washington was not only by race but by gender. Even the journalistic clubs had no women members, and generally not even women guests. The National Press Club, recognizing that its luncheon speakers made news, permitted women journalists to sit in a balcony. Ohboy!

Washington, D.C., a city where residents pay all taxes and where they can be drafted into the armed forces, had not even a glimmer of home rule. It had no vote for local or federal offices of any kind. It was run largely by city commissioners appointed by the president—and by Congress.

Now it elects local officials, but the president and Congress still can overrule actions of the city government, deciding even how the city spends its own tax revenues. These revenues come from one of the highest state or local income tax rates in the country—as well as from sales and property taxes. And while District residents also pay federal income taxes, they are denied full voting representation in Congress. The early American colonists had a stirring slogan about that kind of taxation.

In the 1940s, before air conditioning was widespread, Washington summers had such a sticky reputation that some governments listed it as a hardship post. Streetcars still operated, quietly and efficiently, among the best in the country. This convenient form of public transportation was later discontinued and the tracks eliminated at considerable expense. By the 1990s, with traffic gridlocks and energy and pollution problems, some cities were actually installing new trolley lines.

No barricades or concrete stanchions ringed the White House. The street between the White House and the Treasury building was open to auto and pedestrian traffic.

Since then, there has been more and more security for officials, if less for residents, who are aware of daily muggings and homicides.

The Secret Service and its functions have become vastly enlarged, not to say bureaucratically bloated. In its determination to protect Vice President Dan Quayle in 1992, these agents blocked off the entire Capitol plaza—until an outraged Speaker of the House Tom Foley sent them packing.

Foley told me of his own more direct experience with protection at a time when the president and vice president were both away. Since the Speaker is next in line for the presidency, a Secret Service delegation suddenly descended on him. They asked what kind of car he used to go to and from the Capitol. When Foley told them that he biked to work, they stared at each other with a wild surmise, visualizing a cycling squad of protective agents around the biking Speaker, making its way from Foley's home to the Capitol. He took them off the hook by acceding to their request that, until one of the two top executives came back, he ride in a car. When the president or vice president returned to the Capitol, the Secret Service left the Speaker as suddenly as they had come—without his bike to ride home.

Among other things different in post-war Washington was Watergate—not then a building, much less a scandal. It was a place on the riverbank where there was a good restaurant, and firmly moored in the river was a concert stand. On moonlit evenings canoeists would glide by, gently paddling their way between the musicians and the audience. Once when a canoe overturned, the couple in the water, anxious to avoid disturbing other music lovers, very softly called "help."

Under even more congressional rule than now, there were odd Washington regulations. One was a ban on vertical drinking. Drinks could be ordered and served at tables, but you could not even hold a glass in your hand while standing or walking. A waiter could move it for you from one table to another, where you could resume seated consumption. Perhaps Congress was trying to prevent the return of the old-fashioned foot-on-the-rail bar—or maybe these legislators felt that a sloshed slide from a seated position to the floor was less unseemly than falling flat on the face from the upright position. This restriction was later repealed.

With World-War-I–vintage temporary buildings lined up along sections of Constitution Avenue, a saying was that nothing was more permanent than a "tempo." Another saying was that Washington, D.C., combined all the charm of the North with the efficiency of the South.

Washington, D.C., whatever its faults—many of them national faults—was an exciting place to work. It still is. Trips to the Capitol were as good as going to baseball openers. And for a young cartoonist to see up close and sketch some of the figures he drew, and to think that they saw his work in the paper, was even more exciting. Unlike the situation at NEA in Cleveland, where the cartoons went to many papers but seldom appeared in that city, the work here was seen every day and the response was immediate. It was like watching the fellows on the bus looking at one of my first cartoons in Chicago. But here many of them were government officials.

Attending a White House Correspondents' Association dinner was an occasion, made more so by a senator who was sitting at the same table as some of us *Post* people. One of the big issues *The Post* had fought for editorially was civilian control of atomic energy, which this senator, Styles Bridges of New Hampshire, had strongly opposed. Like many long-settled issues, it may now seem amazing that it was once a burning question. But with the atom bomb still new and tension with the USSR increasing, the struggle between civilian and military control was vigorous. Eventually, civilian control won.

At the correspondents' dinner, Alfred Friendly, who had written many of *The Post*'s articles on the subject, asked Bridges if he thought *The Post* editorials or articles had made a significant difference in the outcome. Bridges nodded and, gesturing in my direction, said, "The cartoons." This was pretty heady stuff.

But I had learned a lesson from *Washington Post* editor Herbert Elliston shortly after I arrived at the paper. He took me along to a party where, as we were about to enter, a Cabinet member on the way out warmly greeted him with "Hello, Herbert." Elliston replied with an equally warm and friendly greeting, and almost in the same breath, he said to me, "I'm giving him hell tomorrow." Elliston felt that *The Post* should use all the advantage of being at the center of things in Washington, but being civil or even friendly with public officials did not interfere with his editorial judgment.

An early acquaintance was Martin Agronsky, then doing a radio program. Our views were generally similar, and we had in common the fact that during periods of political hysteria we both took losses, his on radio stations and mine in newspaper syndication. Like Elliston he was interested in talking with people of many views and we sometimes had dinner at Harvey's Restaurant, a favorite of many politicians.

In 1948, when President Truman seemed headed for certain defeat, we sat at a table with a sad J. Howard McGrath, then chairman of the Democratic National Committee. I ventured the suggestion that Truman should call a special session of Congress to enact his progressive domestic program. Then if Congress passed his proposals, he would be perceived as a "strong president," and if Congress failed to act, he could still take a strong stance against congressional obstructionists. McGrath thought about this and said, "It's a good idea but it wouldn't work."

Another time we chatted with J. Edgar Hoover, a Harvey's regular, and he explained that the reason for all the "raw material" in FBI files was that he felt the Bureau should not evaluate material. As he put it, "If you sent in a postcard about me, it would go into the file on me." This sounded good in theory, but much FBI raw material was leaked or passed along to others who used it to defame people. These things, as well as Hoover's racism, his reluctance to pursue "the mobs" and his use of FBI files to blackmail officials from presidents on down, had not yet been exposed.

Many years later I was getting a haircut in the Statler barbershop when Hoover sat down in an adjoining chair and much fuss was made over him. His conversation to the barber consisted of denunciations of "those fellows in the press" and the harm they were doing. There was an echo of Hoover, sometime after his death, when I secured an edited version of my FBI file under the Freedom of Information Act. Much of it was blanked out. One of Hoover's notations, which accompanied clippings on speeches I had made that agents had passed along to him, was, "I would not believe anything that fellow said."

102

Back on E Street, an office had been created for me when I signed on at *The Post*. I was later moved into a kind of broom closet and then from pillar to post—sometimes behind *Post* pillars. Finally, I got a little office that provided an excellent view of parades. When President Truman was inaugurated, friends came downtown to share this space and leaned out the open window—in that old building the windows actually opened—to shout greetings to people they knew in the parade cars. Truman smiled and waved as he passed by.

I was still there in early 1950 when the Corcoran Gallery of Art put on an exhibition of my cartoons that must have included a couple of hundred. The Corcoran made something of an event of it by having several prominent women serve tea to invited Cabinet members and congressmen. And director Herman Williams even sent out a courtesy invitation to the White House. To our surprise, President and Mrs. Truman accepted.

For their visit a special showing was arranged on a Sunday morning before the gallery opened for the day. I was up and about early for the occasion, too early for my usual Sunday brunch, so I decided to eat an apple. It was a mistake comparable to Adam's. After one bite, I needed no mirror to verify my tongue's discovery of the great dental chasm. The tooth that had sprung out while I was giving a talk in Chicago had found the perfect time to unleash itself again. With the help of a Washington dentist who hurried downtown to meet me at his office, the tooth was cemented back in place in time for me not only to be there with director Williams before President and Mrs. Truman arrived, but to greet them with a smile.

I wondered what their reaction might be to cartoons that were critical of Truman's administration or people in it. I needn't have worried. He would chuckle and call to his wife, "Bess, you have to see this one of Harry Vaughan." At one point, in front of a cartoon about some right-wingers, I made a comment about the politicians opposing him. Instead of saying something partisan, he made a philosophical and prophetic remark: "Well, one of these days the voters will change their minds and throw us all out and put others in."

The first time I went to a White House "social event" was when President Truman put on a reception and dance. A few of us from the office, with our dates, met for drinks at the home of a *Post* writer. Whether he was blasé about such functions or simply trying to be casual, he was in no hurry to go, and I felt unsophisticated about calling attention to the hour. Finally we took off for the White House. We were very late, the last to arrive, and with the dance in full swing. President and Mrs. Truman were by now seated in a little reception room off the East Room. But as we entered, they stood up and greeted us just as warmly as if we had arrived right on the dot and were their only guests.

I've thought it somewhat ironic that Truman, a "farm boy" who never went to college and was generally considered a rough-cut product of a Missouri political machine, was more of a gentleman than some of his successors who were better educated or came from prominent families. He would not stoop to the campaign tactics of some later supposedly more genteel candidates for the presidency.

Certainly he was a model ex-president. When he left office, he went home on a passenger train and refused to accept high-pay offers from private companies because "the presidency is not for sale."

It's often said that whatever we think of any current occupant at 1600 Pennsylvania Avenue, we should "respect the office." I feel that respect for the office should begin with the person who occupies it—or who campaigns to occupy it—and his respect should extend to the other branches of government too.

But the Big Name incidents are almost Cinderella stuff. The usual routine has always been working over a hot drawing board, hearing "Yer late" from engravers, and, at the old building where everything seemed to be held together by wire and tape, having occasional hassles with building supervisors and production people. We recall not only the little triumphs, but the sometimes more frequent little indignities.

The Post put out a "bulldog edition" to boost street sales and to mail out of town early. On those deadlines, I not only went down to the wire but frequently tripped over it. And the production manager, who used to stick his head in the door to complain, threatened that if the cartoon was not in sufficiently early, he would run it in halftone—like a photograph, with overall dots producing a gray effect, rather than as a "line cut," where the blacks and whites were etched sharply. Line cuts took longer.

The first cartoon on which he made good this threat was one about a gubernatorial election in Georgia in which Eugene Talmadge triumphed over the more progressive incumbent, Gov. Ellis Arnall. In this drawing of a youngster being taken back down Tobacco Road, the gray tone didn't look too bad—it even gave a kind of appropriate nightfall quality to the picture.

But with deadlines moved still earlier, the halftones appeared more frequently, sometimes with the cartoons only partly done. The drawings were given back to me to be finished for later editions. Since this first edition was the one that was mailed around the country, I began hearing from other cartoonists, who commented on this bold, innovative technique in which parts of the drawing were sketched in, parts shaded, and the entire cartoon given an unusual tone.

I hated those halftones. And eventually *The Post* early edition and I got on schedules that meshed. To this day, when I am unusually late, some engraver with a long memory will cry "Halftone!" The zinc cuts or metal engravings of the finished cartoons, made in those days of hot metal newspapering, were saved and used for later reprints. When a new engraver threw one away, I asked if he'd please save them. The next night he handed me the metal cut wrapped in the original cartoon, which he had carefully folded around it several times like wrapping paper.

There were other things to occupy me in spare time.

As the "staff cartoonist" on a paper that at the time did not have its own art department, I was frequently asked to draw special cartoons—aside from the published one—on the occasion of this or that employee who was retiring, getting married, hospitalized, returning or maybe having an anniversary.

Some requests came from employees I scarcely knew. One was from a fellow who did some sorting in the E Street mail room next to my office. He kept after me to draw a picture of him, and, as politely as possible, I kept explaining that I didn't have time. But one Saturday afternoon when I was at the office catching up on correspondence, he pointed out that now I was not making a deadline and this must be a right time. I told him I was not a rapid sketch-portrait artist, but he persisted. I said that for me to do a drawing of him would probably take about half an hour, to which he replied, "That's all right." So, deciding finally to get this over with, I gave in and asked him to sit down. He said, "You mean me sit here for half an hour while you draw me?'' I said, ''Yes.'' To this he replied with a touch of indignation, ''I can't do that—*I don't have that kind of time!*''

Another request was from some man I didn't even know in one of the mechanical departments, who told me his son was getting out of the Army and would be home for Christmas, and would I draw a picture of him for a big family Welcome Back? I had never seen his son and asked for pictures of the boy. He pulled out of his wallet a blurred black-and-white full-figure snapshot of the son, in which the small face was scarcely visible. But I was touched by the home-for-Christmas idea and agreed to do something in time for the event. As nearly as I could make out the face, I tried to reproduce it in large size in watercolors. Around the face I drew a green-holly-and-berry Christmas wreath and lettered Welcome Home, Joe. And I got it to the man in time for the big holiday return. He looked at it, said Okay, and then I heard no more about it. Sometime after Christmas had come and gone I saw him again and ventured a question on how the picture went. He said Okay—they had found a better photo of the boy's face and had it blown up to size, ''and we used that wreath you drew and pasted the photo over the picture you did of him and it looked all right. It was Okay.''

"YOU MEAN ME, HARRY?"

One of the first *Washington Post* cartoons
Jan. 5, 1946

OBBLIGATO ON THE MUSICAL SAW

March 8, 1946

"DON'T MIND ME—JUST GO RIGHT ON TALKING"

Feb. 5, 1947

THE SHOT HEARD ROUND THE IMMEDIATE VICINITY

April 21, 1949

BELL-RINGER

Feb. 4, 1948

108

12

Post *People*

In 1950 the still struggling *Washington Post* made a bold move to a new seven-story building, with new presses and *two* self-operating passenger elevators. Luxury! Here the editorial offices were all in a row, separated only by partial partitions that provided partial privacy. My office was located between Alan Barth's and Merlo Pusey's—Pusey being the associate editor and closest to the fully enclosed office of editor Herbert Elliston.

Elliston was a Yorkshireman who had served in the British army in World War I. Like Meyer, he was an internationalist, and when I first met him at Meyer's home to discuss working for *The Post,* I think it was my pre-war cartoons that had made them feel I was right for their editorial page.

He was a good and courageous editor. To me, one of Elliston's best moments came with the return of Gen. Douglas MacArthur, who had been fired by Truman. Emotions ran high, and adulatory MacArthur fans were lining the streets to welcome him—probably ready to throw rocks at *The Post*. But Elliston never wavered in asserting the importance of the civilian supremacy upheld with MacArthur's discharge.

When I took sketches to Elliston's office, I learned to put my favorite on top because he usually glanced up from his writing to look only at the first one and say, ''Fine.'' Completely unlike editors who thought cartoons should illustrate the editorials, he would sometimes look at the top sketch and say, ''This is fine, but we're running an editorial tomorrow saying the same thing. Would you mind drawing up one of the other ones?''

I generally tried out sketches on people in the newsroom, as I still do, and showed them also to editorial colleague Alan Barth. Barth wrote clearly and forcefully. He was responsible for some of *The Post*'s finest editorials and for much of its reputation as a champion of civil liberties and civil rights. In advocating gun controls, he once wrote 77 consecutive daily editorials on the subject. A man of quiet humor, Barth used to tell me to remember that one word was worth a thousand pictures.

Pusey, unlike Elliston, had been at *The Post* when Meyer bought it. He also wrote a Pulitzer Prize–winning biography of Charles Evans Hughes.

About 1952, *The Post,* with promotional pride and advertising space to spare, ran a full-page ad featuring a photograph of the first books by Pusey, Barth and me—three published authors on its editorial staff!

Pusey was a big Eisenhower fan. ''Fan'' is probably not the right word for this rather straitlaced man whose support might better be described as earnest and determined. When Elliston was away, Pusey occupied his office and I showed my sketches to him. If old Mr. Macmillan on the *Chicago News* had seemed like an unresponsive replacement for an editor, he was a real cartoon buff compared to Pusey. On one occasion, when a government official had been fired— probably during the loyalty-security witch-hunting period—I did a sketch that centered around his being kicked out. Pusey looked at it and said pointedly that nobody had actually *kicked* anyone—all they had done was demand this man's resignation.

Someone else who came with the paper when Meyer bought it was sports editor and columnist Shirley Povich, who remained one of the paper's biggest attractions. Because of his name, he received some mail addressed to Miss Shirley Povich and was included in a who's who of prominent women. He received a questionnaire from an organization compiling items on professional women and solemnly filled it out. When he came to a question about how respondent gets along with male colleagues, he wrote, "I just act like one of the boys."

After noting some less than brilliant sports performance, Shirley recalled a baseball coach's studied evaluation of one player: "He cannot field. However, neither can he hit."

A favorite Povich recollection is of the Redskins football game played in Washington on the day of Pearl Harbor. From time to time the loudspeaker would summon General So-and-So or Admiral Such-and-Such to report at once. But, according to Povich, Redskin owner George Marshall did not announce the actual invasion for fear it would divert attention from the game.

Marshall long refused to include any black players on the team. And Povich wrote a piece in which he described the Redskin colors as burgundy, gold and Caucasian.

It's hard to avoid "Redskin fever" when the team is hot. When they won a Super Bowl, I walked the few blocks to the Georgetown area where the biggest celebration filled the streets. Empty buses were stalled in a scene recalling the end of World War II.

The details and plays of the game are beyond this occasional TV watcher, who still thinks a noseguard is something that's worn when swimming and who focuses only on which direction the ball is going. But the Redskins are the common conversational currency of the District of Columbia. A cab driver can usually be diverted from voicing occupational grievances by asking him, "How about those 'Skins?"

In a season when quarterback Sonny Jurgensen was going strong, I was riding with an elderly and polite cab driver who had tuned in to a game. As we discussed great quarterbacks, I ventured that Sonny Jurgensen might be the best. With the utmost courtesy, the driver responded in a gentle voice, "If I may say so, sir, in my humble opinion Mr. Jurgensen cannot carry the jockey strap of Mr. Johnny Unitas."

In those early days on *The Post,* from time to time I would hear from Mr. Meyer. He did not offer ideas, although it was clear that he sometimes disagreed with the cartoons. Once or twice when I drew a cartoon on the powerful post-war dollar or something of that sort, this former banker and former governor of the Fed would look in to say, "Well, I see you're now an expert on international finance. You must tell me about it sometime."

Meyer was gung ho for *The Post* to succeed, and was always working to promote it. On his cab rides he would ask the drivers what paper they read and try to sell them subscriptions to the *Post*. He was not the first newspaper owner to plug his paper in that way. I remember reading that *New York Tribune* publisher Horace Greeley, riding on a streetcar, noticed the man next to him reading the *New York World*. Greeley asked if he ever bought the *Tribune*. "Yes," the man replied, "I keep that in the outhouse to wipe my ass." To which Greeley replied, "Keep it up, keep it up, and after a while you will have more brains in your ass than you have in your head." Meyer probably wouldn't have said that, but he was competitive on behalf of his paper. Once when the publisher of the *Washington Evening Star* mentioned that he had trouble getting to sleep nights, Meyer suggested that he try reading the *Star* in bed.

A rather flustered writer on *The Post* once told me she had just come up the elevator with Mr. Meyer. Wanting to say something and not knowing quite what, she heard herself chirping, "Fancy meeting you here." Meyer turned to her and replied, "Why shouldn't I be here? I own the place." At that point she would not have minded if the elevator had dropped down the shaft.

Meyer's remarks were generally delivered with a twinkle in the eye. In 1954, just after completing arrangements to acquire the competing *Washington Times-Herald,* he stopped by *The Post* cafeteria but found at the checkout counter that he had no money with him. He borrowed a dollar from an employee, explaining, "I don't have any change—I just bought a paper."

His buying that paper enabled me to buy some souvenir reminders of my days in Chicago. When *Times-Herald* furnishings were offered for sale to *Post* employees, I picked up a large tea table and cabinet (complete with world atlas) that had graced the Washington office of Col. Robert R. McCormick, publisher of the *Chicago Tribune* and bête noire of New Dealers and internationalists. I still have them.

The Meyers often invited me to dinner, and occasionally to join them in their box at concerts. They had some fine paintings, many of

112

impressionists whose works they liked before the artists achieved great fame. And musical friends like Rudolf Serkin sometimes entertained in their home. At one concert, we heard a piano recital by Sviatoslav Richter. An unfortunate side effect of that experience is that ever since, when there is news of earthquake tremors and mentions of the Richter scale, I always think of someone doing practice runs on the piano.

Except for occasional concerts, the music I went to hear in Washington was Charlie Byrd on the guitar at a local bistro and sometimes at Helga Sandburg's house. Despite the fact that my parents played the records of Caruso and Galli-Curci on the early Victrola and took us to see some performances, I never became an opera buff.

Trying to bridge gaps in my music appreciation, I asked *The Post*'s music critic, Paul Hume, to recommend some records. A few days later he presented me with a long list, which he had carefully selected to provide not only a range of pieces but the exact catalogue numbers of what he regarded as the best renditions available. I purchased all of them and got a great deal of pleasure from them.

One morning I was walking along an office hall when he came striding briskly from the other direction, opening his mail as he went. As he read one letter, he stopped and looked at it with astonishment. "Look at this," he said, and asked what I thought. It was a letter from President Truman blasting Paul's review that had panned daughter Margaret Truman's singing performance. He asked if I thought this could be real, and I suggested we take it to our resident authority on the president—White House correspondent Eddie Folliard. Paul showed the letter to Eddie, who read it and smiled. "That's him, all right," said Eddie.

In doing his stories, Folliard said he acted on the assumption that the reader needed to be told—a good point for reporters who forget that the reader may not be thoroughly familiar with the subject in which the writer has been submerged.

Eddie served a term as president of the longtime newspaperman's organization, the Gridiron Club, and at one of its annual dinners he managed to bring together Richard Nixon and Harry Truman. Until then Truman would not speak to Nixon and might not even have attended a party where he knew Nixon would be present. Eddie saw to it that they met. Nixon seized the occasion to get a bourbon and branch water that he handed to Truman, who thanked him. I think Eddie was quite proud of his role in this, which I regarded as a dubious achievement.

Before becoming a White House correspondent, Eddie had been a staff reporter. He was also a reformed alcoholic who finally decided, as he said, that "the stuff was poison to me" and gave up drinking completely. But he told me a story of his drinking period, when he interviewed an aging Andrew Mellon.

After a bad night Eddie had the shakes, but he was able to carry on with his work. He sat across from Mr. Mellon, described by Eddie as being palsied. When the somewhat trembling Mr. Mellon took a cigar from his humidor and put it to his mouth, Eddie managed to strike a match that he advanced with unsteady hand as he and Mellon leaned toward each other. Cigar and match kept moving and shaking but never quite meeting. Finally Mellon withdrew his cigar and rang sharply for a butler to light it. It must have been a scene worthy of some great comic team.

Ferdinand Kuhn, an early *Post* foreign correspondent, told of a different type of interview with an elderly statesman. This was Mohammed Mossadegh, prime minister of Iran, who was later ousted in the CIA-promoted pro-Shah military coup. Ferdie began his interview with a few softball questions to the prime minister and then proceeded to the nitty-gritty ones. At that point the wily old politician said, "My strength waxes and my strength wanes. Now it is waning. Good day." End of interview.

About a week after I joined *The Post* in 1946, Meyer's son-in-law, Philip Graham, came on as associate publisher. And when Meyer accepted the position of president of the World Bank, Graham became publisher. He was a hard-charging but completely charming man, whose approach to the job was quite different from Meyer's. He was active in editorial decisions and, when he wanted to make sure the viewpoint was exactly to his liking, wrote editorials himself. He also had close relationships with politicians, and fit in well with big wheels and wheeler-dealers. Graham would sometimes make a comment—pro, con or joking—about a cartoon, but, like Meyer, made no suggestions.

After we had both been at *The Post* awhile, he asked me to go to the

114

Supreme Court with him for lunch with Felix Frankfurter, a justice Phil once clerked for. During the conversation in Frankfurter's chambers, a matter of my work situation came up. I was still on the seven-day-a-week schedule begun with Mr. Meyer. It was a demanding one that, among other things, made it difficult for me to get away for once-a-month weekends with family in Chicago without getting there D.O.A. And I had been chafing under this routine. Phil put it to Frankfurter, who rendered a decision that was certainly agreeable to me. He said, "There must be leisure for ideas to stroll into the mind." This phrase might have been his or a quotation from some source I was not familiar with, but I liked it. Graham finally conceded that a six-day schedule was enough and that I was entitled to a day of rest.

But life with Phil was certainly not all work schedules or politics. He laughed easily, liked to kid people and loved to come up with a good story.

On a late-in-November day, I ran into him just after he'd had a visit from Walter Winchell. The W.W. column did not run in *The Post,* but on visits to Washington, Winchell sometimes dropped in on Graham. Phil couldn't wait to share an item about the gossip columnist himself, who, Phil explained, had been carrying on an extramarital affair. He said that a weary Winchell had asked him, "Do you know what's the worst thing about it? It's not the sex part, it's not the little deceptions and the keeping track of the schedules—it's the *two Thanksgiving dinners.*" Phil broke up over the idea of this man eating his way through a big Thanksgiving dinner with his wife, then visiting his paramour to find that she had worked to prepare for him a really sumptuous holiday dinner with all the trimmings.

Graham brought in as executive editor J. Russell Wiggins, who had been editor of a Minnesota paper. Elliston, as editor, had confined himself to the editorial page, while managing editors handled the news. Editorial and news functions have been divided at *The Post* and Wiggins was the only executive editor who covered both fields. A Jefferson scholar, he had in common with Elliston a great appetite for books and articles of all kinds.

They were two of the best-read people I ever knew. The fact that neither had completed formal education may have accounted for that. They were always learning, perhaps always "catching up" with graduates whose educations sometimes drop off after the receiving of a diploma.

Wiggins at one point determined that new staff members should be college graduates. I told him that if I were now applying for a position, I'd probably have to work on a half-time basis, since I left college near the end of my second year. He laughed and said that he'd have to rule himself out entirely—he hadn't been to college at all. I think the employment policy was later rescinded, but with an increasing number of college graduates even working as copy aides, it may have become moot.

The Post had a good newsroom staff, and one of its best reporters, Murrey Marder, was sent to Europe, where he became *The Washington Post*'s one-man foreign service. One of the newsroom people I sometimes asked to look at sketches was a knowledgeable young reporter who had done excellent investigative work on a New Hampshire newspaper—Ben Bradlee.

Just outside my office I once heard a shouting match between city editor Ben Gilbert and an apparently headstrong young reporter, Carl Bernstein, which sounded as if it might end with a separation from the paper. Fortunately it didn't.

Even closer to my office was a reporter who wrote engaging pieces that he sometimes illustrated. I thought the articles by this fellow, Tom Wolfe, were very good, but I was particularly impressed by his drawings and hoped he would do more of them. Then he went to New York, and I saw no more of his artwork. But in late 1992, I read that the National Cartoonists Society was giving him its ACE (Amateur Cartoonist Extraordinary) award. I was glad to know that even with those white suits he had taken to wearing, he must still be dipping into the drawing ink at times.

13

After Hours

After New York, Washington turned out to be a fairly turn-in-early city. Most of the action was at cocktail parties and dinners. And without being what anyone would describe as a party animal, I found that the Washington job provided more opportunities to hit up the hors d'oeuvres than the Army did.

On one occasion, Mary Lasker invited me to a cocktail party at her house. I was proud of myself for having finished work early enough to make it. Then I found I had lost the address she had given me, but was soon relieved to find it in the phone book and got there on time. The bar was neatly set up, and a man, perhaps a houseguest, offered me a drink. Shortly after, his wife came downstairs and joined in the conversation, and I supposed our hostess would soon follow. But as the conversation went on—and lagged a little—and she failed to appear, I noticed that other guests had not yet arrived either. Finally, I asked about our hostess, and what had been a mystery to the couple was resolved.

Sometime before they had swapped houses with Mrs. Lasker—

perhaps the kind of thing that could happen only in Washington. They were indeed having a cocktail party that night—but scheduled a little later—and had spent a good deal of time trying in a polite way to figure out who the hell I was and which of them had invited me to their party. They certainly did know her new address, which was their old one, and I got there only a little late.

Many of the most enjoyable parties were given by Alan Barth and his wife, Adrienne. Along with media people, friends of theirs like Fredric March, Melvyn Douglas or Leonard Bernstein sometimes turned up. There were also such legal lights as (Thurman) Arnold, (Abe) Fortas and (Paul) Porter, of the firm of the same name; or Judges Skelly Wright, Henry Edgerton and David Bazelon. Most often there were Joe Rauh and his wife, Olie.

An outstanding lawyer, Rauh successfully fought many pro bono civil liberties cases. And he was sought out by people like Lillian Hellman and Arthur Miller when these playwrights were summoned by the House Committee on Un-American Activities.

During Miller's appearance in Washington, his wife, Marilyn Monroe, stayed at the Rauhs' home. At the time, one of Rauh's young sons was asked for a comment on this houseguest. He said, "Well, it's not exactly like having your brother around."

Another recollection of the M.M. houseguest period came many years later at a 1991 birthday party for Rauh, just after the Persian Gulf War. It seems that at the Rauh dinner table, Miss Monroe had murmured a request for a glass of water. Olie Rauh watched husband Joe and son Michael streak toward the kitchen "like a Patriot missile after a Scud." She had never seen such speed before. Many of us who were always happy to visit the Rauhs would have been even happier if we'd been invited to their home for dinner during that period.

My own entertaining has been extremely limited, partly because anything beyond visits from a few close friends would involve straightening up the house, which might take weeks of effort. But in a sparsely furnished apartment in post-war Washington, where, as the saying went, anyone with a bottle and a box of crackers could throw a party, I put on a few.

A small rotating poker group developed, which included Albert Z.

Carr (author and former Truman administration member) and his wife, Anne; Ed Harris (correspondent for the *St. Louis Post-Dispatch*) and his wife, Miriam; and Jim Newman (a brilliant man who had been counsel to the Committee on Atomic Energy) and his wife, Ruth. Newman also wrote one of the best-selling though not necessarily best-read books of the time, a history of mathematics. We took turns at providing drinks, sandwiches and poker chips. New marvels of the later '40s were my powerful window-unit air conditioner, which visitors sat around, much as they might at a winter fireplace; and Ed Harris's tiny television set, which some of us scorned. He predicted that within a year we'd all have them, and he was right.

The Harrises loved the outdoors and bought a farm near Washington. Later, when Ed left to take an assignment as a Hollywood reporter, I took a trip with them to Yosemite, where we had nearby cabins. We tried what the park brochures listed as numbered "walking tours." At the end of them, the Harris kids ran on ahead followed by Miriam, while Ed and I brought up a distant and dragging rear. After we returned from one of these tours, a neighboring cabin occupant asked what we had been doing that day. Ed replied, "Today we took Death March Number 4."

Two grandes dames of the Washington political scene (as distinguished from glitz hostesses) were Florence (Daisy) Harriman, who had been U.S. minister to Norway under Franklin Roosevelt; and Cornelia (Leila) Pinchot, widow of Pennsylvania governor and Theodore Roosevelt colleague Gifford Pinchot. Both were early and prominent advocates for the rights of women and children.

Mrs. Harriman's Sunday dinners were organized, with guests seated at tables around the room in such a way that when she opened the evening to after-dinner talk, each of us could see everyone else and take part in general discussion. I mostly listened unless called on.

Mrs. Pinchot's dinners were likely to be informal buffets and not held on any particular evening. Guests often included Supreme Court Justices William O. Douglas or Hugo Black.

On one occasion Mrs. Black told me how her husband, as a Mississippi judge, came to run for the U.S. Senate. In his speeches around the state he kept mentioning that many people were asking him to run for the Senate, but he didn't know if he should. She said that one night as they were lying in bed about to go to sleep, she asked him, "Hugo, who are all these people who keep wanting you to run for the U.S. Senate?" And he said, very quietly, "me."

Black once explained that you had to look for people's real motives—not what they said, or even what they might convince themselves of, but the reasons behind the reasons. I'm not sure how he divined these things, but it struck a responsive chord with me. I have always wished that reporters would not shy away from the simple words "he said," instead of writing of some politician that "he thinks," "he believes," "he feels." Most of the time all we know for sure is what *he said.*

Black was one of the most ardent defenders of the First Amendment, but once in a small group he exercised his own right to comment on the press. He said, with heavy irony, that it was wonderful how editorial writers knew everything about every subject and how every situation should be dealt with. Perhaps this came after reading a newspaper opinion critical of a Court opinion.

A woman who parlayed family funds and a flair for publicity into acceptance as a Washington hostess was Gwen Cafritz. A small outdoor afternoon party at her house was nothing exceptional and wouldn't have been memorable except for a postscript. Afterward she let it be known through a column item that she had invited Eric Sevareid and me because she wanted us to see an actual Washington social party. Another columnist had fun with this. He wrote about how nice it was of her to invite a couple of underprivileged boys who otherwise wouldn't get to see upper-class life. And he added that it must be hard for Sevareid to get around anyhow, weighed down as he was with pockets full of money from his broadcasting contracts and royalties on his best-selling book.

Memorable in a different way was a small dinner at the home of Sen. Brien McMahon of Connecticut. I think the only other guest was William C. Bullitt, Roosevelt's first ambassador to the Soviet Union, who had become a complete Russophobe. He spent most of the evening assailing *The Washington Post* as being practically pro-communist and declared that every American should belong to what he called the B.R.N. Club—Bomb Russia Now. At this dinner we certainly made a strange couple.

At a couple of parties during the '40s, I ran into a pleasant, offbeat politician, Glen Taylor. He had made the jump from "singing cowboy" to U.S. senator from Idaho, and I asked how he had done it. He explained that in a state with so small a population, he had made it his aim to meet every possible voter. He and a candidate for governor had driven all over the state in a jalopy, and he'd pumped every hand he could, saying, "I'm-Glen-Taylor-running-for-U.S.-Senate-and-I'll-appreciate-it-if-you'll-vote-for-me."

What was most interesting was his comment on his traveling companion. "Not a good campaigner," said Taylor. "When we'd stop in a town, I'd jump out and go all up and down the street shaking hands. And when I'd get back to the car, he'd still be talking to the first person he'd met. Worse than that," sighed Taylor, "they had talked long enough that they had found something they *disagreed* on."

A variation on this chatting-it-up theme was voiced later by Walt Kelly, creator of "Pogo." At the national editors' conventions, held annually in Washington, the Saturday night windup was a big blast put on by Bob Hall of the Hall Syndicate, which handled Walt's cartoons and mine. Bob would ask us to stand in a receiving line as editors passed through to the main room where there was drinking, dancing and entertainment.

Walt regarded this as a no-win situation. He reasoned that people who liked your work didn't need to meet you. And there was always the chance that some editor—particularly at a stage when he might be well lacquered—would get around to mentioning something on which he disagreed with you. My own observation over years of such conventions is that no editor is more lavish with praise about your work than one who has just canceled it.

Instead of trying to put on some kind of dinner or party of my own, I decided one year to take a table at an annual press dinner. I invited some old friends and a few people who had recently entertained me. These included the ambassador of Ireland, Bill Fay; political columnist Bill Shannon (author of *The American Irish* and years later our ambassador to Ireland); and one or two more who, through no particular plan, gave our table a distinctly Hibernian tilt.

After dinner we sat back for the entertainment, which I had assured them was generally good. But this time there was no Bob Hope or Victor Borge or Danny Kaye. Instead, there were a couple of comedians whose distinction seemed to be that they had an endless repertoire of bad Irish jokes. These caused even less mirth at our table than at the others. I slid down in my chair a little and then took to diverting my guests from the show by asking: Would anyone care for a drink? A shotgun? A rope? A stick of dynamite?

When it was mercifully over, my guests politely found it an interesting evening, a nice dinner. I might have done better if I'd just asked them over to my messy apartment for a drink and turned on the TV.

One of the best and most original hosts in Washington was painter and writer Hugh Troy. His real mission in life was inventing and performing the creative practical jokes that made him a legend. It was Troy and a couple of friends in working clothes who put up a "men working" sign on a busy New York street, which they proceeded to dig up. Then they took their signs and departed, leaving a large hole in the thoroughfare. It was Troy also who bought a park-type bench, sneaked it into a park at night and in the morning started to carry it off. When stopped by a policeman, he asserted that the bench was his, and when taken before a judge, produced the bill of sale.

During a party at his house, I noticed among the pictures on one wall a small and unusual oil painting. It depicted the inside of a submarine with what appeared to be the pope looking through the periscope. This was exactly what it was. Troy explained that he had done this painting to illustrate what was supposed to have happened if Catholic Al Smith had been elected president.

I was not present, but I heard about the party he put on for his British friend Stephen Potter, author of the book *Gamesmanship,* when this humorist visited Troy at his home in Washington. Each guest brought a Potter book for him to sign—all of them by other writers named Potter. I understand that Troy also combed all the agencies in the area to get a butler named Potter, so that throughout the evening he could every once in a while bellow, "POTTER!," to serve something or other—each time causing the guest of honor to jump an inch or two into the air.

On another occasion with an author/houseguest, he supplied each person at the party with a copy of the author's book, which they asked him to sign. And when the party guests took their departure, all the books were noticeably left behind.

There wasn't anybody who entertained the way Hugh Troy did.

14

New Item

There is a point at which people or products are sometimes "discovered," even though they may be no different than they've been all along. A person or an object, whether a backgammon game, a hula hoop, a crusading Nader, a Ninja turtle, a pet rock or a rock performer, becomes some kind of Hot Item and a momentum develops. A story is told about a doorman at a French hotel, resplendent in a gold braided uniform with medals on his chest. A resident notices one day that the medals are authentic and asks about them. The doorman replies, "The first was pinned on me by mistake; the rest followed naturally."

Recognition, whether deserved or not, tends to multiply according to the law of demand and demand, which I have just made up. That is, anything in demand becomes more so when other people realize it's in demand. This may last until the next New Item.

All that is to say that during the early 1950s I seemed to have become some kind of discover*ee* or reached a state of Itemhood that resulted in various offers coming my way, as well as some awards that I hoped did not follow naturally. The offers included one from a man who wanted to incorporate characters from my cartoons into neckties. I couldn't quite visualize people sporting neckwear that featured an atom bomb character or an unflattering caricature of some congressman—and let that golden opportunity pass.

Another seemingly improbable idea came from some high officials of the American Newspaper Guild, who asked me to run for president of that organization. They told me their choice would be sure of election. The prospect of filling the office originally held by Heywood Broun was exciting, but aside from the time-consuming nature of such a position—even supposing I could have it—I had other reservations. I wasn't sure that I would make a very good union leader since I was, for one thing, disturbed by the practice of featherbedding—payment to non-working employees, sanctioned by negotiations between employers and unions. To my surprise, the guild leaders said they understood this view, that it was fair, and that it would make no difference in their support. Fine. But if the position didn't take a lot of time I'd be something of a figurehead, and if it meant real involvement, it would cut into the daily work. So I declined with thanks.

But the possibility of being a candidate for that kind of thing stirred the juices. It is not hard to see how politicians become convinced that they must be "the people's choice." It's also illustrative of what can be suggested when a person comes to be regarded as a Current Thing.

More in line with the regular work were offers from other newspapers. One of these was the *New York Post*, at that time a tabloid with excellent editorials and columns. The *New York Post* ran the cartoons daily and often phoned to ask that I wire a copy of whatever I was working on that day. This resulted in my sometimes taking evening trips to the Associated Press offices to get off a print. I was glad that they were so eager for the work, but the prospect of moving from Washington to New York, and to a paper already using the cartoons full time, seemed no gain except in terms of additional income.

Then a couple of years later the same paper made another offer that was a real grabber. Owner and publisher Dorothy Schiff asked me to come to New York to discuss a new proposal. She offered to make me co-editor of the *New York Post*—a position I would share with current editor James A. Wechsler, who joined us at this meeting. The three of us batted the idea around, and the answer to my inquiries about duties and responsibilities was a write-your-own-ticket scenario. I could do whatever I pleased—draw as many or as few cartoons as I felt like doing, write whatever editorials I wanted, make assignments for articles and investigative reporting—anything and everything. After our lunch, I dropped by Wechsler's office to make sure I knew how he felt about it. He strongly urged that I come aboard.

To understand the appeal of such an offer, you have to remember there were still many papers that regarded the cartoon as an editorial illustration. And while that was not the case at *The Washington Post,* I was at that time still showing sketches to an editor. And even though I didn't submit anything I didn't want to draw, there is a difference between making policy for others and sometimes coping with other people's policies. But in the end what I really wanted was to continue living in Washington, and to keep on doing a daily cartoon, with whatever talks and writings could be fitted in.

Among other cartoon spots that were of interest was one that came when famous cartoonist Daniel Fitzpatrick was getting ready to retire from the *St. Louis Post-Dispatch.* That newspaper had a strong and well-respected editorial page, and the cartoon occupied a space that looked like about a quarter of that page. I felt complimented when Joseph Pulitzer, a man I regarded highly, tendered that job over lunch in his hotel room. After an overnight think, I came up with a suggestion that he take on Bill Mauldin, who at the time was out of cartooning altogether.

A sugar plum vision that danced briefly in my head came courtesy of the director of the Nieman Foundation at Harvard. He let me know that I would be welcomed as a Nieman fellow. The lucky recipient gets a year at Cambridge to sit in on classes if he likes, or write, think or use the time however he chooses. This had a special appeal to a person who had left college midway to begin cartooning. But now it was the same choice—the daily cartoon or something else, like college revisited. The daily schedule won out again.

Much closer to home was the prospect of becoming a member of an Important Club.

I visited occasionally with Lowell Mellett, former editor of the *Washington News,* who did his entertaining at the Cosmos Club. When he asked one evening if I would like to become a member, I was delighted at the prospect of joining this group of what I had heard described as mental heavyweights.

What Lowell had not bothered to mention at the time was that in the Fearful Fifties this club, like the nation at large, was riven by conflicts over political views and patriotism. He later told me that even in this group, with its reputed high intellectual standards, some of the Great Minds were deeply concerned about keeping out what they considered too liberal or subversive members—and even ferreted out "wrong" books from the club library. So I was, inadvertently, a sort of test case—a membership guinea pig. But after considerable delay, I was approved.

Most "exclusive" organizations appear more august from the outside than from within. I sat through a long meeting to vote on admitting the first black member—and later spent a couple more long evenings to vote on the admission of women (who at one time couldn't even enter through the front door as guests). These meetings added up to most of the time I spent in a club I seldom used. And after the second overwhelming vote against women, I dropped my membership. That policy has long since changed; and I sometimes get back to this club's congenial surroundings as the guest of some woman member.

But during that clubman period, something else beckoned—the wonderful world of television. Robert M. Hutchins, former chancellor of the University of Chicago, headed The Fund For The Republic, a non-profit organization largely devoted to preserving American liberties during those witch-hunting days. He proposed a weekly 15-minute television program in which I would appear in living black and white, saying whatever I wanted to say and illustrating the talks with cartoons I had done. Would I do it? You betcha!

In charge of production for this program was Joseph Wershba of CBS, who worked with Ed Murrow and later produced programs for "60 Minutes." We had a good time turning out the pilot films, shot in my apartment. He and the Fund people were enthusiastic about the trial runs. And as the starting date approached, I prepared a script, selected cartoons and did a mental countdown to shooting time.

What followed was a strange silence. I heard nothing from Hutchins or his associates. Shortly before the program was to begin, a lawyer representing the Fund called. He took me to dinner, where he explained that the program had been canceled. One of the right-wing congressmen of the time—I think Francis Walter—had threatened to end the Fund's tax-exempt status if I went on. Since I was supposed to be free to express my opinions—and since any opinion could be interpreted as an attempt to "influence legislation"—the Fund decided not to chance a threat to its tax status. So it was reported that we had mutually agreed to cancel the program—a disappointment to me and to Wershba, by this time a good friend, who had also been looking forward to doing the show.

A couple of years later, Fred Friendly of CBS phoned to recruit me for a one-time-only TV program on the filibuster—then being used mostly by anti–civil rights senators. Would I debate the issue with Sen. James O. Eastland of Mississippi, a legislator who opposed civil rights and strongly supported the filibuster? This program was not to be shot live but to be taped and edited. Friendly explained that I needn't worry about fighting for time because the senator and I could both add to our remarks at the end of the taping and our arguments would be spliced in to make a coherent whole. I agreed to do the debate and spent several evenings with friends more familiar than I with parliamentary procedure. They helped me bone up on the history and precedents involved in Rule 22—the provision for "extended debate" on which the filibuster was based. Briefly, my position was that *at some time* the Senate should be permitted to vote on a measure.

The "debate" itself was conducted in separate studios, mine in Washington and Eastland's in Mississippi, while cameras in both places recorded the discussions.

Since the program was to be edited later, I didn't mind the senator's interruptions or his sometimes rambling discourse, knowing that I could make all the points I wanted to, regardless of sequence. At the conclusion, friends in the studio were ecstatic. "You beat him!" they told me. "You won."

When the show finally aired, I learned about the perils of edited programs. Much of what I had said seemed to have ended up on the cutting room floor. My "extended remarks" were not included. And in the edited program I appeared to be making futile attempts to interrupt the senator, while the announcer commented that here was a debate on the filibuster in which the senator was conducting another successful filibuster.

A different sort of question about a filibuster was answered for me later in a conversation with another senator, Wayne Morse, an Independent from Oregon. He became a current record holder in the nonstop speech department after twenty-two hours and twenty-six minutes of talking. What I wanted to know was this: What about going to the bathroom? Was it true that a tube-and-bottle "motorman's helper" was used? It was not. Morse said that the energy consumed in his record speechmaking left him, if not dehydrated, at least able to hold the floor without any problem of holding his water. Well, it was a question I had heard batted around and he answered it.

The Senate later made some minor modification in the filibuster rule—and finally acceded to letting TV cameras into the chamber.

In television, anything can happen or not happen. Howard K. Smith, excellent correspondent for ABC News, wanted to do an interview in which he would use quite a few cartoons assembled by me. But higher authority intervened with a decision that such a program would not show proper "balance." The head of ABC then was James Hagerty, who, as President Eisenhower's press secretary, had complained about me to the publisher of *The Washington Post*. Hagerty was also among the very few people in public life who could not leave his political prejudices at the door when I ran into him once at an embassy party. Nevertheless, Howard Smith later managed to put together a program on which I appeared with a sufficient variety of commentators to pass muster with the main office.

In addition to the television "feature pieces" and discussions, booktour shows have been interesting—not only because people say, Hey, they have seen you right there on TV, but because of people you sometimes meet on the programs themselves.

Where else could I have met somebody like Metropolitan Opera director Rudolf Bing on one show and, shortly after, Jimmy Hoffa on another? I had done highly uncomplimentary drawings of this Teamster Union boss, and when a program host asked Hoffa if he was acquainted with my work, Hoffa replied, "Oh, yeah—those cartoons can kill ya." But whatever the cartoons did to his public standing, they were not responsible for his permanent disappearance.

At a broadcasting station in another city I ran into famous folk singer and war protester Pete Seeger. His sponsor provided him with a limousine, while my publisher left me to make my way around in cabs. So

Seeger gave me a ride back to my hotel. I enjoyed talking with him and we exchanged anecdotes on the way. How else but through The Miracle Of Television could a person say: Pete Seeger gave me a lift in his limousine?

It was through TV also that I ran into former Reagan Chief of Staff Don Regan—at a broadcasting truck near the White House—where, he explained, we were both now unwelcome.

Unlike busy network anchors who must spend time traveling around the world wearing trench coats in exotic or dangerous places, most of us spend a lot more time watching television than appearing on it.

My favorite TV recollection is of returning to a hotel room after taping some program. With the show scheduled to come on shortly, I turned on the TV—but nothing happened. I phoned the hotel desk and explained the problem. They assured me that their television man would be up right away. Soon "the TV man" knocked on the door. He asked what the problem was and I told him the set wasn't working. He tried it himself—and sure enough it was not. Then he gave the TV console a good kick. It instantly sprang to life, working perfectly on all channels.

The wonders of early television!

15

American Isms

The House Committee on Un-American Activities, which I had cartooned in its earliest days in the '30s, did not improve with age. And the Cold War, with alarm about communist expansion abroad, produced a kind of cold fusion generating intense heat at home. The committee hearings, under the chairmanship of J. Parnell Thomas, were like something out of *Alice's Adventures in Wonderland*. Off with their heads! Sentence first, trial afterward.

Thomas must have been a great publicity lover, because he asked for copies of cartoons about him, which I did not send. The managing editor of *The Post*, Alexander F. (Casey) Jones, was a neighbor of this congressman and kept asking me to send on something just to get Thomas off his back. But the last straw came when Thomas became ill and was taken to the hospital. "For God's sake," said Casey, "please send that guy a drawing. As they were putting him in the ambulance, he said, 'Don't . . . forget . . . tell . . . Herb . . . to . . . send . . . cartoon.' " Thomas survived his illness, as well as the fact that I never sent him anything. And this man who conducted so many "trials" in his committee room later went to trial himself on charges of taking kickbacks from employees, and did time in the penitentiary.

Contributing to his fall, as I heard it from a reporter, was a cold radiator. He had apparently been carrying on an affair with a woman on his staff, and when he did not come home one night and the hour grew late, his wife went to the place where the employee lived and found Thomas's car parked there. Perhaps they had been working late. Perhaps he had just arrived and was seeing the employee to her door. Thomas's wife put her hand on the car's radiator. It had turned cold, and so did she. Her knowledge of Thomas's illegal activities supposedly started him on the way to prison. His behavior as committee chairman was probably much worse than his acceptance of kickbacks. But the money matters were what did him in.

In 1947, Thomas was joined on the committee by a newcomer to Congress who had also found campaigning against "un-Americanism" useful—Richard M. Nixon. One of the best-remembered features of his campaign against Rep. Jerry Voorhis (D-Calif.) was the large number of anonymous phone calls to voters telling them that "Jerry Voorhis is a Communist." The Nixon technique worked. And his political career might have been summed up in remarks after that election. He told a Voorhis aide, "Of course I knew Jerry Voorhis wasn't a Communist. . . . But I had to win. That's the thing you don't understand. The important thing is to win."

Propelled by the committee's investigation of Alger Hiss, who later was convicted of perjury, Nixon ran for the Senate in 1950 against Rep. Helen Gahagan Douglas. This campaign featured a "pink sheet" describing the "pink lady"—who was, of course, no more pink or red than Congressman Voorhis had been. But the technique worked again, and Nixon went on to the U.S. Senate. Here he could share billing with another senator who had worked the same side of the street and had hit the headlines earlier—Joseph R. McCarthy, junior senator from Wisconsin.

McCarthy had been elected in the same "class of 1946" that brought Nixon to Congress. On February 9, 1950, McCarthy made, inappropriately enough, a "Lincoln Day" speech, at Wheeling, West Virginia. He said that he held in his hand the names of 205 people working in the U.S. State Department who were communists. He never revealed the names, and from time to time changed the figures, but in his statements there were always a sizable number of communists in the government.

He got lots of newsprint and was well on his way to re-election in 1952. The first cartoon I did on McCarthy was in the same month as his West Virginia speech and showed him as a transparent figure whose charges were obviously thin. Others followed a few days later and continued through his career to December 1954, when he was finally censured.

The word "McCarthyism" originated—with no thought of creating a new term—in a cartoon in March 1950 that showed Senators Taft, Wherry and others pushing the Republican elephant toward a tower of tar barrels. For want of a better term to summarize the issue, I labeled the top barrel *McCarthyism*. After the word became popular, the senator tried putting it to his own use in a book called *McCarthyism: The Fight for America*. It is amusing to see some of McCarthy's successors apply the term to people who expose them.

Part of the success of the McCarthys and Nixons was due to public fear and frustration over the spread of communism in other countries. When the corrupt government of Chiang Kai-shek collapsed and Mao Tse-Tung's forces took over, the Democratic Party in the United States was blamed for "losing China." And officials who had realistically appraised the course of events were tarred as "pro-communist," despite our government's futile efforts to support the Chiang regime and prevent a communist victory. The Mao forces acquired a good deal of weaponry from supporters of Chiang. Satirist Mort Sahl distilled the problem by saying that we'd have given Chiang the atom bomb but we were afraid he'd sell it.

If a person could not stop an expanding communism abroad, he could scapegoat and destroy people at home. If you couldn't rub out a Russkie, you could nail a neighbor.

There was another factor in anti-communist politics. Many members of the political party that had lost five consecutive presidential elections were hungry to regain power by any means. When McCarthy began tossing out numbers and charges, a senator considered as respectable as "Mr. Republican," Robert A. Taft, told him to keep at it, and if one thing doesn't work, try another. This was the same Taft who

"YOU MEAN I'M SUPPOSED TO STAND ON THAT?"

March 29, 1950

134

called the Marshall Plan a "global giveaway." He had been an isolationist when Hitler was triumphant in Europe but now Taft and many of his colleagues were gung ho for going after Communist China. I called them Asialationists.

It is hard now to conceive of the hysteria—fanned by Nixon, McCarthy and colleagues for their own purposes—that gripped the United States for more than five years. With a reckless disregard for reputations, congressional committees summoned witnesses and guillotined their careers.

These were not, in fact, attacks on communism, although some of the duller congressmen specializing in "anti-communism" undoubtedly felt that they were saving the country from a threat to its existence. But the Nixons and McCarthys knew better. Like the communists themselves, these politicians were primarily after "liberals"—mostly Democrats.

The end justified the means. The purpose was not only to defeat but to destroy. And many reputable people in and out of government were ruined. The Democratic Party had its own version of an "anti-communist" lord high executioner—Nevada Democrat Patrick McCarran. He was head of the Senate Judiciary Committee and its subcommittee on internal security. He worked closely with McCarthy and his methods were much the same. I drew McCarran as a bum trying to look reputable, and heard from a staff member that what particularly bothered him about my characterization was that he considered himself quite a dapper fellow.

One of the legacies of the McCarthy era, enduring even into the 1990s, was the McCarran-Walter Act. Under this act distinguished visitors including Nobel laureates have been barred even from temporary entrance into the United States if they were believed to hold or express views considered "un-American."

But it was McCarthy, with his animal cunning and his instinct for publicity unfettered by any sense of morality or honesty, who personified the intellectual terrorism of the time. More than anyone else, he identified himself with the campaign to "root out," as he and his colleagues always put it, "communist subversion."

Republicans of conscience like Senators Margaret Chase Smith of Maine and Ralph Flanders of Vermont stood up to McCarthyism—

along with such Democratic senators as Millard Tydings, William Fulbright, William Benton, Herbert Lehman and Stuart Symington. They stood against what were, in fact, attacks on civil discourse and decency. But it was a long time before they prevailed.

Something of the McCarthy flavor may be inferred from the way he spoke of others in government. He referred to Fulbright as Senator Half-bright. In campaigning against Gov. Adlai Stevenson, Democratic presidential candidate, he referred to him as "Alger—I mean Adlai" (an oblique reference to the convicted Alger Hiss). In an appearance before an overflow crowd of newspaper editors who had invited him to speak, he accompanied a reference to the U.S. State Department with a wave of a handkerchief in a yoo-hoo gesture. McCarthy was not exactly a class act.

His assistants, Roy Cohn and David Schine, traveled abroad terrorizing U.S. government libraries by demanding removal of books they didn't like and threatening investigations. These vaudeville team junkets might have been funny if they were not so deadly.

Imagine a time when a person in public life might seriously come under suspicion for having on his bookshelf a volume by Karl Marx; or when government employees and others might best receive "liberal" publications in plain brown wrappers; or when book publishers might decide it was unwise to use the color red too vividly on the jacket of a book of commentary. Those who had contributed to such causes as the fight against Franco fascism in Spain were particularly at risk. They now found themselves labeled as communists or communist sympathizers ("comsymps" was the term). Guilt by association— having contributed to the "wrong organizations" or knowing the "wrong people"—was enough to expand the lists of those who could fill the tumbrels.

It has often been noted how close are comedy and tragedy. Congressmen who were going to save us from communism missed no possibilities in their hunts for tell-tale signs of political satanism. One of them cautioned against people who referred to the USSR or the Soviet Union instead of calling the enemy *Russia*—the American way. Another found the clue to journalistic iniquity in newspaper mastheads, as he gave warning to look out for papers with *Post* in their title—*Washington Post, New York Post, St. Louis Post-Dispatch*. . . .

The threat to the nation was generally described as "godless communism''—as if the difference between our society and totalitarianism was not freedom but religion. And there was also the implication that those who were not sufficiently religious were you-know-whats or you-know-what sympathizers.

Meanwhile, the lists of suspected subversives cross-bred and multiplied. It was not necessary to be in government to get into the game. The owner of some grocery stores in Syracuse, New York, set himself up as an authority on Americanism, compiling blacklists of people in the entertainment industry. As an enforcer, he led boycotts of products made by sponsors of broadcast programs that employed people he disapproved of. This might seem laughable if the studios and advertising agencies had not accepted his lists, along with others, as criteria for who was employable.

Mark Goodson wrote of his own experiences as a TV producer opposing what he called "the dark terror of the television blacklisting days (1950–1955)." Demands were made on him, among others, to drop worthy performers because some executive or advertising agency called for their heads. After a while, he wrote, no explanations were given at all. Without even being confronted by accusation, much less accuser, performers suddenly found doors closed. In at least one instance, an actor who had been dropped from a program committed suicide.

One of the many cases where Goodson fought blacklisting involved what must be the ultimate in advertiser submissiveness. He was told to get rid of an actress who, he finally discovered, simply had the same name as another woman who was on a blacklist. When he brought this to the attention of the advertising agency executives, he found that they *knew* she was not the person listed. But they'd had some complaints and didn't want to take any chances. For his insistence on keeping this actress on the show, Goodson himself almost came to be listed as a "pinko."

Another who faced down a blacklisting demand was Robert Kintner, then head of ABC Radio. When headhunters called for Gypsy Rose Lee to be dropped from radio because her name appeared on a list, he simply refused. He might have pointed out that this entertainer, who had gained fame as a stripper, had nothing to conceal, but he played it straight.

The movie industry was a natural for investigators and blacklisters.

I recall having to pass some superpatriot pickets to see a Charlie Chaplin movie.

I did some talks on the hysteria of the time and made blacklisting the subject of a speech in Los Angeles attended by some movie people and politicos. The gist of what I had to say was that blacklisting was an abomination, and that Hollywood, of all places, with its capacity to reach tremendous audiences in its films, should be the last to be intimidated.

The next day screenwriter Dudley Nichols took me to lunch with Dore Schary, film producer, and later author of the play *Sunrise at Campobello*. Schary agreed with what I'd spoken about. He said he had tried to get other film producers to stand together on this issue with no success. But, as an example of the power of movies to resist pressure, which had been my theme, he told of an incident years before when some muscle *had* accomplished its purpose.

It was at a time when an anti-semitic publication called the *Dearborn Independent* was published with the backing of Henry Ford. The studios had been put on notice that Ford—or his publications director and political guru—was about to launch a campaign against Jewish influence in the movie industry. Schary invited Ford's representative to Hollywood to see a public-service movie short he had made. He then rolled the film, which was on the laudable subject of automobile safety. It showed a series of automobile crashes—in which all the cars involved happened to be clearly Fords. Schary said that this anti-semitic campaign against Hollywood was suddenly called off.

But most producers had little stomach for a blacklisting fight as careers were derailed and destroyed while the hunt for "subversives" went on. And the dim lights of the House Committee on Un-American Activities basked in the glow of Hollywood's bright lights. They had "friendly witnesses" and "unfriendly witnesses." One of the friendly ones was Ronald Reagan, former head of the Screen Actors Guild, who testified to communist influence in the union and in Hollywood.

Reagan was not asked to name names. It later developed that there was no need to put him in this embarrassing position. He was secretly naming names to the FBI, which he served as an informant. And under J. Edgar Hoover the FBI worked in close collaboration with the congressional committees that shared his views.

Indeed, some communists did work to seize control of unions, and their principal opponents were mostly the "liberals" who were the chief targets of McCarthy and other committee attacks. James Wechsler, editor of the *New York Post* and an acknowledged member of the Young Communist League as a college student in the 1930s, became a vigorous fighter against communist influence in the Newspaper Guild and elsewhere, as well as a strong opponent of McCarthyism. This prominent editor was subpoenaed to appear before McCarthy in closed session. Wechsler later wrote a rather chilling account of what it was like to face him and associates Cohn and Schine in a couple of hearings that lasted a total of four and a quarter hours.

Ostensibly he had been summoned because Cohn and Schine had found one or more of his books in a U.S. Information Agency library overseas. But at the hearings the book, or books, didn't get a mention. The inquisitors didn't even know the names of the books that had supposedly alarmed them. But Wechsler's loyalty was constantly questioned. He was asked over and over to produce names of college-day associates as a precondition for making public the transcripts of these closed hearings. McCarthy kept asking the editor if he had been intimidated by the committee—a question to which an affirmative answer might seem less than courageous and a negative answer might indicate that the committee was doing benign work.

Wechsler also wrote about McCarthy's first election to the U.S. Senate, when communist support helped him win the close Republican primary election against Sen. Robert La Follette, Jr. Asked about this at the time, McCarthy said, "Communists have the same right to vote as anyone else." And, following his election, he said, "Stalin's proposal for world disarmament is a great thing and he must be given credit for being sincere."

Unfortunately, McCarthy did not find it profitable to give the same credit to people who later opposed his methods. But his tolerant statements on Stalin and communists were made in 1946 before he found pay dirt in the anti-communist line.

McCarthy's followers were numerous and intense. There was nothing they couldn't support in their hero.

At a meeting where someone in the audience asked McCarthy why he wore built-up shoes, he said it was because he carried about ten pounds of shrapnel in his leg. Of course he didn't carry any shrapnel at all. His only wartime injury was a temporary one incurred during a shipboard hazing ceremony. But despite the obvious ridiculousness of the story, those ten pounds of shrapnel carried full weight with his supporters.

During the time of un-Americanism and McCarthy & Co., I can't say that I "suffered for my art" or for my convictions. The blood pressure may have jumped on reading the newspapers, but there was real pleasure in having an outlet for my anger instead of imploding with it. *That* would have meant suffering.

The loss of some subscribing newspapers was not catastrophic, and with the number of competing papers existing then, the newspaper syndicate worked to make up for cancellations.

The Washington Post, like Washington in general, did not then have the security measures adopted later, and I had no "outer office." Callers did not always confine themselves to letters and phone calls; some came by to express their displeasure in person. But despite these occasional visits and the kind of vague threatening letters that must come to just about everyone in the opinion business, there was nothing that might classify as bodychecking. Newspaper columnist Drew Pearson had a different experience. When he repaired to the men's room of a club where he was attending some function, he was physically attacked by McCarthy.

Among letters of that period, one stands out in my mind. It came from a man I visualized as being very busy and probably accustomed to giving orders and having them followed. He gave his unvarnished opinion of my "Americanism" and demanded that I turn myself in to the FBI.

Many of us must have considered how we would respond if we were called to appear before a committee headed by someone like McCarthy. My only thought was that I would demand an open hearing, where I might at least use the forum to comment on the chairman's record. Such a summons never came. Since I have never been a political joiner or followed any particular line, my record must have provided slim pickings for McCarthy. But he felt he had an opening anyhow.

In 1950, I had put together for the State Department a pamphlet of cartoons titled *Herblock Looks at Communism.* The idea for the booklet apparently originated with a woman in the Library of Congress who wrote to publisher Phil Graham. Phil passed it along to Edward Barrett, assistant secretary of state for public affairs, who liked the idea. The pamphlet was printed, and millions of copies in various languages were distributed throughout the world.

McCarthy must have figured he had an angle even in this obviously anti-communist booklet. The State Department put it out in support of the war against aggression in Korea. But McCarthy was at war with the State Department, and he tried to give the impression that I was in its pay.

He said he could not understand "why the State Department should subsidize this man who is actively committed to oppose attempts to drive Communists out of government. . . ." But he miscalculated on that one. I had prepared the pamphlet and given permission for use of the cartoons without any compensation to me or to *The Post*, which paid for some printings of its own.

So the charge didn't stick. But in the soil of McCarthy's mind, new ideas kept sprouting. The charge of being "in the pay of the State Department" could be applied to anyone who so much as accepted travel fare from New York to Washington to take part in government broadcasts or publications.

I often attended congressional hearings, and when McCarthy himself finally became a witness before a questioning committee, the hearing room was jammed. To get the best view of the senator, I sat up front in a room so crowded that I found myself wedged in at a table right next to one of McCarthy's henchmen—I think Don Surine. As I sketched McCarthy, his associate kept eyeing me and looking over my shoulder at what I was doing. Finally he spoke. He leaned even closer and said in a low voice, "You draw good."

I didn't ask him to put it in writing.

"FIRE!"

HERBLOCK
©1949 THE WASHINGTON POST CO.

June 17, 1949

142

THE GREAT ORIENTAL DISAPPEARING ACT

June 27, 1951

"... ADDER'S FORK, AND BLIND-WORM'S STING, LIZARD'S LEG, AND HOWLET'S WING ..."

June 6, 1949

"HERE HE COMES NOW"

t. 29, 1954

"SOMETIMES I WONDER WHAT'S IN THOSE DARN THINGS"

May 31, 1953

"I HAVE HERE IN MY HAND—"

May 7, 1954

144

"HOW DID ATOMIC ENERGY INFORMATION LEAK OUT TO THE DAMN SCIENTISTS IN THE FIRST PLACE?"

"IF YOU ASK ME, IT'S UN-AMERICAN"

Sept. 12, 1948

Oct. 22, 1947

"ALWAYS HAPPY TO TAKE THE WORD OF A LADY"

Sept. 25, 1951

"WE HAVE DOCUMENTARY EVIDENCE THAT THIS MAN IS PLANNING A TRIP TO MOSCOW"

March 25, 1953

16

All Abroad

After publication of my first book, in 1952, I felt that it was time to see more of the big wide world—time for what the memory books used to title My Trip Abroad. The mere mention of a trans-Atlantic trip brought advice from practically everyone I knew who had crossed the ocean. Since I was going by ship, that alone was good for a lot of advice—most of it bad. I followed it by signing up for first-class, which I was assured was the only way to go.

On the small French ship, this was indeed a nice way to travel. But while first-class food was unsurpassed, there was more fun in tourist class. Another fellow and I wanted to explore beyond those gilded confines and discovered a passageway to the tourist section. A door opened to the sound of music and laughter, and a pretty French girl drew me into a passing conga line. By going back and forth, I was able to combine shipboard fun and romance with the upscale but not so lively accommodations.

My first stop was England—and right on to London, which was everything I hoped it would be, though still showing scars of the war.

During those post-war years when things were tight, an arrangement had been made for the London *Economist* to use the cartoons with no payment except a subscription for me. But the editors, wanting to do something more, arranged to put me up in a small hotel that was owned by the magazine. Their hospitality was appreciated, although the room was rather sparse and the loo was down the hall. Better than that, they arranged a luncheon, to which they invited cartoonist David Low and some other newspapermen.

Understanding each other's countries and politics has increased greatly since the *Economist* ran one of my early cartoons that showed the U.S. Capitol in the background. An assistant asked the editor why I had put St. Paul's in the drawing. They also printed some explanations of symbols like the GOP elephant and the Democratic donkey to make these Americanisms clear to the reader.

Before I visited Parliament, Low gave me advice on making more or less surreptitious sketches from the gallery. Seeing Churchill in action was a real treat. I don't know if he sometimes had a little drink while speaking. But the backbenchers kept interrupting with joking questions: Would the prime minister like another glass of water? He accepted the comments with a smile.

On later trips to Europe, I made it a point to visit other parliamentary bodies. The French and Italian chambers were more plush than the British—the Italian one reminding me of an opera house. The surprise was in Greece, where the post-war legislators sat at desks much like the ones in the U.S. Senate. If the British Parliament hecklers sounded strange to a Washingtonian, they were decorous compared to the Greek assembly members at that time. In addition to calling and shouting, unhappy delegates kept raising and banging down the lids of their desks, giving the impression of a schoolroom with teacher absent. Democracy, we know, is not the tidiest form of government, but the raucous behavior in the chamber was still preferable to the military rule that came later.

Back to that first trip, there was lunch at *Punch* with editor Malcolm Muggeridge and staff members and plenty of great sightseeing. Then, on to Paris.

Some helpful, well-traveled friends had selected a place to stay—a real Left Bank hotel, where I would get the full flavor of Paris without associating with any Americans (like me). What they had not considered was the fact that even in school my knowledge of French was not too *bon*.

My friends were right about the small Left Bank hotel. It was so completely French that no English was spoken at all. In my case, the language experience was total submersion.

I tried using the phone to contact friends, but an unfamiliarity even with numbers was a stumbling block. So with each call I would go down three flights of stairs and hand the written number to the hotel operator—and then race three flights back up to my room to pick up the phone. Unfortunately, every call seemed to be answered by a secretary or maid. And when I gave the name of the person I wanted to speak to, I didn't know whether the answer was just a minute, nobody's home, wrong number or what. So I would just repeat the name and hang on until the phone cut off.

I couldn't help thinking of the story about the illegal immigrant who had been taken into the home of a friend who had to leave suddenly. When the illegal asked about food, the friend told him to go to the counter restaurant downstairs and ask for apple pie and a cup of coffee. "Ah-pull pie, cahp cahf-fee," repeated the illegal. After the friend was delayed a couple of days he phoned to apologize, and the illegal asked what else could he order besides the pie and coffee. "Oh, gosh," said the friend. "Sure—go back and ask for a ham sandwich." "Hahm Sahn-wich," repeated the illegal, who rushed down and gave the waitress his new order. "White or rye?" she asked. The illegal looked up hopelessly and said, "Ah-pull pie, cahp cahf-fee."

That was me on the phone. My arrival in Paris couldn't have had worse timing. It was a lovely summer weekend, and everyone who might have answered my calls was away.

On Monday morning I got the operator to call the American Embassy, where I asked for press attaché Ben Bradlee. "The first thing we have to do is get you out of that hotel and into the Crillon," said Ben, who promptly did just that. From then on, spending time with friends made Paris the joy that it ought to be.

Driving around that city with Ben was an experience. On the streets I got the impression that lots of drivers were trying out for the Grand Prix in all directions. When traffic suddenly came to a stop, all the gaps

148

between cars would quickly be filled by bikes and motorbikes. Then they would all be off and racing again. I marveled at the way Ben maneuvered his way through this traffic. He responded, "You've got to be fearless"—which might have been his motto when he became an editor. A modest test of my fearlessness as a passenger came when Ben's longtime friend Bill Blair perched me on the back of his motorbike while he zoomed around Paris squares one night.

Arrival in Italy was easier, partly because no worldly-wise friends had booked me into a hotel where I could not be understood at all. In Rome, I walked out of the hotel into a square and entered a nearby building that, with its great vaulted ceiling and opening to the sky, absolutely bowled me over. It was the Pantheon. Seeing this architectural masterpiece on a tour would be impressive. To walk into it unexpectedly was stunning.

For some reason I had less of a language problem in Italy. When I ordered ravioli in a restaurant to see how it compared with my mother's, the busy waiter brought some other kind of pasta. Seeing my disappointment and watching my efforts to get the waiter's attention, a man in a group at the next table asked in English what the problem was. When I explained, he called the waiter over and told him in vivid Italian and English that he had no business bringing me the wrong thing. If they were out of ravioli, they should have said so. What kind of waiter was he anyhow, eh?

Two people I looked up in Rome were correspondents Frank Gervasi and Curtis (Bill) Pepper. It would be hard to imagine an American more Italian than Gervasi, who spent much of his life in Italy. But he was bothered by the fact that somehow he still seemed identifiable as an American. So, he said, he had himself fitted out from head to toe with Italian clothes—hat, shoes, tie, socks, everything. And when he walked out into the street a boy ran up to him and said in English, "Hey, mister, you want to buy a fountain pen?"

Gervasi really laid it on, hosting a dinner party at Alfredo's. As the specialty was served, he had violinists approach my part of the table, where they struck up their music while fixing me with steady, unremitting gazes. I am not accustomed to being personally played at by violinists, and felt faced with a choice between letting the dinner get cold or seeming to be rude to the earnest musicians. I returned their gaze with what I hoped looked like appreciation, while trying not to miss my mouth with forkfuls of hanging fettucini.

One night in Rome, Bill Pepper and his wife, Beverly, a sculptor and painter, took me to the loft of what must have been a government warehouse. Here, by flickering match lights, we saw various parts of huge stone figures, unassembled or disassembled, of undetermined age—a huge arm leaning here, a great head or torso lying there, all casting enormous moving shadows. It was an eerily beautiful and impressive sight.

In Naples, where Frank had to do a story, one night we went to a carnival that boasted a shooting gallery. He and Bill and I shot all of the targets, clay birds, statues and whatever else was standing or moving. Then, after congratulating each other on our marksmanship, we made a quick deal with the gallery owner and went on to shoot out all the light bulbs that illuminated and framed the gallery. Everyone, including the shooting-place proprietor, was happy. It was a great time to be an American tourist in Europe.

One of the people I became acquainted with on subsequent trips was Hugh Cudlipp, editor of the *London Mirror*. This paper was more like the old *New York Post* than any other tabloid, with good editorial pages. But Cudlipp also had the tabloid editor's mind for the arresting macabre line. Turning to me at a large staff luncheon, he smiled and whispered that not all of these people would be here if I came back in a couple of years. He didn't mean anyone was going to be fired. He had counted the seats at the luncheon table and simply figured that actuarially somebody in this group would no longer be among us.

He spoke of the strong feelings held by readers of the paper. He said that when he took cabs, he gave the address of a building across the street to avoid the flak he might get if he mentioned the *Mirror*.

Cudlipp also told me of a formal dinner he had attended where a beautiful woman, dressed to the nines, had approached him after the dessert and liqueurs. She smiled and asked, "Are you Hugh Cudlipp of the *Mirror?*" He smiled and said that he was. "Whereupon," he said, "she hawked up and deposited on me a large oyster." If Cudlipp's *Mirror* was not as scandalous as it became later, editing it was obviously never dull.

On another trip, when Cudlipp learned that Alan Barth and his wife would also be on the plane, we debarked to find a waiting Rolls with flower-bearing chauffeur who drove us around the city all morning until jet lag caught up with us.

Inviting me to another of his *Mirror* lunches, Cudlipp suggested that we both make speeches. I hadn't really expected to be called on for anything like that and have always worried about preparing a few words from the moment I first agree to speak. I wandered around London's parks giving it some thought, and continued thinking about it that night and the next morning. When I arrived for lunch, I didn't feel entirely easy but as ready as I would get. After we were seated a little while, Cudlipp leaned over and said in one of his asides, "Let's forget the speeches—we'll just have lunch and conversation."

On a trip several years later I received a call inviting me to come to No. 10 Downing Street. Yes, I would certainly be there at the appointed time. I had always been curious about what was beyond the unpretentious doorway and the inevitable bobby, and was given a brief tour on the way to Prime Minister Harold Wilson's office. It was, as you would guess, not just a row house, but the entrance to what must have been several houses put together to provide plenty of depth and all kinds of rooms.

If No. 10 Downing Street was much larger than I expected, Wilson's office was smaller, certainly compared to the Oval Office. It was an informal kind of light-paneled room with working desk. He asked what I would like to drink, opened a cupboard and mixed it himself. This was not like the White House either. He showed me a moon picture that President Nixon had sent him, and we settled into a couple of chairs to talk about anything and nothing in particular. With an upcoming British election he told me of a wealthy American politician who had offered to make a large contribution toward Wilson's election—well meant but with little understanding of the British system. If he spent more than a few pounds for phone calls and such, said Wilson, it would be a scandal—certainly quite different from our elections.

On another visit to London, I remember going to a theater with an American friend. When asked, "Check your bag, ma'am?," she replied that no, thanks, she would just carry it with her. To this the man explained that no, ma'am, it was necessary for him to look into her bag. That was shortly after some IRA bombings. But it was all strictly low-key.

It's a great city and a small world. On one excursion I ran into Bud Trillin and his bride, over from New York. Another time I went walking through London looking for an art store, which I'd heard was the world's greatest—you could find everything including drawing papers, pens and other materials that weren't even made anymore. On this search, I ran into Jonathan Miller walking his dog. I had first met this remarkable man—doctor and Shakespearean director, among other things—when he was in Washington convulsing audiences in the British show *Beyond the Fringe*.

Knowing London's streets better than I, he offered to join in my search for the great art store. We found it. But on the door was a sign indicating that it was closed—not just for the day—not for the weekend—but permanently. It had shut down only a day or two before. This in London, where I thought old and worthy establishments went on forever.

Some time ago I set forth Block's Law: *If it's good they'll stop making it.* Perhaps there should be a corollary: If it's a really great place, it will close.

If it could happen in London, it could happen anywhere.

17

The Ike Era

The campaign of 1952 brought about a minor crisis on the editorial page. *The Post,* under Eugene Meyer, had not endorsed candidates for office. But with Gen. Dwight Eisenhower and Sen. Robert Taft competing for the Republican nomination, publisher Phil Graham decided *The Post* should support Ike. Perhaps he welcomed the chance for the "liberal" (if not downright subversive) *Washington Post* to line up with a popular Republican; and certainly Ike was the internationalist in the race against Taft. However, *The Post* could hardly run an editorial saying, "Ike For The Republican Nomination." So, without waiting for the Democrats to nominate a candidate, it ran an editorial endorsing "Eisenhower for President."

When the Democrats nominated Gov. Adlai Stevenson of Illinois, I had no doubt about which candidate I was for—especially after the presidential candidates chose their running mates. While *The Post* supported Eisenhower (and—uh—Nixon), the cartoons clearly favored Stevenson (and Sen. John Sparkman of Alabama).

Nixon had attended the 1952 Republican convention as a member of the California delegation pledged to the nomination of Gov. Earl Warren and jumped ship to support Eisenhower. The combination of this defection and the fact that he was a young and ruthless campaigner won him Eisenhower's approval. This selection hardly delighted *The Post*. And the disclosure of the "Nixon Fund," through which prominent supporters made contributions to him, gave *The Post* real pause.

When a national uproar threatened his place on the ticket, Nixon, accompanied by his wife, Pat, made the televised "Checkers speech." He shrewdly called for supporters to send telegrams to the Republican National Committee. The success of the speech in producing the desired GOP support was enough for Eisenhower, who declared that Nixon was "my boy."

Eisenhower's mentor, George C. Marshall, five-star general and later secretary of state, had been attacked by McCarthy and his fellow senator, William Jenner of Indiana. Jenner called Marshall "a living lie and a front man for traitors." When Eisenhower spoke in McCarthy's state, he reportedly had in his speech some words in defense of Marshall, but deleted them. And in this campaign Eisenhower even promised to get the "Reds and pinks" out of government.

One day editor Herbert Elliston mentioned that the cartoons-vs.-editorials split was an embarrassment to Phil Graham. I suggested that *The Post* needn't run the cartoons during the rest of the campaign and I would simply mail them out to the syndicate papers.

This seemed like a good solution. But with the cartoons dropped, Stevenson supporters accused *The Post* of censorship. And the *Washington Daily News,* always happy to needle *The Post,* ran an article about the missing cartoonist. They called attention to the work by the same cartoonist appearing in other papers. Phil decided that since everyone knew about our divergent views, and since differing views were, in fact, what distinguished *The Post* from papers where staffers took orders from the chief, it was silly to leave out the cartoons. A few days later they reappeared.

After the inauguration, the cartoons still did not give President Eisenhower the support he generally received from *The Post*.

During this period a friend who had been to one of Eisenhower's stag dinners told me that my cartoons had come up in conversation and Ike had indicated that he didn't read them or wasn't familiar with them.

Shortly afterward I ran into columnist Doris Fleeson. She remembered that President Truman had sometimes showed visitors clips of my cartoons to illustrate how he felt—and that once Truman had answered a press conference question by telling the correspondents to look at my cartoon in that morning's *Washington Post*.

When she asked me about current White House reaction, I relayed my friend's report and at this she let out a whoop. "He doesn't see them!" she exclaimed. "When I saw him in Europe before he was elected, he pulled a sheaf of your cartoons out of a drawer and showed them to me—he thought they were great." Of course, those cartoons were not critical of Ike, but of some figures in the Truman administration and some congressmen, particularly of Sen. Taft, who would become Ike's rival for the GOP nomination.

If the reactions of public figures are interesting, so are the impressions of people who observe them. William Hayes, manager of *The Post*'s TV station at the time, told me of being on Eisenhower's staff at the end of the war, when Ike and his aides prepared for a forthcoming press conference. Someone at this prep meeting brought up the question, "What did you think of the performance of Negro troops, General?" According to Hayes, Ike said, "Good gosh, they're not going to ask me that, are they?" "They might very well," said the aide, and so the staff came up with a good answer: "I never thought of them as Negro troops, I just thought of them as Americans."

Later, during Eisenhower's presidency, an acquaintance suggested that I was being too tough on Ike, a man he admired greatly. He had been a World War II correspondent, and told me how impressed he was when he attended a post-war Eisenhower press conference. "Ike," he said, "was asked what he thought of the performance of Negro troops in the war. And he looked up with surprise and said, 'Negro troops? Why I never thought of them as Negro troops, I just thought of them as Americans."

If the general's answer was not as spontaneous as this correspondent thought, Ike certainly showed his capacity for preparation—which helped to win a war and an election.

In the late 1980s some scholars "reappraised" the Eisenhower presidency and gave Ike better marks than they had earlier. I think much of the reappraisal of this not-best-or-worst of presidents was based on a combination of nostalgia and amnesia. There was an understandable longing for a period of peace, for the days before the Vietnam War, Watergate and a busted Treasury—and forgetfulness about events of the time.

If there were no Watergates or Iran-contras, there were certainly scandals. Conflicts of interest and ethical lapses were disclosed in the Federal Communications Commission and in members of the Eisenhower official family. Closest to Ike was adviser Sherman Adams. He had received gifts from a businessman for whom Adams made calls to the Federal Trade Commission, and it was only with the most painful reluctance ("I need him!") that Eisenhower finally let Adams go.

Eisenhower opposed the "creeping socialism" that he declared had been spreading in the United States since 1932, and he gave encouragement to private power lobbies. He helped a couple of contractors, Dixon and Yates, secure a government contract to compete with the New Deal's Tennessee Valley Authority. But the contract arrangements, when they were finally revealed, involved so many questionable practices that Eisenhower had to give up the Dixon-Yates deal.

So much for the political "crusade" to "clean up the mess in Washington," and an administration that vowed government "as clean as a hound's tooth." I drew it as a hound badly in need of dental care.

Some of the scholars reconsidering Ike's management style came up with a new "hidden hand" theory describing him as in complete command of his White House policies. I've always figured that any president is accountable for his administration.

A plus for Ike was the fact that he did not intervene militarily in Indochina. But at that time it was a French colony fighting for independence—not yet the North and South Vietnam created at the 1954 Geneva Conference as a temporary division. It was Eisenhower's secretary of state, John Foster Dulles, who acted to prevent an all-Vietnam election that would have united the two parts. And Eisenhower sent in the first American military advisers to South Vietnam.

It's hard to see how a unified Vietnam, under an elected and less radicalized Ho Chi Minh, would have been worse than the continued division of the country and the war that followed.

Vice President Nixon said about Dulles, "Isn't it wonderful, finally, to have a Secretary of State who is not taken in by the Communists?"

156

The two predecessors were Dean Acheson and George C. Marshall of the Marshall Plan.

In Asia, the same administration was so virulently and ostentatiously anti-Red that it barred American reporters from traveling to mainland China. The country itself, as well as the government, was not to be seen. The Chiang Kai-shek government on Taiwan had become "China" to the U.S. government. In cartoons I showed the landmass of China as *Terra Incognita,* and also had our State Department scissoring it out of world maps. Dulles, Nixon and others in their party consigned it to oblivion—and tried to do the same for those who sought to recognize its existence.

McCarthy and the Eisenhower administration policies destroyed the careers of government experts on Asia—whose expertise itself made them suspect. Their knowledge might have helped prevent the Vietnam debacle.

Such non-heroic policies under the administration of a war hero occasionally echo in the obituary pages. In October 1992 some newspapers noted the passing of "Haldore Hanson, 80, a former war correspondent, State Department official and economic development executive." He was, *The Washington Post* obituary noted,

> one of the State Department officials attacked by Sen. Joseph McCarthy (R-Wis.) as "pro-communist." The only evidence McCarthy had for his charges were quotes, taken wildly out of context, in Mr. Hanson's writings on China. Despite the fact that Mr. Hanson was cleared by every congressional group that investigated him and exonerated by the FBI and the State Department, he was "asked to resign" from the Foreign Operations Administration in 1953.

Abroad, the administration, with the assistance of John Foster Dulles's brother Allen, then head of the CIA, overthrew the government of Guatemala as well as that of Iran—where it ousted Prime Minister Mohammed Mossadegh and put the Shah back on the throne. And when Egyptian dictator Gamal Abdel Nasser nationalized and shut down the Suez Canal, it was Eisenhower who effectively caused a rollback of the French, British and Israelis who had taken military action against the Egyptian dictator and retaken the canal. Whatever the arguments for or against this policy, it established Nasser as the undisputed Arab leader and the man who organized the Arab nations for a war to annihilate Israel.

The Cold War got colder after Eisenhower attempted a cover-up of the fact that we had spy planes overflying the USSR—without realizing that a missing U-2 had been downed and pilot Gary Powers (with film) had been captured in the Soviet Union. Nikita Khrushchev derided the Eisenhower deceptions and canceled a scheduled summit meeting.

In Europe, Eisenhower's State Department urged the people of Hungary to throw off the yoke of Soviet rule—and then stood by while tanks mowed down the Hungarians.

These foreign policy actions—and inactions—didn't seem to me to qualify as a basis for retrospective raves.

Eisenhower did end the Korean War—reportedly with the threat of using the nuclear bomb, on which we then still had a monopoly. Yet, after all the Republican criticism about the Truman administration having "lost China," it was on Eisenhower's watch that Cuba became a communist country. There was a nice irony in how this helped to elect John Kennedy over a Republican who had built his career on fears of the spread of communist influence.

The Eisenhower administration at home came in for my criticism, particularly on what I considered two major moral issues of the time: desegregation and McCarthyism. If there was a "hidden hand" on the issue of segregation, it was one that might better have been stayed. Before the Supreme Court's 1954 desegregation decision, Eisenhower arranged for a little lobbying during at least one of his stag dinners, where he urged Chief Justice Warren to chat with another guest—John W. Davis, the attorney representing the segregation side in the Court. The president wanted to give the justice a better understanding of the segregationist view.

Another justice, William O. Douglas, managed to duck out of range when he sensed Ike's lobbying on this issue at one of these dinners.

After the Supreme Court's unanimous desegregation ruling, Eisenhower conceded that it was "the law of the land" but pointedly held that you can't change the hearts of men. And my cartoons showed him more interested in deliberateness than "all deliberate speed."

The absence of leadership from the White House gave time for

158

segregationists to launch a campaign of "massive resistance" and to dig in. In 1957, when Gov. Orval Faubus of Arkansas called out the guard to maintain segregation in Little Rock, Eisenhower hesitated a few days and then sent troops only to prevent what might have been mob violence. This was three years after the Supreme Court's decision.

There was an interesting sidelight at *The Post*. Phil Graham later seemed to kick himself and the government for Faubus's course of confrontation. Graham told me that if only they had realized it at the time, Faubus could have been bought off with an appointment of some kind. He felt that what Faubus really feared was losing his job and the limelight, and that the offer of a good position would have satisfied him.

I think the only time I saw this usually ebullient publisher in a gloomier frame of mind about a public matter was when he talked of the possible effects of biological warfare, a new subject he had been studying. He pointed out that it would be more horrible than the nuclear threat represented in my A-bomb cartoons.

His reflections on Faubus and Little Rock were not nearly as apocalyptic, but he felt strongly about a missed opportunity to avert one of the most bitter episodes in the progress toward desegregation.

The fact that Eisenhower regarded the appointment of Warren—architect of desegregation and of the one-man-one-vote ruling—to have been his biggest mistake seemed to me an unhappy reflection on him.

McCarthy and the other hunters of un-Americanism marched on during this presidency. I had done cartoons critical of the "loyalty-security" program begun during the Truman administration. But under Eisenhower it was carried further—with recklessness and great political gusto. Like McCarthy, with his changing numbers of "communists in government," the Eisenhower administration, in what it called an "improved" security system, did its own juggling with numbers. In declarations by Nixon, Attorney General Herbert Brownell and others, the administration stated that it had rid the government of 1,400 or 2,200 or 8,008 "security risks." Whatever their number, most of the verifiable fired employees turned out to have been people hired by the Eisenhower administration itself or who merely transferred from one department to another.

But if the administration did not find and "continue to ferret out and destroy communist influence in government,'' as Eisenhower said, it did drive from public service many worthy employees to keep the numbers game going. Some of its security risks also included people who had previously departed the government, as well as some who had previously departed this world—a little like taking names off tombstones.

Even the Atomic Energy Commission was politicized. And Robert Oppenheimer, one of the scientists who helped create the atomic bomb, was declared a ''security risk''—because he was judged not to display enough ''enthusiasm'' for the development of the H-bomb. Some ''security'' system.

But along with the firings there were also hirings. The Department of Justice hired and paid professional informers who turned out to be professional liars. In a two-year period more than 80 were on its payroll—at taxpayers' expense.

Brownell also brought new zest to the compilation and use of the Attorney General's List, inherited from the Truman administration along with the loyalty-security program.

Like blacklists, this one was used to tag people as subversive and as a basis for demanding names of people who might belong to organizations on the list. Visas were withheld for fear of some kind of foreign infection. Physicist Linus Pauling was one of those denied a travel visa. But he was allowed a visa later when he embarrassed our government by winning one of his two Nobel Prizes.

When McCarthy attacked the administration itself by going after the secretary of the Army, Eisenhower finally came to the defense of his own official. If he had fought the war the way he fought the moral issues at home, he might have sat tight and waited for his personal headquarters to be attacked. Fortunately, he did better as a general.

One of the things that had recommended Eisenhower over a fellow Republican like Taft was that he was not an isolationist. But on domestic matters his administration proved surprisingly conservative. I renamed a fairly new Cabinet position *The Department Of Not Too Much Health, Welfare And Education*. And when it was caught short on the supply of the new long-sought polio vaccine, I did a cartoon on Secretary Oveta Culp Hobby's astonishing statement that nobody could have foreseen the demand for it.

The administration's affinity for private power companies was the subject of several cartoons. One of them showed a TVA installation and one of its plaques bearing the inscription: *Built For The People Of The United States*. A power lobby figure is saying to Eisenhower: "First thing to do is take down those damn plaques." Well, recognizable exaggeration is part of cartooning. But several years later I met a man who had been an official in the Eisenhower administration, and he asked if I remembered the cartoon. I braced myself and said yes I did. He told me that just before it appeared, the administration had actually planned to remove these plaques. Life doesn't just imitate art—it sometimes gets out ahead of it.

In another cartoon during this period I had a State Department employee asking his wife if they shouldn't have their Christmas card list cleared. I soon heard from a former government employee who had served abroad and who had applied for a position in a military part of the government at home. When asked if he had maintained connections with anyone abroad, he said only to send out some Christmas cards. He was asked for his Christmas card list.

Perhaps all presidents suffer from leakophobia—the fear that inside-the-big-house information will get out. But this was accentuated during the Eisenhower administration, which became more restrictive and wielded government secrecy stamps on things having no bearing on the national interest. Secrecy is a subject that probably causes more concern to the press than to the public, whose "right to know" we try to defend. Many people feel that the government, which may be a hated "them" at tax time or when it fails to deliver some service, is a kind of daddy-who-knows-best when it asserts a need for secrecy.

But if individuals don't care about a public right to know, they love to be in on secrets themselves. Once during this period I was on a plane sitting next to a woman who enjoyed chatting about current events. She had something she wanted to tell me, but apparently felt troubled about whether or not she ought to. Finally she ventured that I seemed like a nice man and one who could be trusted. She then reached into her purse and drew out a paper containing the lines she wanted me to read. What she was letting me see was a paragraph in a Kiplinger newsletter.

The Eisenhower administration carried secrecy to an extreme, practically seeking to isolate scientists from each other. And it went beyond secrecy to actual misrepresentation in playing down the range and hazardous effects of its nuclear tests.

It also tried to minimize the significance of the Soviet Sputnik—and a second Sputnik containing a live dog, which may have laughed to see such sport. Nevertheless, the country became sufficiently alarmed about these USSR space triumphs that it got interested in better schooling, particularly in science and in space technology.

Aid to education has always been a favorite subject of mine, and a close ally was Agnes Meyer, wife of *The Post*'s publisher. Before marrying Meyer she had been a newspaper reporter, and she occasionally wrote special articles for *The Post*. She had a keen interest in public education, and if I had needed any encouragement in prodding a reluctant administration toward federal aid, she would certainly have supplied it.

Whatever our criticisms or our urging for government action, a constant was Eisenhower's great personal popularity, largely maintained by seeming to be "above the battle." And his personal health was probably of more general concern than any of his policies.

A little rhyme at the time was:

> *Now I lay me down to sleep.*
> *I pray the Lord Ike's soul to keep.*
> *If Ike should die before I wake,*
> *I pray He also Nixon take.*

The only time *The Post* ran an explanation about a day's cartoon was when Ike suffered a heart attack. The cartoon I had drawn on Friday was for *The Post*'s Sunday editorial section—at that time printed a day in advance. It showed Nixon sitting on Eisenhower's shoulders, urging him to run again; and with the advance printing there was no way we could make a substitution for it. So the front section ran an explanation of the printing schedule.

Ike's recovery cheered the country, and when his advisers prevailed on him to run again, it gave new heart to his political party. A newspaper photographer caught a shot of Adlai Stevenson watching the TV as Ike's decision to run again was announced. His own heart must have sunk as he recognized that 1956 would be another tough year for him and his party.

After Eisenhower's re-election, when I next saw columnist Walter Lippmann, he greeted me with the assurance that "It's all right—you're at your best in opposition." Perhaps opposition does bring out the best in cartooning, but winning isn't so bad either.

THE HELICOPTER ERA

March 27, 1957

164

THE BENT TWIGS

Sept. 6, 1949

RICHEST COUNTRY IN THE WORLD

Sept. 8, 1953

"ROCK-A-BYE BABY, IN THE TREE TOP— LET'S MAKE BELIEVE THE FALLOUT WILL STOP"

March 22, 1957

"WELL, WE CERTAINLY BOTCHED THIS JOB. WHAT'LL WE STAMP IT— 'SECRET' OR 'TOP SECRET'?"

March 13, 1957

"HAVE A CARE, SIR"

March 4, 1954

PRAYER RUG

July 10, 1957

"NOTICE HOW WE'VE GOT THEM ISOLATED"

June 2, 1957

"PLAY IT AGAIN, GAMAL"

Oct. 7, 1969

"NAH, YOU AIN'T GOT ENOUGH EDJICCASHUN TO VOTE"

Dec. 10, 1958

"TSK TSK—SOMEBODY SHOULD DO SOMETHING ABOUT THAT"

April 3, 1956

"HEART ATTACK, POOR CHAP. SEND FLOWERS AND LIST HIM AS A SECURITY RISK"

Oct. 18, 1954

"HURRY UP WITH THAT DRAGON, THE AUDIENCE IS GETTING IMPATIENT"

Feb. 22, 1954

"LATER ON, I'D LIKE TO ASK YOU SOMETHING"

Sept. 30, 1957

168

18

Medic

Whomping up the daily cartoon has always been a one-man job with me. But as the mail, phone calls and clutter increased, I also turned out an occasional paragraph for the help-wanted section. I felt affluent enough, and had just space enough, to hire a part-time secretary. But since most part-timers were looking for full-time work, there was a series of comings and goings and classified column listings.

One of the women who showed up was Jean Jablonsky. She was nice, and her application seemed okay, so I asked if she took short-hand. She said she could, and in my best businesslike-employer fash-ion I proceeded, with some backing and filling, to try to—ahem—uh—frame—a—uh—letter. She took it down on her steno pad and transcribed it on a piece of stationery. Some 30 years later, long after I had asked her to stay on full time, and long after she had become Mrs. Rickard, she recalled this interview. She had been nervous about her ability to take dictation—even more ill at ease than I was in giving it. And, as she reminded me, that was the only time I ever dictated a letter to her.

Instead of using shorthand, she learned the more difficult task of deciphering my answers to letters, which begin with scribbles at the bottom of the letter received and turn corners to run up the side and then over the letterhead and around.

Jean does not let me keep the originals of these letters, which she is sure I would lose. She has known me to lose things on an empty desk moments after handing them to me. What she gives me are photocopies, which can be replaced with other photocopies when I lose the first ones.

And as assistant in everything but the actual drawing and writing, she began organizing the office, previewing letters, giving a first editing to manuscripts, handling reprint requests and just about everything else. She stops short of tying a tag around my neck saying, "If lost, return to . . . "

She couldn't possibly have arrived at a better time. A year after she came, my mother and brother both became ill. Bill died, and three months later so did my mother. But in the meantime, Jean had spent time in Chicago looking after my mother and the practical nurses who were supposed to be fulfilling that function—while I went back and forth on planes. So in addition to managing the office, Jean served as nurse and family companion. But her Florence Nightingale career was not over. The following year, 1959, she had another case.

I had planned a trip to Europe, where I'd meet up with my remaining brother, Rich, and his wife. But shortly before departure time, the owner of the apartment building where I lived served notice that the building was being sold and all tenants—including me and my cat, Bella—must be out within a matter of weeks. I went on a crash course of apartment hunting, up and down innumerable stairs, and developed what is called "chest discomfort." As the discomfort persisted, I phoned my doctor, but he was away for the weekend.

That night I kept a date with a friend but explained that I was not feeling well and had been unable to reach my doctor. She offered to call *her* doctor. Since she and he were part of a group health plan, he could hardly treat me, a non-member. But she came up with an idea. She would phone him and describe the symptoms as her own. Doctor was in, and heard her. Then, probably acting on the assumption that women are less subject to heart attacks than men, he told her not to worry, just rest and see if the symptoms would go away.

170

The symptoms did not. After seeing her off, I spent a restless night, some of it in bed with this invisible foot on my chest. The invisible foot did not remove itself and defied the law of gravity when I got up and spent much of the night pacing around and chain-smoking.

I thought of a medical friend, Dr. Isadore Lattman, a noted radiologist, but hesitated to wake him by phoning too early. At daybreak I called, told him I was sorry to bother him and described my situation. "Just lie there," he told me, "and I'll be right over." He came as fast as he could and ordered an ambulance. While we were waiting, I was about to take a drag on a cigarette when he suggested that I put it out. I did. He went to the hospital with me where the diagnosis was in non-medical terms a heart attack.

On Monday morning, my doctor took over and followed the technique in vogue at the time—keep the patient in bed for several weeks. This had the side effect, or bedside effect, of producing visits from all kinds of callers. With my brother abroad and unaware of what had happened and no immediate family to screen calls, I became something of a captive audience. My formula for successful bachelor living (give all used dishes and pans an immediate rinse) was not of much help in a single-guy-in-hospital situation. And Jean, as a young secretary running the office and casing living quarters for me, could hardly direct hospital room traffic or pull rank on other visitors.

A *Post* editor did an organizational job, getting up lists of people to take turns coming to see me. These callers included some assorted office managers I scarcely knew. Many ignored the doctor's injunctions to come individually and stay briefly. One man settled in for a long conversation full of amateur medical advice and instructions on who I should write to and what I should do with what he seemed to think of as spare time I didn't know how to fill. He brought along his wife, who also dispensed advice, telling me I should not be eating from the fruit basket and other things that were sent to me. They stayed about an hour and a half, and I'm sure congratulated themselves on being with me in my time of need. I thought about a greeting card I had once seen which unfolded to about five feet in length. It showed a scowling harridan, with umbrella in hand, leaning over the foot of the bed and saying, "Your doctor is a quack!"

One man, figuring that since I was a cartoonist he ought to make conversation on this subject, told me I had better look to my laurels

171

because there were some darn good cartoonists coming along. I finally asked the doctor if there was a way to limit these self-sacrificing people who were generously giving of their time and efforts to make me more of a hospital case.

Of course, there were good friends I was glad to see. But there ought to be a leaflet on hospital etiquette politely issued to other visitors and enforced with iron discipline. It would advise them that a patient for whom rest is prescribed is not just goofing off—nor is he waiting for people to spend the maximum time telling him what chores they want him to perform.

Depending on the reasons they're hospitalized, some patients are more active than others. Correspondent Clark Mollenhoff told about the time he had successful brain surgery and was soon sitting up in bed writing to colleagues—among them a delightful friend and fellow correspondent, Edgar Allen Poe of the *New Orleans Times-Picayune*. When the surgeon came by to see Mollenhoff and asked what he was doing, he said, "I'm writing a letter to Edgar Allen Poe." The surgeon's face revealed that he was thinking, Where did I go wrong?

However my six-week stay in the hospital may differ from present procedures, it served one good purpose: no smoking there. I had started with cigarettes about the time I began working in Chicago. During attempts to stop, I had the common experience of thinking I couldn't get the work out without starting a fire in front of my face. Eventually I got up to four or five packs a day—about all the smoking it's possible to do—filling smelly ashtrays at bedside, smoking between meal courses, and in the morning holding a cigarette in one hand while brushing the teeth with the other.

When it came time to go home, I asked the doctor what I could and could not do—like in the way of work and, uh, sex—and smoking. He told me I could continue doing whatever I had been doing, but suggested sensible moderation, as with cigarettes. I hadn't been smoking moderately and didn't think I could, which he left up to me. But with the six-weeks no-cigarettes start (even though it included eating baskets of grapes or working my jaws on entire packages of gum), I figured it would be foolish to give up this lead time. And that's how I came to kick the habit.

For quite a while I resisted doing cartoons on the subject, not wanting to be a reformed smoker calling on others to conform. But with the health hazards increasingly obvious and tobacco companies showing a callous irresponsibility, it was clearly an issue worth working on—along with drunk driving and other self-produced hazards.

In addition to the hospital stay there was a recommended recuperation period at home. But now it was a new home. Jean had found an apartment for me, moved my worldly possessions, laid down the carpets, arranged furniture, books and whatnot, so that when I got out of the hospital, the new living quarters were already set up.

But recuperating at home presented some of the same problems as the hospital stay. People who had never visited me in previous apartments began coming by. They dropped in to chat and made themselves comfortable while I hopped around fixing drinks and snacks for them.

Finally I decided to make the great escape—to Puerto Rico. It was just right—a nice climate in the latter part of the year, carefree surroundings and people I could see when I wanted to. In addition, I got acquainted with Governor Muñoz Marín, a remarkable and charismatic

CIGARETTE BOX

AMERICAN CAR BOMB

Jan. 14, 1964

Dec. 16, 1983

man, sometimes called the Puerto Rican FDR. Besides the governor's palace, he had a tree-shaded outdoor retreat for relaxed conversation over drinks on warm evenings. Visiting with others was much more restful than being host to people visiting me. And I got back in the swing of things playing a little golf—no better than before but hardly worse—with a partner in an electric cart for the fast getaway from topflight players waiting to tee off.

I had been laid up in September and with the leisurely recuperation prescribed then, was ready to go back to work at the end of the year. The office schedule that had started with seven cartoons a week, and then six, was now shortened by one more. I had finally arrived at the five-day week.

There was one other change at the office—a couch. Phil Graham had sent it down from his office when my doctor suggested that I lie down for a while each afternoon. At first I was somewhat self-conscious about this daylight zonk-out time. Calvin Coolidge used to take naps and it was said that he slept through his presidency. I had mixed feelings—happy that people were concerned about my experience, like a kid who can boast a bandage or scar, but unhappy about anyone wanting to dwell on it as if I were an invalid.

But I felt better about the "Coolidge syndrome" when I heard that Winston Churchill had said man was not meant to go from morning to night without a rest period. Later, Lyndon Johnson claimed he could get in two days' work by starting over after a nap. There really is something about blunking out completely, even if only for a few minutes, that seems to recharge the batteries and provide for a fresh approach.

So I became an out-of-the-closet-and-into-my-dreams unabashed napper. Well, almost. When people phone during this brief sack time, Jean says, "He's not in right now." In a way she's right. Every day for a half hour or so, I'm out of it.

19

New Frontiersmen

The first cartoon I did after I came back to work in January 1960 was of Vice President Nixon as a witch asking the mirror, "Who's the fairest one of all?" Phil Graham was somewhat unhappy with it—partly because, as he put it, the drawing seemed to say, "I have returned." And he could have been bothered by a description of it in *Time* magazine as a return to the old tough cartoons about the Nixon that publication seemed to admire. But if Phil had any reservations about the cartoons, they were not evident in memos and letters to outsiders in which he promoted my work, defended it against critics and praised me. He was in close touch with all kinds of politicos and corporate CEOs. "You don't know what it's like," he once told me, "to be needled by people asking, 'Are you running the paper or not?'"

Time magazine had Graham on its cover in a 1956 issue, with his smiling face against a background montage of my cartoons. Phil had asked if this was okay if *Time* paid me for use of the cartoons, and I had no objections. But it was an odd combination cover for a piece completely on the publisher.

In 1960 this magazine asked me to do a cover on Soviet Premier Khrushchev coming to the United Nations. The editors were quite happy with it, but what pleased me more was learning that Groucho Marx wanted to buy the original drawing. As a long-time Marx Brothers fan, I was even happier when Groucho phoned me to chat and express his feelings about the '60 election. He said, with Grouchian hyperbole, that he was probably the only person in Hollywood who was for John F. Kennedy.

The first time I met Kennedy, a U.S. senator at the time, was at a *Washington Post* book lunch where we and a couple of other authors spoke. His book was *Profiles in Courage*. And in his talk, he pointed out that anyone who thought my cartoons were tough should see the kind that were done about politicians in the earlier days of the republic.

In the 1960 primaries, my choice was Hubert Humphrey, and I also still admired Adlai Stevenson. But I had no problem with Kennedy as the Democratic nominee, especially considering the alternative— Nixon, who, in planning his campaign, said he had to "erase the Herblock image." During a debate with Kennedy, he also had a TV image problem.

As far as cartooning is concerned, the TV giveth and the TV taketh away. Because people seem to spend more time televiewing and less time reading long newspaper accounts, the cartoon, as another visual medium, can still compete for attention. But in another sense, TV may have diminished the influence of cartoons. Whether a Reagan or Bush or even a Nixon, the image projected in a cartoon is now up against the carefully constructed image politicians present on television, where they can lie convincingly. They and their handlers create their own images. And in spot commercials, they also create their own caricatures of their opponents. A Boss Tweed today would probably be well groomed and well coached as he told viewers of unfair attacks on him by his opponents—and, of course, by the media.

When Charles de Gaulle controlled French television, he was the butt of many cartoons in his country, but he knew he had the all-pervasive medium.

Kennedy was particularly good on television and with the press in easy give-and-take where he came across as natural and spontaneous. As a presidential candidate, he answered questions on an evening TV interview show. And at the end, the host asked if there was anything Kennedy would care to say to fill the few seconds remaining. JFK replied that he was recently inducted in an Indian tribal ceremony, and now when he saw old cowboy and Indian movies he cheered for "the guys on our side."

During the campaign Graham had Kennedy to an office lunch, where he came across as likable and forthright. In response to a staff member's question, he was quick to say he would welcome debates. Later, at a presidential press conference, he went on record as being willing to debate his opponent in the next election.

Graham pressed JFK to choose Lyndon Johnson for the vice presidential spot, and Kennedy accepted this as a means of strengthening the ticket. After the JFK-LBJ ticket won, Nixon suggested that voting irregularities in Chicago had cost him the White House—*but* that for the good of the country he would not challenge the result.

This was vintage Nixon—the false innuendo coupled with the noble refusal to claim his due. It was in keeping with his style that suggested: I could point out that Insert Name is a lying S.O.B. who has consistently robbed children's piggy banks, *but* I am not going to say that.

It ranks right up there with the Nixon false alternatives, in which he rejects "the easy thing" to do. These might be summarized: There are those who want us to get into nuclear war immediately, and there are others who believe we should unilaterally disarm completely; but I believe we must follow neither course.

There was a good reason why the 1960 election was not challenged by anyone. Republican poll watchers in Chicago were out in force, in far greater number than the Democrats could muster to watch polls in the hardly pristine GOP-dominated downstate area. And no one wanted a recount.

More importantly, the Nixon innuendos didn't add up as well as the 1960 electoral figures. These didn't lie—Kennedy 303 to Nixon 219, a margin of 84 electoral votes. A shift of Illinois' 26 electoral votes to Nixon would still have left him short another very large state or some smaller states. Win or lose, Nixon could never seem to get through a campaign without some measure of fraud.

On a very cold January 20, 1961, I watched the inauguration while squeezed in at a press table—actually a rather long wooden plank—and felt like a fish in a freezer. As the ceremony proceeded a flask of brandy sustained life for a colleague and me. And when some electrical malfunction caused smoke to rise from the podium during Cardinal Cushing's seemingly endless invocation I hoped his eminence was about to descend into hell—and would have been happy to join him there for a little fire and brimstone.

Even in a near-frozen condition I felt warmer than I had while attending the Eisenhower inaugural eight years before. Then, as I watched the incoming and outgoing presidents, I found myself next to a woman I didn't know and ventured that I thought we might miss Truman. She replied icily that perhaps the fellow had done the best he could considering his limitations. Some conversations just don't get very far.

I saw Kennedy a few times more, at a small party or two, some White House dinners and press affairs. He didn't regard the press as the enemy, and in my case at least, seemed to recognize that criticism was not simply carping.

One afternoon I, along with two or three others including a member of Kennedy's staff, took part in a panel discussion before an audience. The staff member took his seat on the stage after the program had begun, and when I whispered, "You're late," he replied in a low voice, "On account of you." He later explained that "the boss" had seen a somewhat critical cartoon of mine that morning and had called him in to ask, "What *are* we doing about this situation?" This, he explained, required him to find out and report back to JFK immediately—causing his delayed appearance at the afternoon meeting.

The JFK press conferences were always worth attending or watching on television. When the Supreme Court ruled against prayer rituals in the public schools, there immediately arose a wail that God was being driven out of our children's schools. Responding to a question on the subject, Kennedy dryly observed that fortunately there were alternatives, like praying in churches, praying at home, etc. He could also have added that individual silent prayer has never been—and couldn't be—prohibited anywhere.

President Kennedy's humor was among his most attractive assets. When a reporter asked the newly elected president if he had a favorite song, he said he liked "Hail to the Chief" pretty well. He also recognized that remarks kidding himself or his family members took a lot of steam out of criticism by others. At a big press dinner JFK read an imaginary election campaign telegram from his father saying that he would pay for a presidential election victory but not an additional cent for a landslide. JFK also said that he was appointing his brother Bobby attorney general to give him some legal experience.

What relationship I had with Bobby Kennedy was far from instant affection on either side. He had earlier served as an aide on Sen. Joseph McCarthy's committee staff, which hardly recommended him to me; and he may well have regarded me as someone who made life difficult for government people doing their duty. I think the first time I saw him was at a party where we ended up across a small room with maybe one or two others. He asked for the original of one of my cartoons. I was sorry I couldn't oblige. He then took me by surprise by asking, what if his brother (the president) wanted one? To this I guess I replied that the drawings were all kept on file.

As time went on we saw each other much more favorably. And I think Bobby kept growing in stature. Like JFK, he also had a good deal of humor. At one party, in talking to a friend, he simulated jealousy of brother Jack by jumping up and down in small-boy fashion, saying, "If I'd been the oldest I could have made it." When he met strangers, he would introduce himself. He didn't assume that everyone knew him, and he gave the other person a chance to provide his own name. To put us on a first-name basis, he kept repeating "Herb, Herb" persistently until I called him Bob or Bobby.

There is always the question of how close a journalist should get to political figures. I've never been all that close to any of them, but there's a natural tendency to see more of the ones you feel are generally fighting the good fight than to spend time with those you don't regard highly. It is not a matter of your views being influenced by those who seem friendly but of feeling closer to those who share your views. I don't think such acquaintanceships have influenced the cartoons, which offer criticism or poke fun where I feel it is needed. The Kennedy administration, which I liked better than most, was no exception.

Visits to Bobby Kennedy's Hickory Hill home—where you might meet Sammy Davis, Jr., one time or former Prime Minister Harold Macmillan another—were always interesting. But I was critical of

Department of Justice bugging, whether authorized by J. Edgar Hoover or approved by RFK. And when Bobby Kennedy ran for president in 1968, I did a cartoon showing Sen. Eugene McCarthy having staked out a "peace candidate" claim first. Opinions on RFK were sharply divided. He was in some ways politically bolder than JFK. And I thought he offered the prospect of inspiring leadership; Eugene McCarthy's followers regarded him as an interloper; and *Post* editor J. R. Wiggins, a Lyndon Johnson supporter, told me that if RFK were nominated he would personally campaign against him.

In the years since John Kennedy's presidency there have been reappraisals of the "Camelot" days, which were not called that at the time, And there are the inevitable what-ifs, particularly concerning Vietnam. Long after that war, I talked with Gen. Harvey Jablonsky, who had been sent by Kennedy to appraise the situation in Vietnam. He reported back to the president that the war, as it was going, would very well last 10 years—an estimate that had a Defense Department official snorting and striding away in disgust. But the next time the general came to the White House he had an extra star on his shoulder.

Kennedy associates have expressed conflicting opinions about what Kennedy would have done in Vietnam had he lived. He felt a need to show strength against Khrushchev. But after the failed Bay of Pigs invasion, Kennedy became quite skeptical of estimates by the Joint Chiefs and the CIA. And while most of JFK's advisers were retained by Johnson, one of the closest and most important, Bobby, was not. Kennedy successfully handled the Berlin crises and the explosive Cuban missile crisis, in which Bobby argued strongly against the military and other advisers who urged bombing. Considering these JFK-RFK efforts, it's possible they might have avoided going down the road taken by Johnson that made Vietnam an ever-expanding U.S.-run war.

President Kennedy's most surprising lapses in judgment seem to have been in reported presidential dalliances, sometimes shockingly ill-considered. The idea of a president of the United States or even a candidate for that office having assignations with the mistress of a leading Mafia figure is boggling.

Yet if there was an unusual amount of lust there was also a good deal of luster. And a president who was no angel could still be, in his public life, on the side of the angels.

180

The Kennedys brought an excitement, an intellectual stimulation and a desire to serve that hadn't been seen since the days of Roosevelt. Bobby Kennedy's stewardship as attorney general stands out particularly when one considers such successors as John Mitchell, Edwin Meese, Richard Kleindienst, Dick Thornburgh and William Barr. And remembering the Kennedy phone call to the wife of a harassed and jailed Martin Luther King, Jr., we recall that Bobby's bitterest enemy was J. Edgar Hoover—the FBI chief whose hatred of King was so great that he hoped to drive the civil rights leader to suicide.

I remember arriving early with friends at the bleachers in front of the Lincoln Memorial for the August 1963 March on Washington. We watched Washington's entire Mall fill up all the way around the Tidal Basin to the Capitol as far as we could see. Some had feared that this march might lead to God-knows-what. What it led to was one of the greatest and most integrated peaceful assemblages ever, with songs and speeches, including King's "I have a dream. . . ." I stayed as long as I could and then hotfooted it back to the office to do a cartoon. It was a time when people came together for civil rights and we all shared a dream, and we joined hands in singing "We shall overcome."

We believed, as President Kennedy had said a couple of months before, that "the time has come for this nation to fulfill its promises." And then, a little more than three months after the march, the promising life of John F. Kennedy ended unfulfilled.

As one who had doubts about a Lyndon Johnson presidency, I was relieved and cheered when he followed his statement "We shall continue . . ." with a strong push for civil rights and social programs.

With the excitement of the Kennedy presidency and the Johnson achievements that came quickly afterward, the early '60s were a halcyon time. Life was good. In an art group that met once a week, with each of us contributing toward the cost of a model, I did some sketching and painting.

I played my usual ragged game of golf, generally at East Potomac Park, where three public courses were located right in the city. They were open every month of the year to all players regardless of race or sex—or ability. Here it was possible to get out weekends or even play the nine-hole "G course" before going to the office. On these rounds, an occasional partner was June Bingham, wife of the New York congressman. She would toot the horn as she drove by my house, and we were off to play a two-and-a-halfsome. The fractional part was her well-trained poodle, who would sit while we teed off, then trot along behind and sit again when it came to the edge of each green.

But the most regular partner continued to be Fred Blumenthal of *Parade* magazine. For about $500 he and I purchased an old Karmann-Ghia that we used almost exclusively for transportation to and from golf courses. The driver's side was his half, and I explained to friends that I owned a Ghia. My major contribution to our new/used car was a little surprise for Freddie. When he said, "Let's see what's in the glove compartment," and unlatched it, an assortment of all kinds of gloves tumbled out.

In 1964 that convenient nine-hole in-city course was threatened by a proposal to build an aquarium on its site. I wrote an open letter to Secretary of the Interior Stewart Udall, pointing out the benefits of this

1964

182

access-to-everyone course and challenging him to a match for its future. He accepted in a telegram:

> Dear Fellow Trudger: Since I regard you as the District's leading duffer and defender of open space, will be glad to join you for a few holes at East Potomac Park this Friday for a summit discussion of the "doomed course." However, suggest you leave your wedge at home as I will not be responsible for any damage you should do to our open space.
>
> Stewart L. Udall
> Secretary of the Interior

And we played a round that would make any true golfer shudder. At one point, when we were making simultaneous approaches from opposite sides of a green (not exactly the PGA approach to the game or the green), cameras caught our two golf balls colliding in mid-air. During the few moments that shots of this game were shown on TV, no one tuning in by accident could have mistaken this for the Masters at Augusta.

Udall won, and at the end of the game announced that the course would nevertheless be spared—a decision he had reached well before we teed off.

In the '80s, with the Interior Department under the stewardship of James Watt, there was no good-natured play or discussion of plans about the course. The fences surrounding it were one day simply knocked down by front-loaders, which moved in and bulldozed the greens. The course was then left unplayable for a year or two while plans were considered for some other use.

But eventually justice and the rights of duffers won again. A retired government worker and her husband, who had done the G course every playable day for years, enlisted others in a persistent fight. I wrote another piece, this time not addressed to the secretary of the interior. The man who actually brought about the resurrection was Rep. Sidney Yates—a golfer who was concerned about a public recreation area and had the drive and follow-through to bring that nine-hole public course back to life.

In the mid-'60s a Cabinet colleague of Udall's came up with a suggestion for me that involved only the swinging of pen and brush. Postmaster General Lawrence F. O'Brien asked if I'd design a stamp commemorating the 175th anniversary of the Bill of Rights. The stamp went on sale July 4, 1966, in a ceremony at Miami Beach, where O'Brien and I spoke our pieces—and where I learned about things like first-day covers, some of which still arrive at the office from collectors.

My only previous experience with stamps was licking and pasting and wondering if there were enough of them on parcels. I had heard about the surprising value of some stamps from a friend of my dad's who'd had an unusual experience with a new stamp. This was Captain Benjamin Lipsner, an early pilot who became superintendent of the first U.S. airmail service. He knew nothing about philately either, but he knew planes. When the first airmail stamps rolled off the presses, he was shocked and angry to find that the Jenny biplane on some of those two-color sheets was printed upside down, with its landing gear on top. This, he feared, was just the thing to make his fledgling airmail service look ridiculous. He immediately put a stop to the printing and sale of this piece of engraving. Lipsner said he was glad to put this potential embarrassment behind him. Alas, he didn't keep any of those stupid stamps to remind him of it.

There was nothing rare or valuable about my stamp, which brought its face value of five cents. And with postal rates steadily increasing, its value on envelopes has depreciated.

Postmaster General O'Brien promoted the idea of removing the Postal Service from government operation and reorganizing it into its present corporate-independent-semipublic-but-monopoly-who's-on-first? status. The purpose of this policy, later adopted by the Nixon administration, was to get the system out of politics and put it on a paying basis. This must have seemed like a good idea in theory, but O'Brien later had misgivings about the management and operation of the new Postal Service.

From time to time I saw other members of the original Kennedy team. Pierre Salinger returned from Paris occasionally, and generously helped exchange greetings and books between me and *L'Express* cartoonist Tim.

Shortly after leaving office, Orville Freeman, who had been

secretary of agriculture, and his wife were invited to a dinner. Mrs. Freeman arrived on time, but quite a while passed without Freeman appearing. When inquiry was made, it turned out that the recent cabinet member, who hadn't had to drive for some time, was busy parking the car. *Sic transit!*

The knights of the Round Table didn't have to worry about quartering their steeds.

"LET'S GET A LOCK FOR THIS THING"

NUCLEAR WAR

HERBLOCK
©1962 THE WASHINGTON POST

Nov. 1, 1962

186

"SADDLE UP. WE CAN STILL HEAD 'EM OFF AT THE GULCH"

March 28, 1961

"PRAY KEEP MOVING, BROTHER"

Aug. 14, 1960

"AND THIS IS OUR OWN LITTLE TRACKING OPERATIONS ROOM"

Feb. 26, 1962

"LEAVING RELIGION TO PRIVATE INITIATIVE IS UN-AMERICAN!"

June 28, 1962

"SORRY, BUT YOU HAVE AN INCURABLE SKIN CONDITION"

July 4, 1963

20

Lunch Break

Lunch, whether people have it, do it, get together for it or just plain eat it, is a pause in the day's occupation. I generally have it at my desk, and having started out at a dining table with a couple of hungry older brothers, I learned to avoid dawdling. But I don't always stay at my desk. And on one occasion, at least, I've eaten at someone else's desk. That was my lunch with Admiral Rickover.

He had phoned to invite me to his office, an unelaborate place in one of the Navy's old "tempo" buildings. He spoke at some length and eventually called for lunch to be served. The two lunches did not require a lot of space on his desk. My mind rejects the exact menu—I think it was something like a boiled egg and a couple of lettuce leaves, but this is probably an exaggeration. It was in keeping with his Spartan ways, but I felt like the Spartan boy trying to disregard a wolf gnawing at his innards. There are those for whom a light repast puts hunger to rest. In my case it only arouses a dozing monster that awakens to cry, "More!"

It was Rickover's pursuit of excellence that inspired the title of

Jimmy Carter's book *Why Not the Best?* My stomach asked only, Where Is the Rest?

I fared better, and had better fare, sometime later when I found myself part of an informal lunch group that got together about once a month. Founders of this group were author Herman Wouk and Franc Shor, associate editor of the *National Geographic*.

Early "regulars" were John Walker and J. Carter Brown of the National Gallery of Art; Richard Scammon, political statistician and former Census Bureau director; Tom Wicker of the *New York Times;* Henry Brandon of the *London Times;* correspondent Ed Morgan; the ambassadors of Canada and Italy; Louis Wright of the Folger Library; and David Lloyd Kreeger, philanthropist and patron of the arts. Later participants included attorney Clark Clifford and Daniel Boorstin and James Billington, successive librarians of Congress.

A favorite recollection is of a lunch in Kreeger's bright and spacious home where paintings by great artists fit beautifully but unobtrusively. Kreeger, wanting to get the national pulse on some current subject, said earnestly, "Look, we're an average bunch of guys; what do you fellows think?" Just as earnestly the others were about to respond, when I looked around the table at this high-priced bunch of average guys I had fallen in with and guffawed. Kreeger conceded that this might not exactly be considered a man-in-the-street poll.

After publication of *The Winds of War,* Herman Wouk wondered if the group might have some thoughts about a title for the sequel. But such suggestions as *The Warmer Winds* and *The Warring Windbags* didn't exactly make it. And when someone came up with *The Breaking Winds,* Herman's "Thanks a lot, fellows" repeated a couple of times managed to bring to an end the efforts of the eager helpers.

Wouk's meticulous concern for accuracy sent him on travels to all the scenes of his novels. In his home, large detailed maps made his study look something like a war room. And when Yitzhak Rabin—at that time former prime minister of Israel—came as a luncheon guest, he studied these maps, reliving his own history and military campaigns.

During the filming of concentration camp scenes in Europe for *War and Remembrance,* Wouk observed the shooting of a night scene. He saw freight trains bring in the victims, as stolid guards stood watch under the glare of lights. He looked at the local actors and found the re-creation itself chilling.

Because of his intimate study of the war, I once asked him why, with the information we apparently had on the Japanese government's plans, Pearl Harbor took place. He gave the classic answer: "Intelligence is only as good as the people who receive it."

There was not always general agreement on political issues, but the discussions never became heated. When Clark Clifford was defending President Carter's Budget Director Bert Lance, I was drawing cartoons aimed at Lance's removal. We each stated our views and went on to other subjects.

I had a special interest in talking with John Walker and Carter Brown about the National Gallery of Art. On a visit to Washington in 1941, a colleague took me along to its opening when President Roosevelt made a speech in the shoulder-to-shoulder crowded foyer. At the time, some critics described the gallery as being more marble than masterpieces, but Walker and Brown made the art collection one of the world's greatest.

When I asked Walker about the special joys or problems of directing the gallery, he told me that, after closing time, he would sometimes walk through the empty rooms by himself, pausing to savor favorite pieces of art. There is literally a downside to gallery collecting of great art. That is the storing somewhere below of unsolicited gifts of not-so-great art that does not reach the level of gallery walls. But the securing of a masterpiece is a real triumph. Carter Brown was responsible for the acquisition of the gallery's only Da Vinci. And I learned that despite the apparent hazards, air travel is the preferred method of moving a master painting across the ocean because of the shorter traveling time between controlled environments.

But there were a few nervous moments in transporting the Da Vinci, which was brought from Europe by plane in a suitcase occupying a seat next to the man escorting it. The specially constructed suitcase had, among other features, special temperature controls to ensure its survival; and arrangements had been made for it to proceed through customs on arrival. However, in mid-flight the courier was startled to hear that the plane might not make its designated landing but would have to arrive in the United States at another airport. This would mean different customs officials, who would want to open the suitcase. He was relieved when conditions cleared enough for the plane to follow its original landing plan; the suitcase was sped through customs and on to its destination.

I always enjoy visiting the gallery and have learned to see special exhibitions as soon as possible because the weeks or months that invite procrastination soon slip by. With good exhibits, time is fleeting and art is not long enough.

I marvel at Van Gogh, who must be a favorite of just about everybody. And I have a special admiration for Cézanne and the way he laid on the paint. While standing in front of one of his works I once heard Carter Brown give a brief explanation to a guest who had asked what it was the impressionist movement had done. Running his hand in front of the painting, Brown said, "They took you into the studio and let you see the brush strokes."

In the lunch group anything can come up for discussion—art, music, books, the state of the world or a current political situation. Scammon's knowledge of demographics and the political nuts and bolts of districts around the country lead us to ply him with many questions before and after elections.

We learned from the librarian of Congress that a big problem was not collecting and cataloging new books but devising methods to preserve some old ones—not the *very* old ones that were printed on rag paper, but books of a certain age when wood pulp came in and began deteriorating.

Lunch group founder Franc Shor, as editor, writer and constant traveler, was the only person I knew who could claim to have been to every country in the world. He loved good dining, good wine and good conversation. And the "bunch of guys" (maybe ten or a dozen at a time) consisted of people Shor liked talking with. He delighted in tossing out for consideration as possible regulars the names of prominent officials who had come as invited guests, and then ruling them out. He also occasionally played devil's advocate or invited a little brain cudgeling by asking, for example, why classical music that "we" liked should be subsidized while rock concerts paid their own way.

When Shor died he left some of his vintage wine to be set out at a farewell party for various friends and colleagues, who got together with no formal speeches or agenda. One associate of his, twisting the stem of a wineglass in his hand, looked up to observe, ''There were some who thought he was a son of a bitch and some who loved him, and I was one of the latter.'' Just the kind of tribute the late editor would have appreciated.

At the next gathering, Wouk recalled that Shor, after thinking about his writing and editing and wide travels, had said that if there was one thing he might be remembered for, it was the lunch group. From then on, invitations were for ''Franc Shor lunches.''

21

LBJ

President Lyndon Johnson was a mixed bag. Perhaps most presidents are. But Johnson was a Texas-size mixed bag of big achievements, big mistakes and tall tales. As a senator, he hardly seemed like a civil rights champion, and I was not enthusiastic about him as a vice presidential candidate. But as president following Kennedy, he pressed for the 1964 and 1968 Civil Rights Acts and the 1965 Voting Rights Act. He delivered a speech to Congress using the well-understood phrase "We shall overcome"—and overcame opposition.

His War on Poverty and Great Society programs may not have been as great or as victorious as optimists could have hoped, but they had unquestionable successes. His education and health care programs like Head Start, Medicare and Medicaid accomplished a great deal. Surely he was far more an "education president" and an "environment president" than George Bush, who said in 1991 that the Johnson domestic initiatives were failures and responsible for some of the ills of the 1990s. But Bush didn't move to repeal them or replace Medicare and Medicaid with a comprehensive health care plan.

In the 1964 election, it was easy to be for LBJ. He seemed more progressive and less inclined to shoot from the hip than Barry Goldwater.

But when it came to Vietnam, LBJ's capacity for pushing through legislation became the bull-it-through war policy that would end his presidency.

Originally, I was, and I think most Americans were, what columnist Stewart Alsop later described as hawks. There were some notable exceptions. While Kennedy was president, I remember a conversation in which Ben Cohen, famous New Deal brain truster, warned against even the comparatively modest involvement of the time. And Senators Ernest Gruening and Wayne Morse voted against Johnson's substitute for a declaration of war, the Gulf of Tonkin Resolution. This, we later learned, represented a gulf between fact and official statements. It was during Johnson's term that Murrey Marder of *The Washington Post* wrote of a "credibility gap."

Johnson's words about the Dominican Republic in 1965 gave me doubts about his policies in Vietnam. For me, the moment of truth came with presidential untruths about our intervention there. Johnson spoke vividly of Dominican atrocities and reported that our ambassador had to hide under his desk—all false.

In an almost literal sense, Vietnam marked the end of innocence. Of course we knew that politicians didn't always tell it straight. But, in a foreign struggle particularly, we wanted to believe that our government was at least on the side of right and honesty.

The escalation of our involvement in Vietnam was officially reported as representing no change in the situation. But Johnson's privately expressed policy was more in line with his earthy view of the advent of pantyhose, which he regarded as something designed to spoil one of life's pleasures. He described his Vietnam policy as being like first putting a hand on a girl's knee.

Johnson's general deviousness prompted someone to describe him as a man who thought that the shortest distance between two points was a tunnel.

The Post supported Johnson and his policies. I think editor J. R. Wiggins, like many of us, was conditioned in part by the recollections of aggression left unchecked before World War II. But the war in

Southeast Asia was different from World War II and from North Korea's outright invasion of South Korea.

As I became increasingly unhappy with the war policy, there was some more or less delicate maneuvering on the editorial-and-cartoon situation—this time of longer duration than a presidential campaign or a Supreme Court nomination. When I brought in sketches to editor Wiggins, he would sometimes hold forth on the war or other policies on which we disagreed. But he would often end up good-humoredly saying, "All right, but God knows I tried to reason with you."

In a way, this began the transition toward my doing cartoons without submitting them to an editor at all. When a new editorial page editor later lopped off a cartoon caption, I told executive editor Wiggins I'd had it with the new man and was not going to stay on if it meant working with him. Wiggins had a quick and calming solution. "Keep your shirt on," he said, "and just continue showing sketches to me." When he was not there I simply tried them out on others. Eventually the break with the old method of submitting sketches for approval became complete. But each day, as soon as I've hit on the "sketch of the day," a copy of it is sent to the editorial page editor. *The Post*'s policy on LBJ and the war took longer to change.

I saw Johnson a few times at White House affairs and at press dinners and a couple of times at homes where he would put in an appearance. Whatever his concealment on policies, in his feelings toward people he sometimes wore his spleen on his sleeve. If I had done something critical, he might glare at me as he walked around the room shaking hands. At other times, Johnson could be expansive.

Early in his administration, Katharine Graham took a few of us to the White House for lunch with Johnson. He answered some question of mine rather coolly while picking his teeth. Before we left, he presented Mrs. Graham with some memento for her to give to her children because "their daddy had so much to do with my being here."

Only when Mrs. Graham began writing her memoirs did I learn that after *The Post,* under her management, had published something Johnson disapproved of, he stopped speaking to her for about a century. So much for the woman who succeeded her children's daddy.

LBJ's use of this southern term for father must have been infectious. After the 1964 Democratic nominating convention, Hubert Humphrey spoke about the trip there. He said that Johnson kept talking about his daddy, and Hubert found himself talking about *his* daddy. The president and soon-to-be vice president of the United States were flying on majestic Air Force One talking about *"his* daddy and *my* daddy and *our* daddies."

The working relationship that Humphrey and Johnson had formed in the Senate probably gave the Minnesota senator a little more clout with conservatives and provided Johnson with an ally who inspired the confidence of liberals. But the presidential treatment of the vice president struck me as shameful, even extending to making sport of him as a horseman.

Before an annual press dinner—which the president customarily attends and where he makes the closing remarks—the White House let it be known that President Johnson would not be coming. Speaking in his place would be the vice president, who prepared a talk suitable for the occasion. At the last minute, Johnson strode in, with his own speech in hand. I never got to hear or read what Humphrey described as his great lost speech.

A low point in my not-very-close relationship with Johnson came in 1965. The *New York Herald Tribune* had run a story about a speech by presidential assistant Jack Valenti, which seemed to me a bit much. He was quoted as saying that LBJ is "a sensitive man, a cultivated man, a warm-hearted man. . . . I sleep each night a little better, a little more confidently because Lyndon Johnson is my president." Long after, when someone asked Valenti about that speech it turned out this line was a paraphrase of something said by or about Winston Churchill. But despite the admiration of his aide, I couldn't help thinking of the hard-driving executive with his considerable ego, and I did the cartoon "Happy Days on the Old Plantation." A columnist in close touch with the White House immediately wrote a piece saying that people around the president were irate about the cartoon but that Johnson had found it amusing. Nice try by the columnist, but it didn't seem to mesh with actual events.

Shortly afterward I went to a National Press Club luncheon where some visiting cartoonists were doing chalk talks. Johnson made another unscheduled appearance. He began his remarks by glaring at me and saying, "I've just come over from the old plantation." He later added, "I don't feel about cartoonists like the man who said, 'We couldn't find the artist so we just hung his picture.' " Then, again glowering at me in the audience, "I don't feel that way—just occasionally." And from there he went on to heap praise on the other cartoonists. His remarks were not lost on the members of the audience, who commented afterward that he seemed to have something on his mind.

But this was not all. President Kennedy had established the Presidential Medal of Freedom as an annual award based on recommendations of a committee. The awards were made on the Fourth of July each year, a custom continued by Johnson. At a reception at Walter Lippmann's home, Lippmann told me that I had been scheduled to receive the Medal of Freedom and that Johnson had canceled it. He added, "I'll bet they wish they could take mine back too." The story about this incident surfaced as an item in *Newsweek*. And this prompted a statement by the White House press secretary that it was his "guess" the story was totally wrong. He added that the award committee was simply slow with its recommendations. But no awards were made on that Fourth of July or the following ones. And a colleague's check with a staff member confirmed what Lippmann had told me. Historian Eric F. Goldman, who served as special consultant to LBJ, wrote, in his book about Johnson, that Johnson "did not . . . appear to comprehend that by honoring a sometime satirist of himself, who happened to be an American of extraordinary talent, he would be adding flavor to his Administration."

The Medal of Freedom became more and more simply the president's medal—sometimes even awarded at the end of a chief executive's term to loyal followers or staff members. In Vietnam, Johnson reportedly carried medals of some kind in his pocket and once offered one to an officer to whom he had already given one.

I didn't really know Jack Valenti at the time, but he later told me that when Johnson saw one of my cartoons he didn't like, he would ask, "Did you see what *your friend* did this morning?" Valenti said jokingly that I had made him famous, and we did become friends.

LBJ's moods and appearances could be unpredictable. At an Averell Harriman dinner party, one guest listed as Ambassador or Earl or Duke Some-name-or-other was late in arriving. The guest, whose identity was kept secret by the foreign-dignitary name, was President Johnson.

But at this dinner there was also a guest whose artwork the president didn't like. This was Peter Hurd, who had painted an official portrait of Johnson which LBJ declared to be "the ugliest thing I ever saw." Also on the guest list was the person who had recommended Hurd for the portrait job. And to make matters worse, I had just done a cartoon *about* the painting, and what Johnson would have found more acceptable—a radiant kind of godlike figure. But the unflappable Harriman made some humorous remarks that put everyone at ease and may even have softened the LBJ view of artists and cartoonists.

With all the evaluations of the Great Society programs and Johnson's escalation of the war in Vietnam, LBJ's influence—for good and for bad—on the Supreme Court shouldn't get lost in the shuffle. His nominations were Abe Fortas, a brilliant lawyer; and Thurgood Marshall, one of the most notable appointments in the history of the Court.

I met Marshall once, when he was solicitor general and we were seated together at a large dinner. A vacancy had just occurred on the Supreme Court and, by way of conversation, I asked who he thought might be nominated. He gave some kind of noncommittal response. I felt pretty foolish when I picked up the daily paper shortly afterward to find that the new nominee was Thurgood Marshall.

But, in evaluating Johnson's effect on the Court, there was, as so often the case with him, a dark side as well as a bright side. In 1965 he convinced Justice Arthur Goldberg to trade his Court robes for the position of U.S. ambassador to the United Nations. His argument was that Goldberg, a man of outstanding ability as a negotiator, was the one person who could bring about peace in Vietnam. The presidential appeal was so convincing that Goldberg resigned to accept the U.N. position.

There was a story that he had been promised a direct line to the White House, but it turned out that the line worked in only one direction. Whether or not this was literally so, it summed up the situation. But this injury would later be salted with insult. I'm indebted to former Justice Brennan for an account of a Goldberg-LBJ incident.

When Goldberg was on the Court, he had given Johnson a portrait of Oliver Wendell Holmes that had been painted by Goldberg's wife, Dorothy. And Johnson sent them a silver set.

We come now to a moment years later when Goldberg is reading a book by the former president. In this, LBJ said that he had heard rumors that Goldberg was restless on the Court and would like another position. Johnson said that when he and Goldberg were returning from the funeral of Adlai Stevenson (previous U.N. ambassador and presidential nominee), Goldberg "told me these reports had substance." LBJ—according to his account—soon learned that Goldberg wanted the U.N. vacancy. On reading this version—and remembering how LBJ had twisted his arm to accept the U.N. position—Goldberg became so angry that he promptly phoned Johnson and said he was returning the silver set and wanted back the portrait he and his wife had given LBJ.

Johnson's persuasiveness must have been remarkable, especially considering his influence on the lifetime appointees to the Supreme Court. Earl Warren opposed members of the Court serving in any other capacity, and he resisted LBJ's entreaties to head the commission to investigate the assassination of President Kennedy. Johnson argued that only a man of the Chief Justice's stature could give the investigation the absolute credibility it needed. The fruit of the LBJ arguments can be summed up in three words: The Warren Commission.

Colleagues, stunned by Goldberg's resignation from the Court, asked how it could have happened. He is said to have reminded them of Chief Justice Warren's own experience in yielding to LBJ's urging—a clincher.

Incidentally, the prestige of the Chief Justice did not prevent the endless controversy over the assassination and the three-volume Warren report.

The consequences of Johnson's changes in the Court were far-reaching. He had appointed his friend and confidant Abe Fortas to succeed Goldberg. When Earl Warren decided to retire, contingent on a successor being named, Johnson nominated Justice Fortas to be Chief Justice. But Senate Republicans succeeded in delaying confirmation of the lame-duck president's nominee. And eventually disclosure of Fortas's acceptance of funds from a questionable foundation became his undoing. Even though there was no evidence that it influenced any of his decisions, it certainly seemed improper. And it was with regret that I did a cartoon calling for an explanation. Fortas not only wasn't confirmed for Chief Justice, but also resigned from the Court. And the GOP senators prevented confirmation of a Warren successor until after Nixon took office.

Eventually the Court would change anyhow. But the Goldberg resignation began the breakup of the Warren Court. I'm sure Goldberg would have considered his giving up the Court seat worthwhile if Johnson's bright scenario of his bringing peace had any hope of fulfillment. It did not, and the American involvement in Vietnam became wider and deeper.

One evening, in a conversation with a Johnson Cabinet member, I asked why the Vietnamese were not doing more of the fighting themselves. My question must have seemed naive to the official, who said quietly, "I don't think we want them to do their own fighting"—which was of course the case. Whatever policy John F. Kennedy would have pursued, he had once said of the Vietnamese that the war was theirs to win or lose (but that we must stay involved). LBJ felt that with our know-how and power we could do it better.

One of the leading and most influential critics of the war policy was Walter Lippmann, who more and more became the target of derogatory remarks by Johnson and his aides. In 1967, I wrote a piece for *The Post* called "The War On Walter Lippmann" and illustrated the article with the drawing shown on the next page. I was later astonished to read in a book about leading newspapers that I had pictured LBJ and a fleeing Lippmann—just the opposite of my article and drawing.

Arguments raged about the 1968 Tet Offensive, which some observers maintained was the Viet Cong's final all-out effort. But whatever the military situation, there had been too many misleading reports, too many victories in the offing, too many deceptions, too many lights at the end of too many tunnels and too many Americans brought home in flag-draped caskets for the country to retain confidence in this administration's war policies.

Nevertheless, LBJ's announcement, at the end of a speech, that he would not run again came as a complete surprise. While taking in the broadcast from a reclining TV-watching posture on the couch, I snapped into an upright position when he threw that punch line and then phoned friends to ask if they had heard what he had said.

Toward the end of his tenure, Johnson was becoming reconciled to events and criticism. At a White House dinner in honor of British Prime Minister Harold Wilson, LBJ introduced me to Wilson with the highest praise. Johnson said that I was "our best" and added, "Oh,

1967

he'll come over and eat your cookies, but then he'll go back and draw a cartoon giving you hell the next day."

Recalling that early new-boy-in-town cocktail party when editor Herbert Elliston provided the example of keeping the work separate from any hobnobbing with the high and mighty, I felt this was as good a compliment as I could have had.

Better than a medal.

HOUSE DIVIDED

March 5, 1968

"THANKS—THANKS A LOT—THANKS AGAIN— CAN I LEAN BACK NOW?"

July 13, 1965

July 6, 1966

"OUR POSITION HASN'T CHANGED AT ALL"

June 17, 1965

"THERE'S MONEY ENOUGH TO SUPPORT BOTH OF YOU—NOW, DOESN'T THAT MAKE YOU FEEL BETTER?"

Aug. 1, 1967

"EVERYTHING'S OKAY—THEY NEVER REACHED THE MIMEOGRAPH MACHINE"

Feb. 1, 1968

Jan. 28, 1968

THE BUILT-IN BOMB

July 17, 1966

HAPPY DAYS ON THE OLD PLANTATION

June 30, 1965

"ALL RIGHT NOW, TEAM—HEADS UP—WE CAN WIN THIS OLD BALL GAME"

Sept. 5, 1968

22

Capital Visitors

All kinds of people come to Washington for all kinds of reasons, and it may have succeeded the outdoor Paris cafe as the place sooner or later to see everyone in the world. There are heads of state, demonstrators, people making reluctant visits at the invitations of the IRS or congressional committees, sightseers, celebrities and old friends.

Among long-time Chicago friends who called on me from time to time was one I had sort of inherited from my father—Dr. Albert Tannenbaum, who headed the cancer research center at Michael Reese Hospital in Chicago. He was the first to publish a paper on a matter now taken for granted—the relationship between obesity and life-threatening diseases. His experiments and findings were later summed up by a magazine writer in a piece titled "The Thin Mice Bury the Fat Mice."

When I saw Al during World War II, he mentioned that he was doing some work at the University of Chicago. This, I learned after the war, was the atomic bomb Manhattan Project. He later went to Eniwetok for the nuclear blast there. But his own laboratory experiments involved countless generations of mice. And people knowing of his research asked the same questions so often that he finally developed surprising answers for them. In response to the question "Do you think there will ever be a cure so that people won't die of cancer?" he would reply, "I'm not interested in people. My work is with mice." When he was in the mood, he would give a more elaborate answer: "Oh, the cure for cancer is no problem, I have that locked up in the safe. What I'm working on are the *causes* of cancer." This would send his questioners into a tizzy, explaining to him that he owed it to society to take the secret out of the safe and make it public. They would then verge on apoplexy when he insisted that this must be done in an orderly scientific way—first find the *cause, then* come out with the cure.

Al was visiting one evening when the early edition of the morning paper came through the mail slot. While we talked, I took a quick look to make sure nothing had gone amiss with the cartoon. Something had. The typeset caption from the day before had been left on top of the new cartoon that had no relation to it. Al told me later, "When I saw you looking at the paper, I knew there was something wrong even before you threw it across the room and dived over the couch for the telephone."

Another midwestern visitor was a lively young woman from Wisconsin named Eppie Lederer. She came to Washington and dropped in at *The Post* from time to time because she was interested in everything that was going on. One of the things going on was the performance of the junior senator from her state, Joseph McCarthy. She was outspokenly opposed to him and worked tirelessly for his defeat.

She later shared her views and insights with many more people when she began writing for the *Chicago Sun-Times* under the name Ann Landers. I don't know if she ever passed along to them the incidental intelligence I learned in an early conversation—that her father, who had run a motion picture theater in Sioux City, Iowa, was the man who married motion pictures and popcorn. He installed the first popping machine in a movie house.

A friend and fellow artist from high school days named Hank Brennan was a frequent visitor. One day when I was beating out the deadline I got a call from Brennan, who wondered if we could get together for dinner. My old school friend had just been in town a few weeks earlier, and I explained that I was really busy right now. But perhaps some other time—how long was he going to be in town? He said that he was going to be living here now. I suggested that since he was going to be in town regularly, we could get together some other time. He was awfully nice about it, knew how busy I was, and of course would be glad to make it another time.

After I put down the phone and got back to the drawing, it occurred to me that my friend had been pretty casual about mentioning he was going to be living in Washington now. And then the little light bulb went on over my head. This was not my artist friend Hank Brennan—this man had said he was *Bill* Brennan. Good God! Bill—as in William J. Brennan, the new associate justice of the Supreme Court of the United States. Aaargh!

Despite what must have seemed a pretty cavalier attitude on my part, this great and genuinely modest man had not been put off at all. Later on, we did get together from time to time, always a particular pleasure for me. But I was too mortified about that long-ago phone call ever to tell him about the mix-up by a guy who does not get invitations from Supreme Court justices every day of the week.

No possible confusion could exist about names of stage and movie people who turn up here, as many do. There is a certain affinity between Hollywood and Washington, both of which produce people who appear on TV—and a certain mutual fascination between political people and movie people. I think, incidentally, there's also some connection between cartoonists and actors. It is no coincidence that many actors sketch or paint. And it's possible to read in a cartoonist's smiling, frowning or angry face the expressions on the characters he draws, as he acts them inwardly. Outwardly, cartoonists often ham it up where there is an opportunity to do skits. As for politicians who play to audiences, the acting connection needs no elaboration.

At movie preview parties in Washington, the stars sometimes come with the pictures. If there are people who are unimpressed by meeting a Gregory Peck or a Carol Burnett or a James Earl Jones, I'm not one of them. Film producer and founder of the American Film Institute George Stevens, Jr., and Motion Picture Association head Jack Valenti both live in Washington and operate on both coasts. Valenti has screening parties preceded by large dinners and light remarks. And the Stevens home manages a marvelous mix of journalists, playwrights, TV people, authors, politicians and actors. Pamela Harriman is one of the most charming and politically knowledgeable people on either side of the Atlantic, and practically any party at her home is a Washington Event. When President-elect Bill Clinton came to the capital for his first two-day trip after his victory, a dinner party at Mrs. Harriman's was on the agenda. More surprising than seeing celebrities at such places has been the occasional meeting—while hurrying from my office to the newsroom—with an Elizabeth Taylor or Robert Redford that Katharine Graham has been showing through the building.

The movies really moved into *The Washington Post* during the filming of *All the President's Men,* when Redford and Dustin Hoffman spent time in the newsroom getting the feel of the paper and talking with the people they were portraying. Nobody wanted to intrude, but a remarkable number of *Post* people found reasons to see someone or other at desks near the ones occupied by the two stars. Hoffman remarked that either these newspaper people had little interest in Hollywood actors or else they had good peripheral vision. When he took a break from the relatively well-ordered newsroom, he stuck his head into my cluttered office and observed, "It sure is different."

At a Washington gathering, a hostess mentioned to Ed Asner that I was from Chicago, and he volunteered in his trademark gruff voice that at one time he drove a taxicab there. I told him I thought I remembered him and had a bad ride in his cab; and he immediately said, "Yeah, but you were a bum tipper."

Not to make a big deal of big names, but we're all interested in seeing famous people up close. And when they turn out to be regular people and not taken with their fame, that's bingo.

An actress who wins applause offstage as well as on is Katharine Hepburn. While appearing in a play in Washington, she put on a benefit performance for Planned Parenthood. A mutual friend active in that organization framed a print of a cartoon I had done on the subject and asked if I would present it to Hepburn after the play. Would I ever! She couldn't have been nicer. She talked a little about the play and liked the cartoon, but wanted to know if I'd take it out of the frame, sign it and send it to her. The inscription expressed admiration, and she wrote a lovely note in reply. There is a little footnote to that visit here. A friend told me of being with a small group of people who insisted on waiting after a performance just to see Hepburn as she left the theater.

My friend embarrassedly stayed with them. When Hepburn came out, they were delighted that she smiled in recognition, and completely flipped when she stopped and talked with each of them. A classy lady.

Any appearance by Lauren Bacall brightens the scene. And Carol Channing's visits to Washington bring their own excitement. I don't know how she came to be on Nixon's enemies list, but assumed that the threat to the government must have come from her appearance somewhere on behalf of a Democratic candidate. Young son Channing Lowe was a budding cartoonist who soon came to town on his own, and he later became a full-time editorial cartoonist on a daily paper.

It's also a treat when friends entertain the endearing Kitty Carlisle Hart—singer, actress, author and widow of playwright Moss Hart. Among her many admirers was Thomas E. Dewey, who had been twice Republican nominee for president. Their differing political views did not affect their interest in each other. And people who had considered him a stuffy fellow revised their opinion when they met the "little man on the wedding cake" who had proposed sharing a wedding cake with Kitty.

An interest in government and issues brings Hollywood people to testify before Congress on behalf of causes. Congressional politics has also brought some to the Capitol.

Judy Holliday apparently aroused the suspicions of the House Committee on Un-American Activities when it learned that she was a very intelligent woman who only *played* dumb blonde roles in movies. When some friends escorted her to her accommodations atop the Statler Hotel, she exclaimed, "It's the set from *Born Yesterday!*" The set was probably patterned after that penthouse suite.

Myrna Loy spent time in Washington when she was a member of the U.S. delegation to the United Nations. And I was happy to find that she was as unaffectedly delightful off-screen as on. When she became a Kennedy Center honoree at a ceremony in 1990, the general affection for her was palpable.

On one occasion I lucked out to find my dinner partner was Marlene Dietrich, past her movie career but still unquestionably beautiful. She had staunchly stood up to Hitlerism and strongly disliked her early co-star Emil Jannings, a man she described as a Nazi.

Another actress strongly opposed to dictatorship in her country was

211

Melina Mercouri, who made occasional visits here while Greece was run by a military junta. In Washington she expressed her appreciation to those she felt kept alive the spirit of democracy in Greece. She and others told me that my cartoons on her country had a wide underground circulation there. At one party the lovely actress said to Sen. William Fulbright, "I wish I could think of some way to thank you for all you've done." And Fulbright, with almost a straight face, replied, "I hope you will try very hard."

After the fall of the military junta, a more formal appreciation came at the Greek Embassy where the prime minister's wife, Margaret Papandreou, delivered a talk in flawless English. I felt as I had on my first trip abroad about the provincialism of people like me who had no knowledge of a foreign tongue, when someone like the Greek leader's wife spoke our language as if she were a native. The guilt feelings subsided when I learned that Mrs. Papandreou *was* an American native—born and raised here and graduated from the University of California.

Writers also turn up in Washington, whether to express views to Congress, to attend ceremonies or just to visit. The only time I met Truman

"WE TOO HAVE TROUBLEMAKERS WHO DON'T APPRECIATE AUTHORITY"

"DID YOU SAY THE MAGIC WORDS, 'LAW AND ORDER'?"

Oct. 19, 1971

April 15, 1970

Papa

Sketch of Mama

LEFT: *With older brothers Bill and Rich*
ABOVE: *Herb, Bill and Rich, later*
BELOW: *Dad (right) in early laboratory*

Herbert L. Block, Nicholas Senn High School, Chicago, honorable mention.

And So's Your Sister Carr

Herblock, DailyNews cartooni noticed Theodore Dreiser wa ing between trains at the Nor Western station and stopp long enough to make th sketch. Dreiser was advising roup of friends to "vote co unist."

First office (with view of Cleveland Stadium) and the beginning of clutter, 1934

Army war-map poster, 1944

BEYOND SUNNY ITALY!

Corcoran Exhibition, 1950

1950s and '60s
LEFT: *More Clutter*
BELOW (Left): *Still more*
and (Right): Aaargh!

Herbert Elliston

Eugene Meyer and Phil Graham

Russ Wiggins

Alan Barth

Katharine Graham

Katharine and Don Graham

Movie and TV men . . .

. . . and Hepburn

Secretary Udall and the golf game

Secretary O'Brien and the stamp

Norman Rockwell on space travel

Beach travel on the mighty three-wheeler

1957: The National Cartoonists' Society "Reuben" from the designer and namesake himself—Rube Goldberg

Walt (Pogo) Kelly

A couple of the drawings by other cartoonists at Fourth Estate Award Dinner, National Press Club, 1977

Jeannie and Sparky Schulz

Chuck Jones

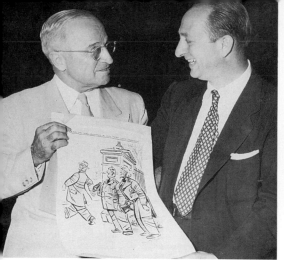

*Authors! Authors! Mary McCarthy and a
senator from Massachusetts*

Former president

Harold Wilson and Lyndon Johnson

Clinton

Capote was when he came down from New York for a party at Katharine Graham's house. Since we were leaving at about the same time and both going in the same direction, she had her driver take us in her car. We had a good conversation on the way and Capote was quite complimentary of my work. When we dropped him off where he was staying, he waved, blew kisses and called before the car moved on, "Kisses, Herb! Kisses!" "Good night, Truman," I called back. This could have been Capote's equivalent of "Well done" or "Good evening," or a variation of a Hollywood agent's calling everybody "sweetheart baby," but more unconventional than I was accustomed to.

A more frequent visitor from New York was Joe Liebling, wonderful writer on food, boxing, the press and whatever other subjects went through his typewriter. At lunch he would remark on the melon or vegetables as being a good year, much as he might comment on a wine. Late in his career, when we got together for a drink after he gave a speech, the ailing and more slow-footed than usual Liebling was besieged for autographs by attractive women. As we sat down for the drinks, Liebling, who had a stutter, said, "When I was y-young I didn't m-make out so well with g-girls, and now that it's t-too late, th-they're all over me."

I once met Robert Frost and found him to be an engaging man. Talking about poetry, he spoke of layers beneath layers, meanings beneath meanings. Somehow the conversation must have moved to the subject of religion, and he told a story that, for all I know, may be somewhere in his writings.

It was about three simple and rather saintly men who lived on an island helping each other and their fellow men and reciting some little saying or prayer they had made up about "we three." Eventually a ship came bearing civilized people with true religion. These church people taught what actual prayers—true religious church prayers— were supposed to be and the three humble men were grateful. Later, after the truly religious men had boarded the ship and sailed off, the three on the island were distressed to find that they could not remember the exact words to one of the real prayers they had been taught. So they ran across the top of the water to the departing ship to make sure they would have it right.

On meeting author Kurt Vonnegut there was instant rapport when he

213

asked if I had known a cartoonist named Gaar Williams. Growing up a *Chicago Tribune* reader, I was a special fan of Williams, who had been a friend of the Vonnegut family in Indiana. From cartoons our discussion somehow got to earliest drawings on the walls of caves. He said matter-of-factly that these were all done by one man, and I agreed. It was a guy called Oomlat-the-Non-Hunter, who traveled from cave to cave with his paint, enjoying choice ribs prepared by the cave women, while the other guys were out hunting and gathering and coping with the animals he drew.

A young writer named Benchley spent much time working in Washington. At a friend's home we were sitting on a couch that was next to a small fish tank, when Benchley began pointing out things of interest in it. I am not big on fish except as they appear on dinner menus, but this fellow not only knew all about them but talked about them in a way that was fascinating. Many others found his knowledge of fish and his way with words of unusual interest when he wrote *Jaws*.

Artists come to town too. At a Corcoran exhibition of three generations of Wyeths, I met Jamie, who had painted a picture of a beautiful pink pig. He had studied these animals and declared they were actually very clean—something I hadn't known, but a fact that hasn't kept me from using them in cartoons to depict less-than-clean political situations. In pointing out political injustices, cartoons may sometimes do injustice to animals. And if tigers, bears, hogs and hippos wrote letters to the editor, they might rightly complain of being stereotyped.

At Alice Longworth's home, I was admiring artist Peter Hurd's famous portrait of her when he pointed to the background and said that if he were doing it over, he might handle the strokes in back a little differently. This came as a happy surprise to me. I had always supposed the creator of such a painting had no afterthoughts on seeing it much later. And it was encouraging to know it is not just an occupational hazard with some of us who work on daily deadlines.

An artist who seemed to have no such doubts was Thomas Hart Benton. When I had visited former President Truman at his library in Independence, Missouri, I saw a mural Benton had done there. Shortly afterward, I met Benton and expressed my appreciation of the painting. He said, "Yes—and that mural *made* that library." It wasn't the response I expected, but I did like his work.

One attraction that brings people from all over the country and beyond is a White House state dinner. On the few occasions I've been to these, I learned that you don't come "fashionably late" or late at all. Everyone is assembled in kind of a semicircle when the president puts in his appearance.

During the Kennedy administration one dinner invitation specified White Tie. I have never been able to get gussied up for a formal affair without fear that something will come unsprung—and with everyone looking on. When a follow-up notice changed the dress to Black Tie, this was easier. At the pre-dinner lineup with all guests present, waiting and viewing each other, I was standing next to Michael DiSalle, governor of Ohio, when my cummerbund fell to the floor in front of me. DiSalle saw and acted at once. A man who made up in girth for whatever he lacked in height, he stepped in front of me and opened his jacket. Behind this protective screen I retrieved the offending article and refastened it—just as the nation's leader made his entrance. DiSalle was a quick thinker and a real gent.

Meetings with fellow journalists are easier and usually informal. With its large newspaper contingent, Washington may be home to more journalists than any other city, and it is a second home to others.

When Bill Baggs was editor of the *Miami News,* he didn't wait for editorial conventions to make his appearances. In addition to visits, he kept up a running correspondence with Pogo cartoonist Walt Kelly and me and, among others, Harry Ashmore, then editor of the *Arkansas Gazette*—sometimes sending copies of his letters to each of us. Once when he heard I was hospitalized, he wired: "If alive, please reply; if not, don't bother." H. L. Mencken is said to have answered critical letters: "There may be much in what you say." Baggs had his own way. He used a rubber stamp that said, "This is not a simple world, my friend, and there are no simple answers." When I inquired about it, he sent me a note that said, "Dear Herb," followed by the rubber-stamp observation, and then signed by him. I had a rubber stamp made up for a one-time-only use, a reply to his stamp. It said, "It is too and there are so."

Walt Kelly was one of the most frequent visitors, and he sometimes put me up at his New York apartment. In correspondence, he signed his letters George B. McClellan, Herbert Hoover, John Q. Adams,

Officer Pup (from the Krazy Kat strip) or any other name that came to his mind.

In a parody of a request-to-cartoonist letter (signed Persepone Partiridge, Secretary), he wrote, asking for a special cartoon for an organization (and of course, misspelling my name): It went, in part:

> We'd like this in oil, 18″ by 56″ at once. We'll display it in the lobby where you will get some very favorable, I guess, notices. Also if you can make it up here, most of us would be glad to see you. There's a bus that leaves from Ithaca, overnight, getting here just in time for the evening services. We intend to serve sponge-cake and prunes at about 11:06 p.m. so it will pay you to "stick around." Please do come.
>
> Naturally there will be no pay for this job, but in the interest of being fair, we have arranged with the Playhouse Proprietors that they will not charge you anything for the display.
>
> If you'd like to stay on for the entire convention (it ends in March), we would like to squeeze you in somewhere to say a few words. I am sure that a number of us will be up at that time of the morning and will be on hand to hear your interesting remarks. In the event that there is nobody about at your scheduled speaking time perhaps you could speak rather loudly and awaken your neighboring tent mates. They will be happy to give you some attention I am sure. . . .

The letter ended with a postscript: "PS: Many of us here have some other good ideas for you."

I never entirely understood Kelly's logistics or lifestyle, which seemed to consist of weekdays in New York with Steffie, his wife at that time, and weekends in Connecticut, where I think there was a former wife and kids. He evidently maintained studios at both places and also sketched some of his strips on the trains in between. Once he left the drawings behind, and the railroad people made a fast search of the train yards to recover them. At another time, he gave me a new phone number where he could be reached in New York. When I asked where this was, he said it was a Chinese restaurant. I thought this was said jokingly until one day I wanted to reach him and tried the phone number. When the party at the other end understood that I was not making a reservation or calling about a carry-out order, he said in pidgin English that Ah, yes, he would get Mister Kelly upstairs.

His last marriage was to Selby Kelly, and it came long after they had first seen each other, when both were working on animated Disney cartoons. They told me that they only saw each other through open windows then because Disney felt he could get more work done by keeping the men and women separate. Selby, a good cartoonist in her own right, kept the strip going. And she arranged for book publications after Walt went on to wherever is the next stop for what Pogo's friends might call great human beans.

23

Fateful Year

"I'M AFRAID TO LOOK"

Dec. 27, 1967

The year 1968 was so bad that—well, if it was a wine, you'd have sent it back. It brought Soviet tanks into Czechoslovakia to crush freedom's "Prague Spring." And it brought the demoralizing Tet Offensive in Vietnam and violent conflicts at home.

Among the less consequential casualties of that year was another *Time* magazine cover I did, featuring columnist Russell Baker. It was scheduled to run before the November election, with a major piece on political humor and satire that even contained complimentary words for some of us who had not previously been among that magazine's favorites. When President Johnson pushed for a Paris conference on Vietnam, the peace-offensive story took over; and the political satire story, along with the cover, was scrapped. *C'est la guerre*. And so much for the lighter side of a tragic year.

Johnson's peace effort might have given some belated help to candidate Hubert Humphrey, though at the time Johnson seemed more determined to control Humphrey than Gen. Nguyen Van Thieu, to whose war he had committed so many American lives. When Johnson finally arranged a peace conference, which Thieu resisted, it might have seemed in LBJ's character to tell this beneficiary of American aid to get himself to Paris or else. But by that time, maybe the lame-duck president felt he didn't have very much *or else*—especially if Thieu felt he could get a better deal from a Nixon administration.

It has always seemed a likely possibility that Flying Tiger Gen. Claire Chennault, his wife, Anna, and others acting on Nixon's behalf helped to talk Thieu into sitting tight. And in 1991, when Congress decided to investigate whether the Reagan campaign had agreed in 1980 to trade arms for hostages in Iran, articles about the 1968 Nixon campaign and Vietnam contacts appeared in print again.

Former Assistant Secretary of State William P. Bundy wrote about this. He said that Claire Chennault, South Vietnamese Ambassador Bui Diem and Nixon campaign manager John Mitchell came together in Nixon's apartment. Nixon, he wrote, determined that "Mrs. Chennault would be his channel to Mr. Thieu." Bundy said cables showed that in late October Gen. Chennault was urging Thieu not to participate in the process. Johnson associates have said that LBJ urged Humphrey to use this in the 1968 campaign, but Humphrey wouldn't bring it up.

During that '68 campaign, Nixon successfully worked both sides of the street—he would prosecute the war *to win*. And he had an undisclosed peace plan, which he didn't reveal at the time—or ever.

In that unhappy year violence and tragedy struck closer to home. On April 4, the Rev. Martin Luther King, Jr., was assassinated, and a wave of racial resentment and violence broke out. On June 5, Robert F. Kennedy was murdered just after leaving a rally celebrating his victory in the California primary.

For years Alan Barth in editorials and I in cartoons had campaigned for gun controls—and against the leaders of the National Rifle Association (NRA). This powerful lobby opposed any limitation on any kind of firearm. It even resisted measures connected with detection devices for explosives and weighed in against restricting the sale of armor-piercing "cop-killer" bullets. In the wake of the Bobby Kennedy assassination, public outrage at last produced an attempt at gun legislation—a watered-down version that banned interstate sale of rifles, shotguns and ammunition.

I did a cartoon listing the names of senators who voted on a stronger bill that went down to defeat, and titled it "The Vote To Kill." (This, incidentally, was the cartoon that precipitated a falling-out with a new editorial page editor, who dropped the title in later editions.) The title plainly meant that the vote to kill gun controls was also a vote to permit the continued gun carnage. The NRA not only trained its editorial sights on me, but 19 U.S. senators signed a letter to *The Washington Post* complaining about the cartoon. Not surprisingly, 18 of these senators were listed as having been against the bill.

Along with their letter, *The Post* published an answer backing the cartoon and followed with a letter from me pointing out misrepresentations in the senators' letter.

As late as 1991, the NRA was still trying to repeal the modest legislation barring the general sale of machine guns and resisted any restriction on assault weapons. It even opposed the Brady bill, named for Reagan's press secretary, James Brady, confined to a wheelchair after being shot in the head when a would-be assassin also hit President Reagan. This bill called for a modest seven-day waiting period to check out handgun purchasers—later reduced to only five days. The NRA also fought a 1993 Virginia law limiting the individual purchase of handguns to one a month per person.

Regardless of opinions or candidates, the 1968 assassination of another civil rights advocate, another Kennedy who was seeking the presidency, was an added horror. In the 25 years following the assassination of Bobby Kennedy, another half million people in the United States met death by handguns—and a larger number by firearms of all types.

The handgun is the American plague, the black death that takes more than 20,000 lives every year.

In the half century from 1932, a majority of our presidents—five out of nine—were at some time assassination targets: candidate Franklin Roosevelt in 1932, President Harry Truman in 1950, President John F. Kennedy murdered in 1963, President Gerald Ford targeted twice in 1975, and Reagan shot in 1981. These were in addition to the two prominent 1968 presidential candidates: Robert F. Kennedy, killed; and Gov. George Wallace, who became a paraplegic. Countries that some call banana republics have better records than that. But then they don't have powerful, well-heeled gun lobbies that contribute millions to political candidates and are eager to push sales of guns into as many hands as possible—with no waiting. The NRA ranks among the nation's top campaign contributors.

I used to say that I was against capital punishment except for people who littered golf fairways with crumpled cigarette packs and paper wrappers—and I still have reservations about such punishment.

But there is something incongruous about our attitude toward life and death and the government. We send hundreds of thousands of people into battle to kill and to be killed because of perceived threats to our national interests or security—while assassins can successfully wage war against our entire democratic system and alter our govern-

SHOOTING GALLERY

March 20, 1988

April 10, 1981

ment. With one or two bullets, they can nullify millions of ballots. They can do what Hitlers and Tojos were unable to do—deprive us of our free democratic choices.

Where there is no possibility of convicting "the wrong man" or discovering a conspiracy, there might be some sentence that would at least spare the country the periodic obscenity of a known assassin appearing on TV and in newspaper articles demanding parole on the grounds that he is a "political prisoner." If it were possible, my preference would be for the names of assassins to be expunged from memory.

The loss of Robert Kennedy was very possibly decisive in the '68 election. I think that had he lived, he or Vice President Hubert Humphrey—whoever won the nomination—would have supported the other in the race against Nixon. As it turned out, the leadership of the "peace movement" remained entirely with Sen. Eugene McCarthy, who sat on his hands while Humphrey tried to close the gap in the polls—and almost succeeded.

In 1968 the murders of political leaders and the riots following the King assassination ironically played into the hands of those whose advocacy of "law and order" had racial overtones.

At the Democratic National Convention in Chicago, there were also the "police riots"—the violent confrontations between police and antiwar demonstrators who baited them.

And finally, there was the election of a president and his chosen vice president, both of whom would later have to resign in disgrace.

After the election I called on defeated candidate Humphrey in his vice presidential office. I had first met him when he came to Washington as mayor of Minneapolis and, after his election as senator, at various gatherings where he always provided lively conversation and humor.

This was, I think, the only time I ever sought an appointment with a political figure. I had no particular reason except that I felt he was a remarkably good public servant who still had much to offer—despite the enervating and even emasculating effect of a vice presidency under Lyndon Johnson. Humphrey had been the innovator of many social programs, the originator of the idea for a Peace Corps and an early and vigorous champion of civil rights. Along with serious purpose he had a buoyant and sometimes seemingly boyish enthusiasm. And if, as he good-naturedly acknowledged, his speeches tended to run overtime, it was usually because his mind was busy turning out ideas.

I had covered the 1948 Democratic convention where Humphrey issued his ringing call to come "out of the shadow of states' rights and into the bright sunshine of human rights." And I hoped that as titular leader of his party he might even now come out from the shadow of Johnson and the Vietnam War to exercise his own full capacities. He was realistic and I guess he knew that his chance at leadership was over.

As we talked, we could hear the constant hammering of construction workers putting up the inaugural stands; and Humphrey, noting that this went on day after day, commented that it sounded like the erection of a gallows. In a way it was a gallows for the political idealism that had gone with the New Deal–Fair Deal–New Frontier eras.

There is something sad and wasteful about the fact that able political figures become presidential candidates, almost make it to the pinnacle and then seem to fall into an abyss. In the '90s there was a story that Walter (Fritz) Mondale, the 1984 Democratic nominee, runs into George McGovern, the 1972 standard-bearer. "George, when does it stop hurting?" asks Mondale. "I'll let you know, Fritz," replies McGovern.

In what was probably the most remarkable comeback in American politics, the candidate who lost the 1960 presidential election and 1962 race for governor of California ("You won't have Nixon to kick around anymore") had been elected president of the United States. To his supporters he must have seemed a risen Phoenix, and to non-admirers a Dracula returned from the political grave. But he had made it.

Art Buchwald mentioned that with this president in office, he and I should have a ball. When I expressed worry about a Nixon presidency, he deadpanned: "Herb, you've got to stop putting the country ahead of your work."

There was a cartoon postscript to the campaign. I had a character wearing a "Dick and Spiro" button sitting atop a pile of unreported campaign contributions and thumbing his nose at the Corrupt Practices Act. The title: "We were busy making speeches on law and order."

But they were *in*. And who was going to make a big deal out of some campaign practices by an elected president and vice president?

24

The Pits

If I felt uneasy about the result of the '68 election there was also uneasiness at *The Post* about the cartoons, or at least one aspect of them. This was the Nixon "five o'clock shadow" that fit in with the political thuggery he and Joseph McCarthy often represented in my cartoons. Phil Graham long had fretted about it. And editor Russ Wiggins, who enjoyed writing light verse, once presented me with a razor and a poem, which closed with the lines:

> *. . . join the good and kind and true*
> *The faithful, just and brave,*
> *And grasp this razor in your hand,*
> *And give that man a shave.*

To which I replied:

> *He's shaved with new Gillettes 'n' Schicks 'n'*
> *Still he is the same old Nix'n.*

Despite the editor's and publisher's concerns about this depiction of Nixon, I saw no reason to change it, particularly in view of his uglier political campaigns.

In 1954, when, as vice president, he conducted a mud-slinging, Red-smearing campaign against some of the most respected senators up for re-election, it occurred to me that he was traveling the country by sewer, and I pictured him climbing out of one, traveling bag in hand. It fit. It described what he was doing.

But even with such a past it seemed to me that an incoming president, particularly at a time of national division and crisis, was entitled to his chance to lead. So I did a sketch of the "one free shave" cartoon and showed it to the editor. Katharine Graham, who was in his office at the time, let out a whoop and threw her arms around me. All hands seemed to be relieved and happy.

Since Nixon was not yet president, I did a kind of tease routine between election and inauguration. I showed the president-elect in such getups as Santa Claus whiskers and other non-full-face situations, to precede the unveiling of the post-inauguration clean-shaven face, which *The Post* celebrated in an editorial. I never put the shadow back on, even during the worst of the scandals, and didn't feel it was necessary. I think readers who missed the old face knew it was still there underneath.

Nixon as vice president had canceled his subscription to *The Post* because of the cartoons. At the same time he explained to a *Washington Post* reporter that he read the paper at the office and asked him to give me his regards. Then he added, "A lot of people think I'm a prick. But I'm not." Now, in an expansive mood, the newly elected president introduced his Cabinet members in a televised appearance, where he said that their wives would have to get used to seeing my cartoons.

The honeymoon—well, let's say grace period—did not last the year. Before 1969 was out Vice President Spiro Agnew, serving as Nixon's Nixon, had been sent around the country to attack the press and to intimidate broadcasters—pointedly reminding the latter that their stations operated under government license. He read speeches complaining about "instant analysis" of presidential speeches and spoke of an unchecked media elected by no one wielding vast power. This had a superficial appeal to those (in Ring Lardner's words) named Legion, who were unhappy about anything that displeased them in the press. They were not likely to shout back that Thomas Jefferson, James Madison and a few other fellows had elected to have a free press, separate from government, to keep an eye on elected officials—like Nixon and Agnew.

Meanwhile, the Department of Justice, under John Mitchell, had already begun wiretapping and bugging citizens and trying to curb dissent in the name of national security. As time went on, it seemed as if the administration's idea of "law and order" was to make crime a government monopoly.

Agnew may have taken special pleasure in delivering speeches attacking "effete snobs" of the eastern establishment, since *The Washington Post* had expressed reservations about his record as governor of Maryland and the *New York Times* had warned against putting him on the ticket in 1968.

I had met him early in the Nixon administration when I went to an Apollo launch at Cape Canaveral, to which Agnew had come as an official representative. At a pre-launch lunch that Walter Cronkite and I and a number of other press and NASA people attended, Agnew made a little after-lunch speech. His remarks included a smiling observation that anyhow I had not drawn him with a five o'clock shadow. But a year or two later he was in full cry, denouncing me as a "master of sick invective."

His verbal assaults on statesmen such as Sen. William Fulbright and Ambassador Averell Harriman were downright vicious, implying a lack of patriotism. For example, he referred to the Ho Chi Minh Trail as "Harriman's Highway." On the evening of one of these attacks, a number of guests at a dinner spontaneously rose to express their high regard for Harriman and their feelings about the vice president. I was moved to say that Spiro Agnew had now become not only a household word but an outhousehold word.

Agnew, who even received envelopes of money in his vice presidential office, later had to plead nolo contendere to an income tax violation to avoid prosecution on a 40-page portfolio of charges. But during the two presidential campaigns and the years in the White House, he acted as Nixon's point man.

In the election, Nixon had followed a "southern strategy" to attract disaffected white voters. As president he displayed a lack of vigor in enforcing the Voting Rights Act, and his attitude on desegregation can be surmised from the fact that he urged a constitutional amendment to forbid school busing.

At a Gridiron Club dinner in 1971, Nixon and Agnew took to the stage to put on a number of their own—a piano duet based on the "southern strategy" idea. Nixon played various themes on one piano while Agnew pounded out Dixie on the other. At the end of their performance, I said to Frederick (Fritz) Beebe, then chairman of the board of *The Washington Post*, "Well, we've never seen anything like this before." He replied, "No, and I hope we never see anything like it again." But later on, when the cartoons on Nixon became tougher and more frequent, Beebe complained to Katharine Graham that they were too much. She passed this along one day when she dropped in to my office, looking harried, and said something like "I'm not trying to tell you what to do, but FYI, Fritz says . . ." Shortly before her retirement as publisher, when we were discussing those earlier years, I reminded her of this visit and she was astonished that she had even passed along Beebe's comments. I think it was the only time she had relayed a complaint from inside or outside the paper, although she must have received plenty of them.

In 1969, when Nixon made a nomination to the Supreme Court, there was one of those occasional divergences between editorials and cartoons. Nixon named Judge Clement F. Haynsworth, Jr. *The Post* supported his confirmation, and I opposed it. Judge Haynsworth's financial ethics seemed to me to be less than adequate, particularly his sitting on a case involving a vending machine company in which he had an interest. After the Senate voted down the Haynsworth nomination Nixon came up with G. Harrold Carswell, easily a worse nominee. He had earlier endorsed white supremacy and racial segregation, and the number of his cases reversed on appeal raised other doubts about his qualifications. On this, *The Post* and I were in complete thumbs-down agreement. I drew seven cartoons on the Haynsworth nomination and 24 on Carswell's—almost one every other day. After two defeats, a furious Nixon nominated Harry Blackmun—proving that Senate rejection of nominations does not necessarily mean going from bad to worse.

I did more and more cartoons on Vietnam. If there was no secret plan for ending the war, there seemed to be one for expanding it. We learned of the "secret war in Laos"—hardly a secret in Indochina—and the not-so-secret bombing of Cambodia. This began the destruction of that peaceful country and millions of its people.

Elsewhere, Agnew, while not delivering attack speeches at home, operated as a kind of unofficial ambassador to the Greek military dictatorship, which the Nixon administration found congenial. The junta gave the vice president a medal representing its highest honor—or as much honor as those dictators were capable of. And there were the continued administration attempts to suppress dissent at home.

In June 1971 a journalistic Rubicon was crossed. After the Department of Justice obtained a restraining order against further publication of the "Pentagon Papers," by the *New York Times, The Washington Post* secured its own copy of the papers and decided to publish them. I didn't know at the time the exciting details of the quick assembly of staff members at Ben Bradlee's house to go through those papers or of the phone conversations with Mrs. Graham, who made her "go" decision in the face of threats to *The Post*'s interests. But we were all at high pitch, and I did several more cartoons on these latest attempts to curb the press.

About three months later I drew the first cartoon on a Nixon scandal—at least something that was shocking to me, although it did not grab the country by the ears. This was the Milk Fund. Briefly, Nixon announced that there would be no increase in the support programs for milk, which brought concerned dairy producers to see him. On successive days, milk-fund campaign contributions began flowing to dummy committees, the meeting with Nixon was held and then price support increases were announced.

If money is the mother's milk of politics, this $2 million milk shakedown of dairy interests was quite a pull on mama. But it was only a beginning. The 1952 vice presidential candidate whose career nearly ended when a secret fund of about $18,000 was disclosed was now into big-time stuff.

Early in 1972, a lesser amount of money attracted greater attention. The ITT Corporation offered some $400,000 toward financing the Republican National Convention—while Nixon was ordering an obedient attorney general to have the Justice Department forget anti-trust charges against ITT. The use of shredding machines in government scandals did not begin with Oliver North and the Iran-contra cover-up. ITT found it convenient to do a lot of shredding at this time, and other shredding machines kept humming a few months later after a burglary job.

In a 1972 wire-service interview, Nixon said, "I wouldn't start the day by looking at Herblock's cartoon." One of many that year that didn't start his day appeared on June 13. It pictured "Nixon Fund Disclosures" as the tip of the iceberg of "Nixon fund secret contributions."

Four days later, some of that secret-funds money came into play when burglars were found trying to change taping machines at the Democratic National Committee headquarters in Washington—in a building complex called Watergate.

MILK RUN

©1971 HERBLOCK

Sept. 29, 1971

230

THE APT PUPIL

Sept. 11, 1968

Nov. 7, 1968

"CALL MRS. BEARD'S DOCTOR—THERE'S BEEN A TERRIBLE ACCIDENT"

March 22, 1972

NEW FIGURE ON THE AMERICAN SCENE

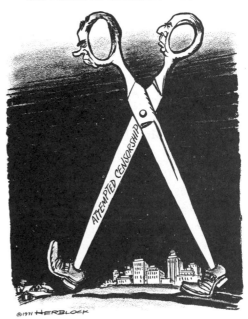

June 20, 1971

25

Scene of the Crimes

There are some politicians I've been interested in meeting, some that I didn't care about one way or the other, and a few that I didn't want to meet at all. Nixon was one of the didn't-wants. But early in the Eisenhower administration, I did meet him at a cocktail party where the host grabbed my arm and said, "You must meet the vice president." We had a brief neutral conversation in which Nixon asked something about drawing what he called his ski-jump nose, and that was okay. *Then* the host insisted on whisking me across the room to meet Mrs. Nixon, who was talking with two or three other women. When we were introduced, she gave a small smile and said to the others that this is the man who hates all Republicans. Of course, this was untrue, but it followed the Nixon line—to make out that there wasn't anything wrong with Nixon, it was the people criticizing him who must be warped. Similarly, people who objected to the depredations of the Committee on Un-American Activities were "defenders of Alger Hiss."

Nixon had replayed political items he recalled from the Roosevelt administration. Checkers, for example, was a scruffy story-line descendant of Roosevelt's Fala, who figured in an FDR speech of great humor and originality.

During FDR's administration some people were known as Roosevelt-haters. Whether any of his wealthy peers actually called him "a traitor to his class," some certainly feared he was taking the country down the road to socialism or worse. The feelings of these people were reflected in a joke of that period: Every day a man on Wall Street gave a newsboy a dollar for a newspaper, which he glanced at and threw away. One day the newsboy asked why he bought the paper. "For the obituary stories," the man said. "But sir," explained the newsboy, "the obituaries are on the inside pages." To which the man grimly replied, "Not the ones I'm looking for."

From the FDR days, when the term was appropriate, Nixon And Company came up with the term "Nixon-haters." Those who disapproved of his methods and actions were not "Constitution lovers," or Americans devoted to civil liberties and civil rights or believers in honesty and integrity. They, and not the president with the enemies lists, were the "haters."

Interestingly, despite the virulence of attacks on Truman, Johnson and other presidents, there was no talk of "Truman-haters," "Johnson-haters" or, during the depths of the Depression, "Hoover-haters." This Nixonism was so successful that a British editor, writing in the *New York Times* in 1991, parroted the phrase to describe those who were not reconciled to the disgraced president.

In the course of his career, from time to time the public was given a new Nixon. These were new and improved and much better than the previous Nixons, which presumably kept shedding their skins. Thus, the Nixon who painted his congressional opponents as Reds and pinkos was superseded by the Nixon who said that President Truman, Adlai Stevenson and Secretary of State Acheson were "traitors—to the high principles" of their party, and replaced by the Nixon who voted to override Truman's veto of the infamous McCarran-Walter Act.

Then there was the Nixon who wanted the United States to intervene in Indochina in 1954, and in the same year the one who conducted the sewer political campaign; followed by the Nixon who declared that attempts to limit nuclear explosions were "catastrophic nonsense"; and the Nixon who strongly urged President Kennedy not to recognize China; followed by the desegregation-era Nixon who opposed school busing; and the bugging-and-tapping Nixon; and on and on—to the "elder statesman" Nixon whose batting average was still not outstanding.

Since his 1974 resignation, there have been periodic Nixon rehabilitations, often advanced by magazines and TV programs that apparently found they could tap a public fascination similar to the interest in chainsaw massacres and bloodsucking bats.

Promoting these efforts has been the ex-president himself, who long ago had noted—and profited from his belief—that "the public memory is short." A special resurrection came in 1990 with the unveiling of the Nixon Library, built with private funds. The Library decided that certain journalists would not be welcome and also that some of the incriminating Nixon tapes were not yet available.

Among Nixon's contributions to his rehabilitation have been writings and interviews in which he seemed to regret helping to protect overzealous colleagues who were involved in an incident at the Watergate building complex in 1972.

This is a little like saying that Willie Sutton ran into some difficulty at a bank, or that the Boston Strangler had an unfortunate meeting with a woman. It doesn't quite give the whole picture or take in the scope of the activities.

Watergate was not just an isolated incident. It was the place where events and the law finally caught up with a group of criminals operating under a corrupt official at the very top of the government.

The bungled effort to continue the bugging job on Democratic Party Headquarters at Watergate was not even the first or second break-in. Nixon's team of "plumbers" had previously rifled the office of a psychiatrist in the hope of getting information for use against Daniel Ellsberg, the defense policy specialist who had leaked the "Pentagon Papers." Under this president, such crimes enjoyed his Good Housebreaking Seal of Approval. And Nixon, on tape, had even suggested to his fellow conspirators that they could break into Internal Revenue Service offices at night to get files the IRS might not provide on other Nixon administration targets.

The IRS already had willingly served Nixon's political purposes. It had three times audited Democratic National Chairman Lawrence F.

O'Brien, whose offices the Nixon plumbers bugged at Watergate. And at least one IRS man had been promoted after overlooking discrepancies in Nixon's own tax records and praising their preparation.

When the Watergate break-in became public, I immediately did a cartoon of Nixon and his two successive attorneys general, John Mitchell and Richard Kleindienst, holding their bugging and tapping machines and asking innocently, "Who would think of doing such a thing?" The following day I showed the same trio (all lawyers) holding a door closed and saying, "Remember, we don't talk till we get a lawyer."

The next day I was walking through the city room with another cartoon, this one showing the footprints of the scandals all leading to the White House, when I met Mrs. Graham. She asked, "What have you got? Let's see," and I showed it to her. She looked at it and laughed. Then she paused and said, "But you're not going to print that, are you?" I said yes, I was just about to take it to the engraver's. And true to her policy of noninterference, she said no more about it.

There were a couple of interesting sidelights on the Watergate break-in, which the Nixon White House first described as a "third-rate burglary," and which Nixon later characterized as a "bizarre incident" and still later as "deplorable." I talked with one of the men involved in making the arrest, who said he thought there was something odd when he saw guys showing up wearing $500 suits. I also heard that when the burglary arrests were reported to Attorney General Mitchell, his first words were not something like "Who are these people?" or "What is this all about?" but "Oh, shit!" And one of the break-in team had a notebook containing some White House phone numbers.

In the 1972 Nixon re-election campaign, the politician that Rep. Helen Gahagan Douglas had characterized as "tricky Dick" now expanded and institutionalized dirty tricks. He did this with presidential associates and their henchmen supported by large special funds for illegal activities including political espionage and bribery. Much of the sabotage was done under the direction of Donald Segretti, who along with 24 White House officials and campaign associates went to prison for their crimes. The sabotage techniques included forged letters, ostensibly on stationery of Democratic leaders; invitations to prominent people to attend non-existent parties; communications from committees purporting to support Democratic candidates; cancellation notices of scheduled meetings; "Democratic campaign literature" designed to antagonize voting groups; and undercover workers creating disruptions in that party, as well as conducting taps, bugs and break-ins.

A special target of these "dirty tricks" teams was presidential candidate Sen. Edmund Muskie, who had led the president in some early polls. The Nixon team set out to knock the chief contender out of the campaign and succeeded. While this was not a physical assassination, the figurative bumping off by presidential hit squads did the job. The voters were once more deprived of a choice that should have been theirs.

One of the best-publicized tricks of the campaign was the "Canuck Letter"—a fake pretending to relate how Muskie spoke disparagingly of Canadian Americans. Marilyn Berger, at the time a *Washington Post* reporter, said White House Communications Deputy Director Ken Clawson confided to her that he had concocted the letter.

An article in *The New Yorker* reported that in the same 1972 campaign, when candidate George Wallace was shot, Nixon immediately sent E. Howard Hunt to enter the home of the would-be assassin. The purpose: to plant George McGovern campaign literature there, giving the impression of some connection between the shooting and the Democratic candidate. Nixon was angry to learn that the FBI had already sealed off the living quarters.

Fakery and criminality were endemic to the Nixon team. Former Attorney General Kleindienst gave false testimony and later pleaded guilty to an offense that kept him out of jail. John Mitchell eventually went to jail for conspiracy, obstruction of justice and perjury.

I never encountered Mitchell, but at a large party I did run into his outspoken wife, Martha, who had apparently been considered quite a problem by Mitchell and his associates. She was very pleasant, and her primary interest in what was going on seemed to be to make sure the investigations didn't stop short of "Mr. Big"—the top man, who had brought Mitchell to Washington with him.

The Nixon people had no trouble raising money for all the secret funds that financed their activities. Some of the money that ended up with the burglars had originally been raised by a man who was given a quickie bank charter after coming up with $40,000 for the Nixon cause.

An administration that compiled dossiers on its opponents found that it was also useful to compile dossiers on businessmen. Such records helped in soliciting ''voluntary'' campaign contributions. Nixon agents visited businessmen to inform them what they might be expected to give—as, in one case, ''We have your firm down for $200,000.'' These opportunities to provide financial help were offers hard to refuse. According to a former lawyer for the then-corrupt Teamsters Union officials, they passed Teamster money to Nixon funds willingly.

Following the money trail was a big part of the Watergate story. One of the advantages of working on a newspaper with a great staff is that you not only can try out sketches on newspeople, but can also check details of stories. During the Watergate developments, I checked regularly with reporters Bob Woodward and Carl Bernstein. They took time to fill me in on facts like the correct amounts of the secret stash in the safe of Maurice Stans and John Mitchell. They kept me abreast of the money laundering in Mexican banks, and of which things were definite and which were not yet nailed down. This was as close to the horse's mouth as a person could get without lodging in its deep throat.

But I also followed Nixon's hokey-pokey with his personal finances. After his election as president, Nixon acquired two valuable properties—homes at San Clemente, California, and Key Biscayne, Florida. The improvements on them so far exceeded any legitimate security needs that I labeled San Clemente ''Rip-off Manor.'' The White House had estimated costs for security arrangements at San Clemente to be a little under $40,000. The actual property improvements came to $700,000 of taxpayers' money. Some of these public expenditures that I listed in a cartoon included ''security heating system,'' ''security ice-maker,'' ''security swimming pool heater,'' ''security club chairs,'' ''security table lamps and desk,'' ''security sofa,'' ''security decorating pillows,'' etc. These costs were on the San Clemente property alone.

Even more interesting were his income taxes, or lack of them. Despite favorable treatment from the Internal Revenue Service, he could not conceal that his income tax payments were ridiculously low and that he owed $450,000 in back taxes.

At one time the government allowed tax deductions for contributions of papers, drawings, manuscripts, whatever, to legitimate institutions. The vice presidential papers of a president of the United States would be of some interest. But Nixon's contributions to posterity, for which he hoped to claim deductions, were padded with batches of newspaper clippings.

More importantly, the deed of papers was *backdated* to make it eligible for tax deductions no longer allowable. And while Nixon claimed ignorance of the mistake, his personal tax lawyer testified that Nixon had gone over the presidential tax returns line by line.

Ah, well, what's a few hundred thousand dollars of tax cheating by a president of the United States? Let it be said here, before Nixon's apologists can say it, that after all, there is no evidence that Nixon sold off the White House furniture or rented out his wife and children.

Since I had met Nixon only one time and casually, the cartoons were strictly on his activities, but once I did feel a rather personal resentment. On an October weekend in 1973—less than two weeks after the forced resignation of Vice President Spiro Agnew—I went to the Delaware shore for a brief "vacation," which turned out to be much briefer than expected. What made this trip even more special was a gift from some friends. They had presented me—by now a total nondriver—with a three-wheel "bike" equipped with a huge shopping basket. I was just enjoying being a mobile unit when it—and the "vacation"—were brought to a sudden halt. News came of the "Saturday Night Massacre"—the firing of Special Prosecutor Archibald Cox and the resignations of Attorney General Elliot Richardson and Deputy Attorney General William Ruckelshaus—which left the Nixon Justice Department in the hands of Solicitor General Robert Bork. So it was back to Washington after one of the shortest and last beach visits of the year. That's the kind of thing that hits home.

The congressional hearings, the tapes, the disclosures of crimes of the conspirators and the "unindicted co-conspirator" in the Oval Office—all were cartoon subjects day after day and week after week. And for the record: All of the members of the House Judiciary Committee—*all,* including the most diehard Nixon supporters—subscribed to at least one of the articles of impeachment. In announcing his resignation, Nixon said he was resigning because he might not have the necessary support of Congress in carrying out his difficult duties. He might better have said that Congress would have supported carrying him out.

238

On Nixon's departure, *The Post* ran a full page of some of my cartoons, topped with another Nixon quote about them:

> Years ago when I was a young congressman, things got under my skin. Herblock the cartoonist got to me. . . . But now when I walk into this office I am cool and calm.

After each of Nixon's various defeats, I was glad to be done with him and get on with other subjects. To use an old phrase, I was content to "leave him where they flang him." It has not been people who "hate" Nixon or want to keep kicking him around who keep bringing him back. It is Nixon and his apologists who do that, inviting reviews of the record to keep it from being dropped down the memory hole.

The revisionists find something ennobling in Nixon's capacity for survival. The same might be said for many thugs and other unsavory characters; and some scientists tell us that in the end, cockroaches will outlast the human race. But they don't find that particularly praiseworthy. There is also a determination to find some kind of greatness in a man who was for six years President of the United States.

Those who make no claims for this president on domestic affairs try to see brilliance in foreign policy. Others recall 20,000 more American deaths in four more years of a Vietnam-Laos-Cambodia war, ultimately lost, ended on terms that might have been reached sooner.

They can also recall the overthrow of Salvador Allende's elected government in Chile and its replacement by dictator Augusto Pinochet —and the Nixon administration's cozy relationship with the Greek junta. They remember too Nixon's military aid and warm policy toward Pakistan while its ruler, Yahya Khan, was following particularly repressive and ruthless policies. Missing in all this global gamesmanship was a concern for human rights and the advance of democracy.

The televised signing of an arms limitation treaty with Leonid Brezhnev in the Kremlin was dramatic. But this was the same President Nixon who had made the nuclear multiple-warhead MIRV the superpowers' weapon of choice. And the "opening to China" was made by the same man who had warned against such action and stood ready to denounce relationships with China by Democratic administrations.

Some of Nixon's supporters pin their good-president claims on his signing of bills for domestic programs that included revenue sharing, and for the establishment of the Environmental Protection Agency and Occupational Safety and Health Administration. But he also impounded funds for programs, however worthy, that he didn't like. And accenting the positive requires overlooking heavy-handed racist "law and order" and "southern strategy" campaigns; the corruption of the Department of Justice; the attempts to suppress dissent; the bugging and tapping; the violations of the oath "faithfully to uphold the laws of the United States"; and his politicization of the CIA, the IRS, the FBI and the Secret Service.

All the rehabilitation attempts are variations of the old line: "Outside of that, how did you like the play, Mrs. Lincoln?"

I finally did one more Nixon cartoon when the 1991 resurrection was under way and moving along fine until it came up against—Nixon, or at least Nixon's voice. A new batch of tapes was released that year, which didn't help in refurbishing his reputation.

Those too young to have caught the earlier albums could now get some of the flavor in these new releases. They showed Nixon and his aides up to their necks in the conspiracy, and Nixon distrustful and contemptuous even of many of his own appointees and closest aides. They also showed him eagerly picking up on a suggestion that Teamster "thugs" be employed to beat up anti-war demonstrators: "They've got guys who'll go in there and knock their heads off."

In addition, snatches of dialogue serve as reminders of yet another unattractive facet of this president. In 1971, Nixon had ordered his personnel chief to find out how many Jews were in the Bureau of Labor Statistics because he feared a "Jewish cabal." The newly released tapes included a May 1972 conversation about anti–Vietnam War demonstrators:

> NIXON: Aren't the Chicago Seven all Jews? Davis's a Jew, you know.
> HALDEMAN: I don't think Davis is.
> NIXON: Hoffman, Hoffman's a Jew.
> HALDEMAN: Abbie Hoffman is and that's so.

And later:

> NIXON: About half of these are Jews.

240

But, of course, as his rehabilitators might say: Some of his best friends—well, a couple of his most loyal staff members—were, you know . . .

A final word on Nixon can be left to former Senator and Republican presidential candidate Barry Goldwater, whose credentials as a party stalwart have never been questioned. Wrote Goldwater:

> He was the most dishonest individual I ever met in my life. President Nixon lied to his wife, his family, his friends, longtime colleagues in the U.S. Congress, lifetime members of his own political party, the American people and the world.

And there was that memorable whopper delivered to an editors' meeting—perhaps appropriately at Disney World—"I am not a crook."

THE TUNNEL AT THE END OF THE TUNNEL

April 22, 1970

"I'LL TELL YOU EVERYTHING YOU NEED TO KNOW"

July 2, 1972

CHOPPER

Jan. 31, 1971

"STRANGE—THEY ALL SEEM TO HAVE SOME CONNECTION WITH THIS PLACE"

June 23, 1972

"NOW, AS I WAS SAYING, FOUR YEARS AGO"

Aug. 9, 1972

243

LATEST ITEM PULLED OUT OF THE SWAMP

Oct. 1, 1972

"STOP THE MUSIC"

Sept. 3, 1972

"THE RANK AND FILE ARE RIGHT BEHIND ME"

Sept. 27, 1957

DISASTER AREA

May 11, 1973

Oct. 17, 1973

245

May 24, 1974

DELAYED-ACTION BOMB

Aug. 13, 1973

June 26, 1973

"YOU UNDERSTAND HOW IT IS, MOM"

Feb. 27, 1974

July 14, 1974

247

*"Years ago when I was a young congressman, things got under my
skin. Herblock the cartoonist got to me. . . But now when I walk into
this office I am cool and calm."*

1977 HERBLOCK

May 3, 1977

26

The Russians Are Coming

My relations with the Soviet Union were not very extensive, but in a small way they illustrated changing times. During my first year in Washington, I received an invitation to the Soviet Embassy's annual party celebrating the October Revolution. I was interested in seeing the embassy, had no qualms about visiting it and some curiosity about what must have been a big party there. But I had a hangup that may have been considered quixotic. The October Revolution was not the one that overthrew the czarist regime—it was the one in which the communists hijacked the democratic revolution, and nothing that I cared to celebrate. If they had a party to celebrate the end of World War II or a press party or one for Tolstoy's birthday or almost anything else, okay. Anyhow, without explaining all that, I didn't go. And invitations stopped arriving.

Some years later, when Nikita Khrushchev was coming to the United States, staff members of *Krokodil,* a humor magazine, came here and we went out to dinner. A well-meaning waitress kept pressing them to eat crabmeat, which she seemed to regard as a strictly American delicacy that would be new to them. She kept attempting to force-feed them, while they drew back and made it clear, even in Russian, that no way did they want to open wide for mama-bird and her crabmeat.

They were friendly, and with interpretation, gestures and sketches, we got along fine. They had been scheduled to go to the West Coast, but for some reason the trip was cut short and they were called back. Perhaps they were suspected of being too chummy with the natives.

Nevertheless, along with some other non-Russian cartoonists, I was later asked to do a cartoon for *Krokodil*. I replied that instead of a special cartoon, I had already done one that I thought would be right and told them they could reprint it. They said fine, so I sent the cartoon—done on Khrushchev's visit here—that showed Eisenhower and Khrushchev riding together, smiling, with arms held high and fingers crossed hopefully. The *Krokodil* editors' reaction was not good. I don't know whether they interpreted the cartoon properly, but it wouldn't have made any difference. Caricatures of the general secretary, even good-natured ones, did not appear in Soviet publications. But at the time I didn't know that and they didn't explain. They asked to reprint something else, and I suggested they select something. They picked out cartoons critical of the United States or that showed American slums and hungry children. I told them I didn't find these suitable.

They seemed to be playing some kind of game. Soviet publications had pirated some of my stuff at other times—without regard to copyright or permission. In the end nothing of mine appeared in that special issue.

We come now to the Brezhnev era. The Corcoran Gallery of Art was arranging a tour for members who wanted to spend about a week and a half, mostly in Moscow and Leningrad, viewing the great Russian art collections in the Hermitage and elsewhere. I signed up. In time, visas came through for everybody in the group except one—me. As the time for the trip grew closer, Tom Ross, a California representative, nudged Russian Embassy officials about my non-visa. They reported that all such things were decided in Moscow.

Ross persisted. What was the problem? At last the embassy told him that Brezhnev did not like cartoons I had done. One in particular, showing a writer's pen stuck in the general secretary's rear end, may also have stuck in the Kremlin craw.

ANOTHER TROUBLE SPOT

SOVIET WRITERS' PROTESTS ON CENSORSHIP

"WHAT ELSE IS NEW?"

McDonald's

GORBY SPEECH TO THE PARTY

June 13, 1967

Feb. 6, 1990

I wrote a tongue-in-cheek Open Letter to Brezhnev, which ran in *The Post,* expressing surprise that my visit to the art museums might be regarded as Ten Days That Shook the Soviet World—and ended by assuring him that he would be welcome to visit the United States: "It's a free country." Of course, there was no response. But long after, when I met Gennady Gerasimov, foreign spokesman under Mikhail Gorbachev, the conversation got around to whether I had ever been to the USSR. I told of my non-visit and he smiled. "Ah, yes," he said, "Brezhnev had quite a sense of humor—but not about himself."

During the Brezhnev period most Soviet officials did not seem to be big on humor. Once at a small dinner party I was seated next to USSR Ambassador Anatoly Dobrynin. He asked if I was interested in drawing illustrations for great books, which I was not. But he pressed on, citing Gustave Doré's illustrations for Dante's inferno and others. I kept explaining that I preferred what I was doing. He probably wasn't trying to talk me out of the editorial-cartoon business, but I had a hard time trying to persuade him that I was not interested in turning to illustration.

252

At the same dinner party former Justice Arthur Goldberg took to inquiring of Dobrynin how it was that the USSR had declined U.S. aid during the Marshall Plan period. As he kept boring in on this subject, Dobrynin and his wife excitedly talked about what a great thing the Soviet Union had done rebuilding itself after the war. Goldberg was needling him and enjoying it.

Dobrynin had a sidelight on a recently publicized incident when he had an appointment to see Secretary of State Alexander Haig and literally got something of a runaround. He said that before each visit, his embassy called State and asked when and where to appear. The usual entrance for him had long been a place leading to a private elevator, and once more he was told to come there. But on arrival, his limo was ordered to go to the public entrance. From Dobrynin's account, Haig had contrived a little show of ordering the ambassador around.

When things began thawing under Mikhail Gorbachev, a new group of *Krokodil* staff members visited the United States. At the National Press Club there were lighthearted meetings and informal comments by cartoonist and humorists of both countries. Later, the World Humor Organization invited me to be part of a group visiting the USSR. I passed on that one but only because of the daily work at the time.

As things loosened up in Eastern Europe and the Baltic states, a small group of journalists from those countries dropped by the office. They liked the old cartoons of Brezhnev. And one of them gave me a small free-Estonia flag.

Then in 1990, before the 1991 attempted coup that changed everything, Gorbachev visited Washington. The Franklin D. Roosevelt Freedom Foundation wanted to present him with the FDR Freedom Medal, and along with other previous recipients, I was invited to attend this ceremony. We assembled at the nearby Capital Hilton and, with proper badges and escorts, walked the half block or so to the Soviet Embassy. Outside the embassy was Coretta Scott King with a delegation waiting to follow, and other groups lined up behind hers. The presentation was one of the first of a long series that day. After the FDR committee speeches and his acceptance remarks, Gorbachev exchanged warm greetings with a few people like Justice William Brennan and former Sen. William Fulbright; and the rest of us shook hands and moved on.

As I started out to say, I had this invitation to the Soviet Embassy. It turned out to be quite a place—spacious, ornate, impressive. Best of all, I felt that I finally got there on an occasion worth observing—and just in time to enter the door under the old hammer-and-sickle flag and close the books on my limited experience with the Soviet Union.

27

Politics and Presidents

There is a myth that taxicab drivers are possessed of great wisdom—something not borne out by the ones I generally ride with. They are more often given to words of routine complaint. The classic story in this genre is of the cab driver who is asked by a charming woman to take her to the pier where an ocean liner is docked. She then invites him to come along on her European vacation, with the meter running all the while. He accepts. The lady is lovely. The vacation is wonderful. And finally when it's over, the cab is loaded onto the cruise ship and they return to New York. At the dock the lady tells the man to drive her home and gives him her address in Brooklyn. At this, the cab driver shouts, "Brooklyn! Jeez Christ, I'll never get a fare back into town from there!"

I've never encountered one quite like that. But early on, I had a Washington cab driver who grumbled a political opinion I've remembered. "The Democrats take your money and spend it," he growled. Then, after a pause, "The Republicans take your money and *keep* it."

Maybe the Democrats should stop fighting the "big spenders" label and just add to it the rest of the cab driver's comment.

Of course, this driver might have had an experience with a fun-loving Democrat who had his own way of promoting his party. On leaving a cab, the Democrat would make a grand gesture of giving a nickel or dime tip as if he were bestowing largesse while solemnly adding the verbal tip, "Vote Republican."

The nice thing about political observation is that any number can play, and in the capital it's a major occupation. For political cartoonists president-watching is part of the job.

"Pressing the flesh" is a campaign custom whose value I have realized but have never fully understood. The fact that a candidate has shaken hands with someone hardly seems an adequate reason to vote for him—unless the voter whose flesh is pressed is already sufficiently in the candidate's corner to turn out to greet him. But there must be something to the this-is-the-hand-that-shook-the-hand idea. A reader in a midwestern state who was particularly unhappy with Nixon mailed frequent notes cheering my cartoons about him. But eventually he wrote taking issue with these cartoons. Nixon had toured his state and had shaken hands with him, and he felt I should be less critical.

That incident was nothing compared to one I heard about from a shaken reporter who had been feeling the public pulse in Iowa, where Sen. Burke Hickenlooper was up for election. A rural resident, asked who he was going to vote for, replied emphatically, "Hickenlooper." When asked why, he said that it was because this candidate was such a godly man. The puzzled reporter asked in what way, and the voter replied, "Because when his plane went down in the Pacific and he was floating around in that raft, he prayed—and God saved him." After a moment's thought the reporter exclaimed, "That wasn't Hickenlooper—that was *Rickenbacker!*" To which the voter replied, "Some call it Rickenbacker and some call it Hickenlooper, but that's the man I'm going to vote for."

As good a political lesson as I've learned came when I'd been working in Chicago for just a couple of years and shared an airport limo with a man named Flynn, who was one of Franklin Roosevelt's campaign managers. Missing no opportunity to tap an opinion from anyone however callow or shallow, he asked how I thought people felt about Roosevelt. With all the wisdom and self-importance of my brief newspaper experience, I felt obliged to tell him that I did not detect any great enthusiasm for his candidate; but I added that I thought perhaps people had a feeling of hope. To my surprise, he seemed perfectly happy with this appraisal. Of course!

Hope! During a depression it helped elect FDR even as he was campaigning against "loose fiscal policies."

Hope! It sells hair restorers, magical lotions and potions, secret-of-success books and products that will make you attractive, successful and rich while cleaning your house and improving your tennis and golf—all with minimum effort.

Hope! It sometimes gives us a religion or a Ronald Reagan—or an Arkansan from "a place called Hope."

If hope elects presidents, incumbency helps to re-elect them. For one thing, when a person is president of the United States he is already "presidential." We don't have to try to visualize him being president and dealing with foreign powers and acting as commander in chief. And we don't have to worry that he will—as opponents of new presidential nominees sometimes suggest—do something crazy like pressing the nuclear button or freeing all rapists and murderers.

In addition, he has all the advantages of free TV time and coverage of just about anything he wants to say anywhere he wants to say it, with a staff to provide proper background props. He can campaign during his entire term in office—personally and with a number of administration officials serving as surrogates making speeches, appearing on TV interview programs, traveling and pushing public funds where they will help politically. And he is not likely to have trouble raising campaign funds.

Harry Truman managed re-election despite all the odds and all the polls against him—and even with less campaign funding. A friend at the Democratic National Committee in 1948 told me that Truman seemed so doomed that networks required payment in advance for broadcasts of his campaign speeches. When he was whistle-stopping, he reportedly had to spend time in one city phoning to raise enough money to get the train out of the station. Then, on the other side of Election Day, a flurry of campaign contributions in the form of pre-dated checks arrived. They came from organizations and people who suddenly found that, for goodness' sake, somebody must have mislaid the letter and contribution because they thought the check was in the mail long before.

Barring unpopular wars or really hard times, sitting presidents are

generally a good bet to remain sitting. But in 1976 and 1980 we had
our first back-to-back losing incumbents of the century—Gerald Ford
and Jimmy Carter.

Ford got off to a better start than many of us had expected, considering a record of partisanship that at one point prompted him to call for
the impeachment of Justice Douglas. For one brief shining month I felt
a genuine enthusiasm for this "accidental president." But then—

On September 8, 1974, I was finishing a book on Nixon that took
him from 1946, when he first campaigned for Congress—a few months
after I began working in Washington—to his departure from office. In
a large conference room at *The Post,* I had just spread out the text and
cartoons for the final makeup when a friend dropped by. "Have you
heard the news?" "No, what news?" "Ford has just granted Nixon a
full, free and absolute pardon for anything he might have done."

It was another Sunday Surprise, like the news of the "Saturday
Night Massacre"—not only a public outrage but a personal intrusion.
I resisted the impulse to tear up anything but called the publisher to ask
for time for one more short chapter.

Ford said he was issuing the preemptive pardon to end our "long
national nightmare" and put the recent trauma behind us. Perhaps
there should be another political axiom: When politicians announce
that they are going to put something behind them or us, they usually
don't. Whatever is put behind keeps coming to the fore.

As part of Ford's efforts to put things behind, he literally dropped
from his vocabulary mentions of Nixon and détente. And in 1975, with
the collapse of South Vietnam and with refugees fleeing by any means
possible, he declared that the Vietnam debate was over and done. So
much for that.

In 1976 the unpardonable pardon may have cost Ford the election—
where he found himself caught between the old Nixon millstone and
the grinding primary campaign by opponent Ronald Reagan.

Ford made an unprecedented appearance before a congressional
committee to maintain that there was no deal. But his pardon still
smacked of a payoff to the predecessor who made it possible for him
to become president. Ford's unsuccessful efforts to provide Nixon with
the White House tapes and documents—and hundreds of thousands of
dollars of public funds—did nothing to dispel that impression.

258

Ford was personally a genial man and a real gain over Nixon. He fell heir to one of the worst recessions of many years, as well as OPEC-created oil shortages with automobile gas lines and inflation.

I never represented Ford as an automobile, although he began his presidency with the ingratiating statement, "I'm a Ford, not a Lincoln." And I didn't show him as a constant stumbler—a trademark with some comics after a couple of unfortunate tumbles.

But I had fun with his WIN campaign. The initials stood for Whip Inflation Now. Ford appeared on television wearing a WIN button that may have been about the only one then in existence. The button and slogan didn't catch on. If anyone still has a WIN button, it ought to be worth a place in a museum, possibly pinned onto a Nehru jacket. After all of the carefully planned secret campaigns, false statements and machinations of the previous administration, the amateurish Whip Inflation Now campaign seemed almost refreshing.

I think presidential selections of vice presidents, Supreme Court justices and other high officials tell at least something about the chief executives.

The political equivalent of the biblical *begats* could begin with their choices for vice president: Eisenhower and Nixon; Kennedy and Johnson; Nixon and Agnew; Carter and Mondale; Reagan and Bush; Bush and Quayle; Clinton and Gore.

Some of Ford's choices for high positions were remarkably good: John Paul Stevens for the Supreme Court; Edward Levi for attorney general. And for vice president: Nelson Rockefeller, identified with the moderate wing of his party. While fulfilling his duties that included representing our country at funerals for foreign heads of state, Rockefeller was asked where he next planned to go abroad. He replied, "Well, that depends on who dies."

A happy, down-to-earth man, he did not have the poetic nature of former Senator and presidential candidate Eugene McCarthy. At a party attended by both, McCarthy was asked to read some of his poetry. After reading for a time he stopped, and Rockefeller was quick to lean forward and say, "Hey, that was good, Gene," and turning to me, "Wasn't that good, Herb?" McCarthy, who had only paused for effect, gave him a long, cool look and continued with the rest of the poem. A still-smiling Rockefeller ebbed back into his chair.

By 1976, Ford, challenged for the nomination by the farther-right Ronald Reagan, dropped Rockefeller to select Sen. Robert Dole as his running mate. In a debate with Mondale, Dole referred to Americans killed and wounded in this century in what he called "Democrat wars," which confirmed an impression that he was a mean fighter.

Ford lost to Jimmy Carter, who had seemed an unlikely nominee. Candidate Carter indicated his difference from "imperial presidents" by carrying his own garment bag, a gesture that may have been as politically effective as it was unnecessary. He also said he would never lie to the people and would be squeaky clean good good good. After Watergate that was good good good enough to win a close election. Hope! Unfortunately, Carter's pledges of goodness served only to magnify any political gimmicks and shadings in his administration.

Since every election has winners and losers, it's obvious that a candidate's team and tactics good enough to win a party nomination are not necessarily what's needed to win a presidential campaign. And some presidents find out to their sorrow that a team capable of helping to win the presidency is not the best to help govern—much as may be owed them.

Jimmy Carter campaigned as an outsider and tried to remain an outsider while he was in the White House. Speaker of the House Tip O'Neill told of trying to help Carter by advising him which members of Congress to talk with to push his legislation. O'Neill was told that no, Carter speaking directly to the American people was enough. This was not the best way to deal with the U.S. Congress. Carter was not the ultimate public communicator either.

When *Los Angeles Times* bureau chief Jack Nelson asked Carter about improving relations with Congress, Nelson said Carter replied that he knew more about what was going on than they did, and "They just waste my time."

The Lone Ranger approach also didn't help abroad, where governments sometimes found Carter's policies to be unpredictably changeable. At a time when we heard much about a neutron bomb that would destroy enemy people without demolishing buildings and cities, I did a cartoon of the president as the Cartron bomb, hitting its friends while leaving its opponents standing. He kept losing stature in the cartoons.

Carter negotiated the Panama Canal treaties, which he had seemed to oppose in murky statements when Ford haltingly attempted such negotiations. And Carter deregulated the airlines, trucking and oil industries and the railroads. With another OPEC oil shock and more automobile gas lines, he proposed an energy policy in which he managed to arouse opposition from defenders of the status quo without going as far as some of us supporters would have liked. But it was nevertheless a *policy* and a real move toward meeting the energy problem.

Then, after many highly publicized meetings with people of all kinds—followed by a long delay—Carter took to the airwaves to tell the country that it suffered a "crisis of confidence." After all the buildup, it was a complete letdown.

In politics, style can seem as important as substance, a fact not overlooked by Carter's successors. Even when advocating good policies, Carter managed to convey a less than forceful manner. Whether being interviewed for a magazine article about times when he had felt lust in his heart or delivering an energy speech in which he referred to this issue as "the moral equivalent of war," he invited parody. The moral equivalent phrase originated with William James, but as a Carter policy, it had the unfortunate acronym MEOW.

I wrote a Carter address, "The Moral Equivalent of Energy," as it might have been delivered on December 20, 1941. It began:

> Many of you have heard by now of the unfortunate bombing of Pearl Harbor that took place on December 7, a date that will live in many memories as a sad one.
>
> I had planned to speak to you nearly two weeks ago but rescheduled this broadcast to provide time to prepare a program and to have further meetings—involving extremely delicate negotiations—with representatives of the Imperial Japanese government who are still in this country.
>
> Our talks, which have been useful and hopeful, have covered a wide range, including the need for a Japanese military homeland in Hawaii, and our need for repairs at Pearl Harbor and to our vessels there. We intend also to ask that they consider, as a matter of urgent priority, the return to us of the Philippines, Southern California and Oregon.

> These are matters of concern to all of us, even if we do not live
> in Pearl Harbor or the Philippines or Southern California or Or-
> egon . . . (etc.).

This, however, was less succinct than the editorial caption that a
Boston Globe staffer wrote as an in-house joke and was dismayed to
find in print in early editions. The title, "Mush from the Wimp," was
later replaced by the more prosaic "All Must Share the Burden."

In the Middle East, Carter found triumph and disaster. The Camp
David agreements ending hostilities between Egypt and Israel were the
triumph. That and his emphasis on human rights were his great legacies. I think Carter deserves much credit as a Johnny Appleseed of a
human rights policy that continues to bear fruit.

Then disaster occurred in Iran. In November 1979 the U.S. Embassy
in Tehran was seized and 63 Americans were taken hostage. At that
time the Ayatollah Khomeini was not yet in Tehran but in Qom. A
daring but not impossible reply to this violation of U.S. sovereignty
would have been to send a force to seize Khomeini or others of his
group and hold them until our people were released. We would have
been no less a great Satan.

Carter made himself and the nation hostage by announcing that he
would not leave the White House while our people were held captive—
and then complained that the American media played up the hostage
situation. He later characterized his concern for the hostages as something of an obsession—in this case one that was politically fatal.

Meanwhile, in December 1979, a month after the hostage crisis
began, Soviet troops moved into Afghanistan. Carter expressed an
almost naive shock and disappointment that Premier Brezhnev would
do this after they had met and engaged in a fraternal embrace.

On the Iran front, Carter did not break relations until five months
after the invasion of our embassy and just a couple of weeks before
Desert One—the failed rescue mission of our hostages that cost eight
American lives and the injury of several others.

It's difficult to understand how Carter, as a former naval officer and
as a president too often absorbed with detail, could not have done
better in overseeing such a mission. It was calamitous. In addition to
the deaths of American servicemen, it resulted in the loss of planes and
helicopters in the desert.

The only time I met Carter was at a White House dinner for a dozen or so media people late in 1979. We dressed comfortably for the 65-degree energy-saving temperature. And after drinks on the "Truman balcony," we ate in the family dining room and were taken on a tour of the second-floor rooms by the Carters, who were friendly and gracious.

At dinner we were free to ask questions. One that I did not ask but often wondered about when doing cartoons of him was: Why, during his time in the White House, had he changed the part in his hair from one side to the other? I suppose it might have been the idea of some media adviser, but it was another one of those things that conveyed an odd impression.

Carter told something interesting about the 1976 primary campaign. He had assumed that Sen. Ted Kennedy would enter, and when he did not, the Carter campaign was temporarily up in the air. As it developed, Carter eked out a narrow plurality in the New Hampshire primary with 29 percent of the vote. My favorite candidate was Rep. Morris Udall, who ran second. And were it not for the other candidates in that race, he might have won, might have seen himself on the covers of the newsmagazines and might have been the man with momentum. Udall later wrote a book, *Too Funny to Be President*. But it may have been political fate that was funny.

Some of the candidates I've liked best—Humphrey, Udall, Muskie and Mondale, for example—have not ended up on top. But then, the idea is not to guess winners. And when the occasion calls for it, you have to criticize your favorites.

Much as I admired Humphrey and Muskie, in 1972, when they challenged the California primary victory of George McGovern, I felt obliged to show them trying to pull off a burglary. And later I had to show candidate McGovern suffering from some self-inflicted wounds.

In 1980 my favorite candidate was a Republican—Rep. John Anderson of Illinois, who ran in his party's primaries and then as an Independent in the general election. I preferred him to Carter and Reagan and regarded him as someone more than just "neither of the above."

A question mark hung over that year's successful Reagan campaign. Committees in the U.S. Senate and in the House gingerly decided in 1992 to investigate whether the Reagan people had made a deal with Iranian leaders to hold the hostages until after the election. A basis for this suspected "October Surprise" was the timing of the release of the Americans and the Reagan administration's subsequent shipment of arms to Iran. A final congressional committee report in January 1993 found no convincing evidence. But the principal figure in such negotiations would have been Reagan's campaign manager, the devious and secretive William J. Casey, who died in 1987.

On January 20, 1981, Iran released the U.S. hostages just as Carter departed from office and Ronald Reagan became the fortieth president of the United States. The revolutionary leader of Iran had, in whatever way, helped to give us the Reagan Revolution over here.

Dec. 13, 1974

"THEY CAN'T SAY I'M NOT DOING ANYTHING"

July 22, 1975

"YOU HAVE JUST SAID THE MAGIC WORD, AND HERE'S ANOTHER UMPTY BILLION DOLLARS"

Oct. 6, 1976

"FORD IS ROCKED BY A LEFT TO THE JAW— CARTER TAKES A HARD RIGHT TO THE MOUTH — BOTH MEN ARE HURTING —"

Oct. 13, 1976

THE BLOB

Nov. 28, 1975

266

Nov. 8, 1977

Sept. 12, 1979

April 16, 1978

Feb. 2, 1979

"IT COMES OUT FUZZY"

©1978 HERBLOCK

May 21, 1978

268

28

A Clutch of Cartoonists

I like cartoons. And the way people draw is hardly a mystery to me. Yet, whenever someone sets pencil to paper, across the table, in a chalk talk or on television, there is no kid more fascinated than this one in watching where that line goes and what is going to happen next. Still, I'm a little surprised when people inquire about my lines and a work schedule that seems to me pretty routine.

For example, in starting to do the finished drawing I use a thin blue pencil—a whole jar of them, in fact. And when I'm pushing the envelope on time, the clock does not allow for saying, "O fiddle dee dee," and leisurely hoping for the best from a pencil sharpener. Well, people who drop by naturally want to know what's with all the blue pencil work on a black-and-white drawing. The reason is that after inking and erasing and applying the crayon shading, whatever is left of the blue sketch lines doesn't register, as black or gray lines would when photographed for reproduction.

Then there is the matter of time spent on completing the cartoon. There never seems to be enough time, and I nearly always end up doing some last-minute touching up in the hallway, on newsroom desks, in the stairwell on the way to the engraving room and then on the engraver's table until it is yanked away from me. But I have not yet tried adding touches to each printed copy as it rolls off the presses. The actual drawing usually takes about three and a half hours. But with an earlier start and more time, I have dawdled and started over and taken six hours or more. And I've turned out the work in less time when there is late news or early deadlines.

The record for speed came when I had just finished a day's work and learned of two tragic events: the Air Florida plane crash in ice and snow at the bridge near National Airport and a local Metro rail crash, also due to the weather.

I asked how long I could have to substitute something on this subject. The answer was "twelve minutes." That's twelve minutes to get up an idea, draw it and turn it in. I did a picture of snowflakes against a solid black background and titled it Bad Day In Washington.

I like to work large and draw the cartoons about four times the size they appear in the paper. The normal procedure then is to take the cartoon to the engravers, who make several negatives and prints, from which I try to select the best one. This alone takes a good deal more than twelve minutes. On this Bad Day, time was even more than usual of the essence. I drew the cartoon the exact size it would appear in the paper, handed it to the make-up man who pasted the drawing itself on the page. The cartoon came out all right, but the schedule was one I wouldn't care to repeat.

One of the many pleasures of this business is meeting other people in it whose work I enjoy. And I'm always interested in how they work. Some of them draw quite small, and some tell me they bat out a drawing in an hour or so. They have different styles, temperaments, views and work habits. But with or without shop talk most of them are fun to be with.

A cartoonist who lives not too far from Washington is Bill Rechin, who collaborates with Don Wilder on the comic strip "Crock." When the irrepressible Rechin first teamed up with the solemn-looking Wilder, he wondered how they would get along. By way of conversation, he asked if there was anything Wilder had always wanted to do.

270

"Yes," was the reply, "to yell 'Theater!' in a crowded firehouse."
They got along fine.

The earliest cartoonists I met were the *Chicago Tribune*'s John T.
McCutcheon and Carey Orr. They occupied studios at the very top of
the *Tribune* Tower and were generous with their time, drawings and
encouragement. When I went to work on the *Chicago News,* the senior
cartoonist was Vaughn Shoemaker, who had studied under Orr.

Shoes was very religious—an evangelical Christian who followed
his beliefs so rigorously that he would not even go to a movie. Once,
he did a chalk talk in which he emphasized the letters DEVIL and
EVIL in the word "vaudeville." He tried without success to save my
soul, but I was impressed by the pragmatism of his clinching argument
for religion. "Look at it this way," he said. "If you join the church
and there's a heaven, you'll get there—and if there isn't, you're not out
anything."

After moving to NEA Service I met George Clark, who produced a
daily panel and whose drawing was much admired. The story goes that
George, who had never taken lessons, felt he had missed out somewhere and decided to enroll in an art class. He was about to enter the
classroom when he heard the instructor telling the students to study the
drawing of that excellent artist George Clark. Whereupon he turned
around and went home. I think this ended his feeling about formal
training containing some magic that had escaped him.

Among the strip artists at NEA was a long-time cartoonist named
Woody. His father was a real pioneer type—a New Englander who had
cleared the land and worked it. According to Woody, his youthful
decision to take up drawing came as a blow to the old man. "Artists
and fiddlers!" said the stricken father. "Artists and fiddlers." He
could hardly believe his able-bodied son would fritter away his life on
one of those occupations.

There is no behavioral pattern among cartoonists in their work habits
or in their personalities, which range from totally extroverted to almost
mousy.

A prime example of the latter was a small baggy-eyed man we'll call
Charlie, who drew one of the NEA strips in Cleveland. He looked like
an aging jockey, and in fact spent much of his well-regulated time at
the track. He arrived at the office at the same time every day. He

started for lunch at the same time each day. And through some compulsion or superstition he immediately came back, circled his drawing table and left for lunch again. Then he resumed his clockwork schedule, taking time out only for low-key grumbling to colleagues. Charlie worked at a drawing table next to one of NEA's huge plate-glass front windows. A particular subject of his muttering was the monthly appearance of a burly window washer who set up his ladder next to Charlie's chair. As he stood on the ladder facing the window, he would remove the dirty water from his squeegee with a backward whipping motion, depositing drops of water on Charlie's drawings.

Charlie was not slow to anger but slow to speak up. After months of grumbling, he finally worked himself up to a point where he would make his complaint.

The window washer came, mounted his ladder and went to work as usual. This time as he flicked his squeegee behind, Charlie called up: "Hey, you! Look what you're doing!" and held up a drawing spotted with the dirty water. The large man turned his head, looked down at the diminutive artist, made a rude suggestion about what Charlie could do for himself, and returned to his washing and squeegeeing. It was a funny-but-sad moment. After all this time, Charlie had finally faced his nemesis and was reduced to muttering more than ever.

Completely different from Charlie was one of the most up-front people I knew—editorial cartoonist John Fischetti. His affections were strong, his dislikes were not concealed and he had no hesitancy about speaking his mind.

When he was with the *New York Herald Tribune,* he sent in his cartoons from Connecticut. While I've always tried out my sketches on friends in the newsroom, Johnny, working at home, tried his on his wife, Karen. They told me of how she would gently suggest that something he had sketched up needed more work or was not quite on target. At this he would pick up his sketch and stalk off, saying, "What do you know about cartooning anyhow?" Then he would later make the changes she had felt necessary.

During his freelance days he had done some drawings for a man who always had some excuse for delaying payment. After repeated visits and requests, Johnny one day marched past the man's secretary into his office and demanded payment. When the man stalled again, Johnny said, Okay, he would take out the money coming to him in the man's office equipment, which he would throw out the window. And so saying, he began rocking and moving toward the window a file cabinet that he estimated was worth $100. As he told me about this, I began laughing non-stop. What had crossed my mind was a possible discussion with the deadbeat, in which they haggled over the value of each item to be tossed out the window: "Wait a minute—that file cabinet is worth at least $150" and "Maybe, but it's used and a little scratched up; when I toss it out the window I figure it'll be worth $110." "Look, John, make it $115 and out it goes," etc. John and I convulsed ourselves going over all the possible dialogues. As for the incident itself, Johnny had the advantage of determined action over hesitation. The man wrote a check for the full amount owed and saved his furniture from defenestration.

When John won the Pulitzer Prize, his paper's owner, Marshall Field III, put on a special lunch "upstairs" for him with some editors and colleagues. On his way, Johnny passed the office of Jacob Burck, long-time cartoonist and Pulitzer winner of many years before. He asked if Burck was ready to leave for the lunch. When he discovered that Jake had not been invited, he notified the publisher that if Jake wasn't invited, he wasn't coming either. They asked Jake to come too.

Burck was himself a delightful person. In earlier days he had drawn cartoons for the communist publication *The New Masses,* and nobody seemed less like a firebrand than this short, gentle man of quiet humor. Working right up to the last minute, he would hand the drawing to the engraving-room cameraman, who locked it into a frame to be photographed. John told me he feared that one day in the rush, Jake and his drawing would both be locked into the frame—with Jake flattened out in the glass when they shot the picture.

John pioneered the modern-day horizontal-shape editorial cartoon in this country. It was popular in England and elsewhere, but for a long time the standard American editorial cartoon had been vertical. Characteristically, he persisted in drawing this horizontal cartoon even though it would have been easier to syndicate his work in a different shape. Later, when Pat Oliphant and others came along with horizontal cartoons, they became more and more popular. John persevered against the herd instinct of editors who resisted the shape of his cartoons. And he probably would have been amused and outraged to find another generation of sheeplike editors feeling that a political cartoon was somehow unfashionable or didn't "fit" if it was *not* horizontal.

The *Baltimore Sun* had two cartoonists—Edmund Duffy, who drew vertical cartoons; and later "Mocha" Yardley, who did horizontal ones.

Duffy is said to have batted out his cartoons early in the day in time to go to the afternoon races. As a young cartoonist, I was so impressed by Duffy's crayon work that when I noticed a watermark in the shading of one of his cartoons, I bought large sheets of bond paper to get the same effect.

Yardley drew more whimsical cartoons. He frequently included a beret-topped character representing himself, and a cat. Readers noted that when a pretty girl appeared in a Yardley cartoon, the cat's tail was not horizontal, but vertical.

On an early trip to California, I spent some time with Bruce Russell, cartoonist for what was then the arch-conservative *Los Angeles Times*. The opposite views expressed in our cartoons made no difference at all in our friendship. At his home he showed me what had started out to be his dream study. His space had been reduced to one corner just big enough for his drawing board, after constant inroads by his wife and daughters, who found the bright room an ideal sewing place.

Another cartoonist living in California was George Lichty, creator of the panel "Grin and Bear It." George, who had earlier worked in a cluttered section of a Chicago newspaper, also had dreamed of the ideal study. And when he built his home on the West Coast he finally realized that dream—a magnificent and spacious room with two-story windows and perfect light. He sat down to work in this ideal environment—and nothing happened. George had grown accustomed to the clatter and busyness of a newspaper. So he went to the local paper that carried his work and asked if they would please give him a corner someplace.

I found him there working happily at a desk next to a radiator. He had his own filing system, which consisted of jamming correspondence behind the radiator. George's delightful loose style looked spontaneous—which it was, in a way. His finished drawings were done without

274

the usual preliminary sketching, but they were proceeded by other spontaneous "finished drawings" until he got one to come out the way he wanted. Jules Feiffer has also used this free-style method.

On one visit to Los Angeles, Bruce Russell drove me some distance to a "good dinner place," which turned out to be a surprise party. He had gathered a group of cartoonists from around the state—including the great animators Chuck Jones and Walt Disney—for what was one of the best evenings ever. Karl Hubenthal, who was doing editorial cartoons for the *Los Angeles Examiner,* and wife, Elsie, took me for a day at Disneyland. Disney's people had provided him with some kind of pass that enabled us to try everything in the park we could manage in one day as fast as we could get from one attraction to another. I still have one of the quacking Donald Duck caps we wore.

Among other cartoonists who found the California climate congenial was Jimmy Hatlo, creator of "They'll Do It Every Time." He had a home and a lawn just off a green on the Pebble Beach golf course. This green was not only on a water hole but also seemed to be almost an island. As some of us were sipping drinks on Hatlo's lawn, I watched the distant golfers tee off, each ball clearing the stretch of water easily and plunking down right on the green. I made a mental note that when I got home the first thing I was going to do was put my golf clubs out for the trash collector. But I felt better when I learned that we were watching a qualifying round for something like a national open.

Despite the fact that most cartoonists are, or ought to be, individualistic, a National Cartoonists Society was begun in New York by some of the best in the profession—notably Walt Kelly, creator of "Pogo"; Rube Goldberg; and Milt Caniff of "Terry and the Pirates" and later "Steve Canyon."

Milt Caniff's wartime adventure scenarios were so ingenious that the Pentagon asked him in to make sure he was not privy to their plans.

I had read Rube's comic strips as a kid—"Boob McNutt," "Mike and Ike" and all the wonderful inventions. He made a successful switch to editorial cartoons, and for some additional fun, he later turned to sculpture. On his first attempt in this medium, he stayed up late working with clay until he had the modeling just where he wanted it and went happily to bed. The next morning he found that his creation looked something like a melting snowman. It was then that this self-taught sculptor learned about armatures and wires or whatever sup-porting materials go beneath a clay exterior.

When the Smithsonian decided to have a resident cartoonist, like a resident poet, it invited Saul Steinberg. He was supplied with a house, where we had dinner prepared by a resident cook. Steinberg made sure his government hosts realized he was the cartoonist *at* the residence, not cartoonist *in* residence—in case they had the idea he was devoting his time here to providing them with his work. But he later did a Washington series for *The New Yorker*.

Sometime in the early 1970s, I first heard about the use of computers to animate cartoons. Cartoonist Paul Conrad's brother, Jim, came up with the idea of a daily animated political cartoon for television. He got together several of us—Paul, Pat Oliphant, Fischetti and a couple of others—to have some of our daily cartoons animated for TV without requiring a lot of extra drawing. Since then I've gone along with a couple of other such projects, and have also seen some editorial car-toons drawn and animated by hand for TV. But even though the animated political cartoon sounds good in theory, it has not yet become the wave of the future. When you see a good political cartoon in print it goes bang. I don't know if animation improves on that. And however many millions see it on TV, it cannot receive the accolade and ex-tended mortality of a place on a refrigerator door. But I'm keeping an open mind. At any rate, the original venture provided the too infre-quent chance to get together with Conrad and some of the other cartoonists.

There have been an increasing number of women in cartooning, and all to the good. I've had a chance to meet a couple of favorites—M. G. Lord, whose editorial cartoons and articles have been a fine addition to *Newsday;* and Lynn Johnston, who draws one of the best strips ever, based on her own family, "For Better or for Worse."

When I told her that I particularly admired a strip featuring the dog Farley, she sent on the drawing, which is a prize. By now her extended family includes millions of readers.

Meeting the slim, attractive Cathy Guisewaite, you wonder how she relates to the charmingly chubby "Cathy," for whom the refrigerator itself is a magnet and who is in constant battle with the scales.

The former managing editor of *The Washington Post,* the late

Howard Simons, at one time had tried his hand at cartooning; and while he later turned to writing and editing, he never lost his enthusiasm for that medium. He got up a dinner to which he invited several cartoonists whose work was reprinted from time to time in *The Post*— and then made it an annual affair. Among the early invitees were Jeff MacNelly, Mike Peters, Tony Auth and Doug Marlette, along with columnist Haynes Johnson, who has a keen eye for cartoons and is a favorite with the practitioners.

The dinners sometimes ran late and were followed by other group activities. One dinner, held on February 11, was running close to midnight, and it had reached the what'll-we-do-now-fellows stage. I made what I thought was simply a funny suggestion. But in about two seconds all the cartoonists had taken it up, piled into cars and were off to the Lincoln Memorial—where we stood in the cold and sang, "Happy birthday to you, dear Abe, happy birthday to you."

Editorial page editor Meg Greenfield continued the annual dinners, which still go on, with other cartoonists coming regularly or appearing from time to time. She added two "honorary cartoonists," humorist Dave Barry and broadcaster Ted Koppel. Koppel generally conducts a sing-along with surprising and generally hilarious lyrics he composes to the tunes of well-known songs.

Each year Meg also invites a couple of government officials, but restricts them to a one-time-only appearance. After the dinners some of these officials have invited us to government offices of one kind or another. Sen. Daniel P. Moynihan, for one, had the Senate hearing room opened to us for a special midnight session of our own. And, sitting in the chairman's seat, I asked Howard Simons, at the witness table, "Are you now or have you ever been a cartoonist?"

At a subsequent annual affair, the dinner and services were, as usual, good. But gradually we became aware that there was something odd—or rather, familiar—about the two people who were waiting on us. Moynihan and his wife, Elizabeth, had contrived a second visit by dressing in the appropriate uniforms and substituting for the waiters. They were welcome rule-breakers.

If we followed the class-reunion practice of citing member-who-came-longest-distance, it would probably be Gary Larson, creator of "The Far Side," who made it from Washington State one year. I think he is the funniest and most original panel cartoonist to set pen to paper. I not only chortle over his cartoons, but often tear them out and ask colleagues, "Did you see what this guy did today?"

At one of these dinners Mike Peters, who is considerably less hefty than Arnold Schwarzenegger, turned up in a Superman suit. His wife had made it for him as part of a gag he had dreamed up to astonish executives at his hometown paper. Mike said that he got onto a ledge outside the executive meeting room, figuring to swoop in on the three-piece-suit men and announce that he was sorry to be late but that he had run into some fog over Toledo. But the meeting itself was delayed. And, as Mike told it, he found that standing on a ledge on a cold day was no fun, especially with pigeons fighting him for the space. Worse, people gathered at the windows in surrounding buildings; and some impolite ones pointed and called out, "Jump." When the three-piece suiters finally arrived Mike was relieved to be back inside.

A lower altitude but equally high comedy Peters performance came at a Pulitzer anniversary ceremony at Columbia University, where Mike sought out its president, a man he had never met. He told this distinguished gentleman, "My name is Mike Peters. I was fortunate enough to win a Pulitzer Prize a few years ago, and I hope I'll have good fortune in the future." Then, shaking hands, he repeated slowly, "I hope you'll remember me; my name is Peters—Mike Peters." After the prolonged handshake, the university president opened his hand to find in it a five-dollar bill.

Some years ago Jeff MacNelly took time off from cartooning on a more or less indefinite sabbatical. Maybe I can put that better in Jeff's own words when he reappeared at an annual dinner later: "Some of you may have heard rumors that I ran off to Alaska with my secretary. [Pause.] Well, they're true." Anyhow, during his absence his syndicate found a replacement in Jack Ohman, of the *Oregonian,* who succeeded in holding a large number of papers and is today widely syndicated on his own.

As Jeff and I, Mike Peters, Jim Borgman and a couple of others were leaving one of these annual ninth-floor dinners at *The Post,* we crowded into the elevator, and the lobby button was pressed. As we started the descent, there was a long silence suddenly broken by someone saying, "If this elevator goes down, Ohman picks up 900 papers."

For years these annual meetings have closed with an Elvis Presley routine by Mark Stamaty of the *Village Voice* and the *Post*'s weekly "Washingtoon."

During a 1993 White House visit by this group of cartoonists, Vice President Gore, who had attended an earlier *Post* cartoonist meeting, urged Stamaty to do his Elvis. The performance may have been something of a first in the Oval Office. President Clinton remembered that he had a necktie with a picture of Elvis on it, had it produced from his living quarters and presented it to Mark. There have been rumors that Clinton at times had done a pretty good Elvis imitation himself.

Chuck Jones, premier animator of Bugs Bunny and creator of Pepe LePew, Road Runner and other characters, sometimes makes it to these dinners. An ace Mark Twain fan, he will recall nuggets from Twain's books that are often overlooked—like the incident where Huckleberry Finn and his raft mate enter an abandoned house and find the previous occupant's wooden leg, and Huck mentions that "we never found the other one."

Jones is not only a fascinating storyteller, but also one who encourages others to talk. One evening he told me of a practically infallible ploy he had developed to start a conversation with any child. He would ask, "Have you ever been stung by a bee?" It worked like magic on this somewhat older kid because it immediately reminded me of a bee incident.

At a picnic, I bit into a sandwich that had already been staked out by a bee and was stung. Not having any idea what to do about a bee sting on the tongue, I phoned my doctor to find out. His wife answered and said she was sorry he couldn't come to the phone right now, perhaps she could help me. I told her no, I really wanted to talk to him. She then explained that he couldn't talk right now because while they were having a drink in the garden, a bee must have somehow got into his glass and had stung him on the tongue. For the benefit of anyone who might want to know, the doctor had put ice on his tongue, and I did the same.

During a phone conversation I asked Jones when he was next coming to Washington. And he mentioned a little-known organization that he was sure existed: the Anti-Destination League. These are the people who manage to do everything possible to make sure you don't get where you want to go. I realized immediately that he was on to something. I had often noticed how these people always stop to chat in front of stairways and elevators, and always at the narrowest point in an otherwise uncluttered sidewalk—for example, between a vending stand and a trash bin or any other existing obstructions. At parties with bars, they not only get their drinks but also continue to stand at the bar while others wait. Jones is right. It can't all be an accident. There must be an organization behind all this.

Jones even gets delightful touches into the signs in his animated cartoons. A favorite is:

Acme Manufacturing Company
We make fine Acmes

It was a passing Jones observation that elephants are nice animals even though their clothes don't fit.

Chuck Jones has by now written it in his book, *Chuck Amuck,* but I can't resist passing on a story that floored me when I heard him tell it—about the ultimate in Hollywood timidity and stupidity. While the United States was engaged in World War II, the studio for which Chuck was producing animated cartoons came up with one that featured a hilarious figure representing the Führer. The studio executive hemmed and hawed and delayed giving his okay to this animation job, until finally he was pinned down on what it was exactly that bothered him about it. He said, "After all, we don't know who's going to win the war."

Jones is obviously a good subject for interviews. In one of these, after he had done a series of drawings on Paul Bunyan and his blue ox, the interviewer asked him if he had always had an interest in Paul Bunyan. Jones said no, but he had once had an affair with an ox.

Most of the cartoonists I've known have been nice guys, and generous. One of the best and most deservedly successful is Charles Schulz. On a rare visit to Washington, the creator of "Peanuts" and his wife, Jeannie, dropped in unexpectedly one day after I had gone to an infrequent lunch outside the building. My secretary told them how seldom I go out and how bad I would feel about not being there when they came by. But they said that was all right; if she didn't mind they would sit down and wait. And while waiting, he signed some Snoopy drawings that would delight her children. This is right up there with Chuck Jones, who, when approached for autographs, often throws in a sketch of one of his cartoon characters.

They don't hardly come no better than that.

29

Movie Review

I treasure a "Peanuts" strip in which Lucy announces, as she begins drawing, that she's going to become a political cartoonist "lashing out with my crayon." While Charlie Brown is asking the subject of her work, she strikes the paper with such force that the crayon snaps in half. "I'm lashing out," she says, "at the people who make these stupid crayons."

Unlike Lucy, I don't decide to "lash out" first and then pick a convenient target. But I'm right with her when it comes to holding definite opinions.

The political cartoon generally pokes fun or points out wrongs. Our free press, it's been noted, was established primarily as a check on government. And this critical attitude applies in spades to cartooning—a particularly irreverent form of expression. There are no sacred cows, and no matter how high the official, no sacred bull.

For those who regard this kind of work as "negative," I'd cite the story of the teacher who tried to inculcate in her young charges a love for birds and animals.

One boy told of how he had taken in a kitten on a cold night and fed it. A girl told of how she had found an injured bird and cared for it. When the teacher asked the next boy if he could give an example of *his* kindness to nature's creatures, he said, "Yes, ma'am. One time I kicked a boy for kicking a dog."

In cartooning we often show our love for our fellow men by kicking big boys who kick underdogs. The effort is to promote fairness, to "keep 'em honest"—or to be the kid who says, "The emperor has no clothes on."

So my daily work consists largely of trying to keep up with the latest untoward developments and hypocrisies—to provide in a small space the picture beyond or behind the TV screen. The lines I draw often differ from the lines on the pollsters' popularity charts, and Ronald Reagan was very popular.

One of the first cartoons I did of him appeared when he was still an actor running for governor of California. It showed a campaign worker reaching to set up cardboard cutouts of the movie star, while another aide says, "Wait—not that one—that's the candidate."

Later, when he ran for president, Reagan still seemed to me two-dimensional. But he had 3-D colorful anecdotes: the welfare queen, never found to exist, who picked up her checks in a Cadillac; and the strapping fellow standing in line with food stamps to buy liquor. They could be seen in the audience's eyes, even if nowhere else. The "shining city on a hill" could almost be visualized, before it turned out to be a luxury spa atop hopeless slums and mountains of debt.

Reagan spoke about the "magic of the marketplace." But like most magic, it proved illusory. This "magic" took a debt of a trillion dollars and tripled it. The real magic was in political presentation—TV appearances, the spoken lines and the popular image.

In a 1985 Woody Allen movie, *The Purple Rose of Cairo,* a lonesome married woman finds refuge from reality in continued visits to a movie house. Eventually the star looks at her from the screen, comments on her frequent visits and materializes from the movie screen to spend time with her.

I think something like that happened in the United States in 1980. For eight years, the country became involved with a former actor and entered into an era when fact, fiction and fantasy, reality and silver-screen make-believe, all blended together. Script lines and the good times rolled, and the national, corporate and private debt rolled on too.

In the age of television, Reagan was a political casting director's dream. The scenario was also a dream—more spending, lower taxes and a balanced budget—not only free lunch, but free breakfast, dinner and room service too. Government, which he aspired to lead, was itself bad—as he put it, "not the solution but the problem." Early Marxists, who professed as their ultimate aim the withering away of government, must have been rolling in their graves with laughter as this zealous anti-communist seemed to adopt that goal. They might also have observed that he didn't practice his own preachments either.

Under Reagan, the executive branch, the cabinet, the White House staff and the bureaucracy kept expanding. What withered away was concern for the less well off, and aid to the now overburdened cities and states. He campaigned against Waste, Fraud and Abuse. But nearly eight years after Reagan left office, a White House study acknowledged that the transfer of government work to private companies resulted in wasteful, fraudulent and abusive contracts that increased the cost to taxpayers by many billions of dollars.

The movie man in Reagan was always present. A diplomat who had helped negotiate the Panama Canal treaties during the Carter administration told of giving Reagan a briefing on them. Reagan began by reciting his political mantra on the canal, "We built it, we paid for it," etc. The diplomat went on to give a rather listless Reagan the necessary fill-in on the subject. "Then," he said, "I made the mistake of mentioning a movie." At this, the next president came alive, and discussion of Panama was, for all practical purposes, ended.

Fiction was presented as fact. The docudrama president told moving stories of how at the time of World War II he had visited concentration camps in Europe—though he had actually spent the war period stateside. In speeches, he told of a pilot who, when his plane was hit, stayed with his wounded gunner, saying, "We'll ride this down together." Reagan concluded with the words, "Congressional Medal of Honor, posthumously." No such Medal of Honor winner existed, and the only place the incident occurred was in a 1944 movie, *A Wing and a Prayer*.

But Reagan could be remarkably realistic about his unrealism.

Charles McDowell of the *Richmond Times-Dispatch* related a dinner conversation he had with Reagan in which McDowell told the president he had once seen Reagan during filming in his hometown. The president politely corrected him, recalling that he had not been in McDowell's town because he had not joined the rest of the cast at the shooting of those scenes. When the flabbergasted correspondent apologized for having recounted this incident for years, Reagan told him not to worry, no need to apologize. "You believed that story because you wanted to," the president said. "I do it all the time."

Even when Reagan's own staff pointed out that an anecdote or a statistic was wrong, he continued to use it. Like a piece of movie dialogue, it didn't matter whether it was true. If it was a good line and got an audience reaction, that was enough.

Mark Twain observed that a lie can circle the globe while truth is getting its boots on. Reagan's fictions could circulate around the country with little fear of being overtaken. And it was impossible to catch up with all of them in the cartoons.

People sometimes comment that "you have plenty of material these days." There is always plenty of material. But with the Reagan and Bush administrations my ink bottle ranneth over.

The term "Reagan Revolution" was not just an expression. Early cartoons on his presidency focused on his attempts to dismantle regulatory agencies. More importantly, former football player Reagan perfected the end run around Congress. When he couldn't eliminate an agency he didn't like, he could man it with people opposed to its work. Defenders of civil rights, the poor and the environment, as well as consumers, felt that Reagan was winning one for the gyppers. His administration even went to bat for tax exemptions for colleges that excluded minorities. And it politicized the CIA and the Department of Justice, which put his objectives before their duties to uphold the laws.

Reagan had, if not a holy alliance, certainly a pious one with the televangelists, many of whom turned out to share the administration ethic of get whatever you can while you can. At least one prominent evangelical con man, Jim Bakker, went to jail. Reagan was supported by an organization headed by Jerry Falwell called the Moral Majority, which, some pointed out, was neither.

Reagan felt that "creationism" should be taught along with

"LEAVE THE FACADES — IT'LL BE JUST LIKE HOLLYWOOD"

©1981 HERBLOCK
Dec. 1, 1981

286

evolution. He advocated prayer recitation in the public schools and wanted a constitutional amendment to this effect. He believed in "privatization" of public resources, but not so much privacy in homes and bedrooms. He spoke of family values, although his own family was not the greatest example. He opposed what the Supreme Court had decided was a right to abortion. He favored a "squeal rule" requiring authorities to report under-age girls who wanted contraceptives. And he had his attorney general, Edwin Meese, head an anti-pornography commission.

This morality did not extend to the poor, to the homeless or to victims of racist policies. Nor did it deal with matters of human rights abroad, except where they were violated in certain communist or "leftist" countries. His administration was not big on individual rights except the right to make as much money as possible in any way possible without going to the slammer. Such policies set the tone for business and finance and for the country. We had leveraged buyouts, corporate raids, insider trading, junk bonds, junk politics and a kind of national yard sale.

Reaganomics was a continuing subject. Supply-side economics, as I understood it, sided with those who were well supplied. An article by William Greider, based on many conversations with Budget Director David Stockman, revealed that the administration knew its policies and projections were unreal. Stockman saw looming deficits of 200 billions stretching "as far as the eye could see"—an underestimate. The books were cooked. But the administration policies stayed on—and continued under Bush. What we got was not only an increased financial debt but a Truth Deficit.

Beauty is in the eye of the TV camera. So is truth and strength. Whereas Jimmy Carter came across as something of a wimp, Reagan stood tall and sounded forceful. Yet Carter, for all his faults and Sundayschoolishness, stood for human rights. After the invasion of Afghanistan, he not only stopped grain shipments to the USSR but also began arming the Afghans and started our own military buildup. Even in his bungling of the Iranian rescue mission, he made an effort to do something about hostage-takers.

Reagan, by contrast, sold arms to Iran. It was Reagan who placed our Marines in Lebanon with no mission except to act as sitting ducks.

Six months after terrorists truck-bombed the American Embassy in Lebanon, they truck-bombed the ill-protected Marine barracks there and cost the lives of 241 Americans.

And what happened next? Two days after this disaster, Reagan invaded the Caribbean island of Grenada. His staff proclaimed him a great leader. The military kept reporters away from the invasion on the excuse that they might interfere with the troops' success. This policy met with such widespread public approval that the Pentagon kept the media at bay later when our troops were in Panama and Kuwait.

Whatever Reagan's personal view of the press in general, he took a dim view of my cartoons. At an annual Gridiron Club dinner where Nancy Reagan made a stage appearance, he asked her in his concluding remarks, "How would you like to come home with me? I could show you my favorable cartoons from *The Washington Post*. It won't take but a few seconds."

A writer who spent a good deal of time in the White House told me that Reagan looked at the cartoon one morning and said—seriously— "This guy just doesn't like me." Reagan knew he was likable, and seemed to think that those who didn't care for his policies must base their decisions on some personal dislike of him.

When a White House lunch was put on for some cartoonists, "Doonesbury" creator Garry Trudeau and I were not invited—a precedent followed, with the same omissions, by President Bush. If the lunch non-invites were supposed to embarrass us, they didn't. They became a column item, and when the subject was raised at a White House briefing, a press secretary said that all who were invited came. Not so. When I had dinner with Jules Feiffer a week or so later, it turned out that he had been invited and had not accepted. It was a decision I was spared.

White House invitations are not lightly tossed aside. And to big campaign contributors they are literally more precious than gold. But the political planners of these occasions are sometimes inclined to overestimate the magic of that address. When it was reported that Will Rogers had declined a luncheon invitation with President Hoover, he explained that "I just wasn't *hongry*."

But I did have a certain curiosity about Reagan that would have been satisfied by a chance meeting of some kind. This was partly because of his second-hand references and partly because of an early experience described to me by the late Newton Pratt, cartoonist of the *Sacramento Bee*. Pratt, a trenchant critic of Reagan while he was governor of California, said that at a reception where Gov. Reagan was greeting people, he refused to shake hands with Pratt. I felt sure that Reagan had long ago smoothed such rough edges before he became a presidential candidate, and never heard of such an incident taking place in Washington. I don't think it would have happened to me if I had ever met him.

There was a curious non-meeting incident. One evening I was a guest of some friends at a benefit dinner where a majority of the guests were probably well-to-do "conservatives." The wife of a Democratic senator, who had come unaccompanied, seemed to find in me a comfortable and familiar face. As we were talking, President and Mrs. Reagan entered the room and began shaking hands as they passed among the guests. Mrs. Reagan smiled and nodded as we introduced ourselves. While Reagan was greeting the man next to me and just as he would have turned to me, the senator's wife grabbed my arm and yanked me back, saying, "We don't belong here!" The vacancy was quickly filled by others; the moment—and the president—passed. In Washington, functions involving political mixed company are commonplace, and I still don't know why this wife of a prominent senator suddenly felt that she (and I) should not say howdyado to this president.

People sometimes ask what public figures are "easiest to draw," or even who would you like to see elected president because of his cartoonability? The latter is a little like asking a columnist or editorial writer who would be his favorite candidate on the basis of how his name lent itself to puns. Since such questions are obviously not intended to offend, I resist the temptation to say I hope for the return of Hitler because of his mustache and the way he combed his hair.

Actually anyone can be caricatured, and when you do a high official often enough, you may refine or exaggerate the caricature so that a certain set of lines becomes familiar to the reader as President X or Mr. Y. Also the caricature itself generally expresses an opinion. For example, my George Bush emphasized his upper (easy to read) lip and somewhat crooked smile and close-set eyes, which to me depicted his character better than some of the high-domed, strong-chinned draw-ings featured in other caricatures.

Reagan, handsome and self-possessed, obviously could not be made to look villainous or thuggish despite his misdeeds and misstatements. I pictured him in the situations he created and sometimes quoted him. In the Reagan-Khomeini cartoon he looks straight and strong on tele-vision, but where's the rest of him?—kneeling before the Ayatollah. A few weeks after the Lebanon disaster, when he said that "our military forces are back on their feet and standing tall," I used that quote with a drawing of the graves of all the needlessly killed Americans who would never stand again.

Reagan declared that those who committed this dastardly act would be brought to justice. But even though the terrorists and the govern-ments behind them were known, the threat was an empty one. Al-though other governments were involved, Muammar Qadhaffi of Libya became the Designated Bad Guy.

A varnish company used to advertise, "Save the surface and you save all." Reagan's surface appearance saved him from the kind of charges that would have been leveled at someone like Carter.

As for cartoon characters, there was no short supply of short-on-ethics people in Reagan's official group. When former Reagan cam-paign manager William J. Casey became head of the CIA, he continued trading in stocks even though his position gave him intel-ligence that was useful in his financial dealings. Casey, who as early as 1959 had lost a plagiarism suit, was not known for candor or forthrightness.

In a postscript to the 1980 campaign, it was disclosed that Carter campaign papers and debating points had turned up in the Reagan camp. James A. Baker III said he had received them from Casey, but Casey said he had no memory of them.

Reagan's attorney general managed to prevent any conclusive in-vestigation of Debategate, as this was called. But the purloining or mysterious appearance of the Carter papers gave added credence later to Casey's role in a possible 1980 "October Surprise" deal with Iran.

Casey was so ostentatiously non-communicative that I usually drew him with a paper bag over his head. Perhaps I should have had him putting the bag over the public's head. The IRS found that over four

Nov. 11, 1986

©1986 HERBLOCK

years Casey had taken tax deductions of some $60,000 on an investment of $95.

Reagan's first attorney general, William French Smith, returned questionable funds and tax deductions when they became public knowledge.

Others in the administration showed remarkable profits and tax deductions. In addition, these crusaders against "waste, fraud and abuse" ran up huge bills for office accommodations, hotel rooms, security systems and entertainment—all at public expense.

Secretary of the Interior James Watt cost the taxpayers $300,000 a year for nine "security bodyguards" and used a million-and-a-half-dollar plane for personal and political purposes.

Edwin Meese, successor to William French Smith as attorney general, received friendly financial help from people who later came to hold posts in the Reagan administration.

Investigations of Meese began before his confirmation and continued through much of his term in office. In 1981 a Senate investigative committee reluctantly decided that he was not "unfit to serve" in office—hardly a ringing endorsement. And when he departed, it could be said of the country's chief law enforcement officer that he had never been indicted. I depicted him doing a kind of W. C. Fields routine—pretending to be surprised that anyone could think that he was in any way unethical or less than a sterling character.

After leaving the government, close Reagan aide Michael Deaver was convicted of perjury in connection with his lobbying activities.

Secretary of Defense Caspar Weinberger frequently appeared in the cartoons. He also did innumerable interview programs where he always vigorously defended the administration and its excessive spending policies.

Pentagon deals with contractors became a public scandal. But it was the comparatively small and easily understandable cost outrages that registered most: $435 for a $17 hammer; $387 for a $3 flat washer; $9,606 for a wrench retailing for under a dollar. An airplane toilet seat cost $640. I took to putting a toilet seat around Weinberger's neck, always with the $640 price tag. It became a symbol of the Pentagon waste that ran into billions if not trillions.

Like most prominent officials, Weinberger was civil when I met

292

him, showing me he wore a conventional collar and tie. But I heard that when the Pentagon considered adding a couple of floors to the already huge building, the prospect of a cartoon featuring a toilet-seat-collared secretary standing atop it was something of a deterrent. Of course, the Pentagon continued plans to expand horizontally.

I did a good deal on Reagan's "welfare for the wealthy" tax and budget proposals. And at the end of his term I drew a cartoon on what he was leaving. It showed an empty treasury with IOUs for the trillions of dollars of debt he had run up, while a smiling Reagan says he is not leaving anything for liberals to be liberal *with*. The actual situation was not even wryly funny to some members of Congress. Senators Daniel Patrick Moynihan (D-N.Y.) and Ernest Hollings (D-S.C.) declared that Reagan made sure that social programs could not be reinstituted.

The Reagan-Bush administration's get-what-you-can philosophy and its corner-cutting of the laws spilled over into scandals.

In addition to Pentagon contracts, there were the Environmental Protection Agency scandals, in which the government provided more protection for officials and polluters than for the environment. One EPA official went to jail. And the Interior Department helped "privatize" oil and coal lands on terms remarkably favorable to selected companies—deals that might have raised banner headlines in the days of Teapot Dome. But my cartoons on these subjects were not matched by any general indignation. In the house-of-credit-cards economy, times were considered good, and the very multiplicity of misdeeds had its own numbing effect.

One administration scandal didn't surface until after Reagan was out of office. In 1989, after allegations of corruption in Reagan's Department of Housing and Urban Development, an independent counsel indicted some HUD officials on charges of fraud, influence-peddling and bribery. When former Reagan HUD Secretary Samuel R. Pierce, Jr., was subpoenaed to testify before Congress, he pleaded the Fifth Amendment. In June 1993, the former assistant housing secretary pleaded guilty to two felony counts.

The most publicized Reagan scandal was Iran-contra, involving the surreptitious sale of arms to Iran—a terrorist state and still ostensibly our enemy—in hope of getting back hostages. The arms sale itself was

"WE'VE GIVEN IT TWO OF OUR FAIREST MAIDENS"

March 11, 1983

outrageous. But it was compounded by the Reagan team's decision to defy a congressional ban and divert money to the contras, a group trying to overthrow the government of Nicaragua.

If the hostages were an obsession with Carter, Reagan made Nicaragua an even greater obsession. Anything was justified in the contra cause. In his efforts to rouse the United States to the supposed danger from Nicaragua, Reagan provided some unintended levity by putting a little-known Texas town on the map. He said that Nicaragua was only "two days' driving time" from Harlingen, Texas! I had some fun with this; and later, after the fall of the Soviet Union, did a cartoon showing Harlingen now safe from the Red Tide.

In 1990 the supposedly permanent dictatorship of Nicaragua held an election, which it lost, and turned over the government to the elected leader.

Iran-contra featured lies and cover-up. The unraveling of this scandal began on October 5, 1986, with the downing of a plane in Nicaragua and the capture of its pilot, Eugene Hasenfus, on a mission to aid the contras. The administration at first refused to admit Hasenfus's connection with our government. Reagan flatly denied it, as he also later flatly denied any arms-for-hostages deals. I did a cartoon of a crashed administration "credibility" plane immediately, even before the official denials.

After a Middle East newspaper story that Reagan pooh-poohed, the Iran-contra disclosures surfaced in this country.

Finally, on November 25, 1986, Attorney General Meese announced to the press what purported to be the surprising news of the contra diversion. His supposed determination to investigate came after Meese had interviewed, without witnesses, Oliver North, a chief actor in the Iran missions and contra aid. Meese dallied while North shredded documents far into the night and removed other evidence from government offices. This was under an attorney general in a "law and order" administration.

The congressional hearings on this matter were practically a shambles. Members of House and Senate committees sat in one unwieldy body. They granted immunity from prosecution to defendants based on information disclosed in committee hearings. They set a time limit on their work. The Senate panel's chairman, Daniel Inouye of Hawaii, made the initial mistake of recommending limited immunity in exchange for testimony. Then he permitted witnesses' lawyers to take over the proceedings instead of confining them to advising their clients.

Col. North, wearing his U.S. Marine uniform, made no bones about lying to Congress, shredding documents, doctoring evidence, backdating papers and helping to prepare a false chronology of events. He boasted of such felonious activities, which Reagan-Bush loyalists saw as performed in a great cause by a hero.

Two things that carry great political clout are medals and money. There is a widespread notion that anyone who can accumulate billions of dollars must have sagacity on all subjects including how to run the government. And many assume that the physical valor attested by medals must also signify moral or political courage. They find it hard to believe that a wartime prisoner or brave soldier might be a con man, a criminal or a political nut.

Oliver North provided not only medals but also the adventure of secret dealings abroad and reports to the White House. In the movie presidency, he was James Bond 007—On His Majesty's Service.

At the hearings, he was hardly a lone patriot standing up against an inquisition. Actually, many administration supporters on the committees spoke as if they were part of his legal team. They argued that violations of the law were all right because it only happened to be the law *at that time*—and it was the fault of Congress for having held other views at other times. As for lying to Congress, well, this was in the interest of national security. Regard for an institution is not increased when members don't show any regard for it themselves.

I was really ticked off by the view of some legislators that the country could not stand another "failed presidency." I am boggled by the concern about "failed presidencies"—as if the person temporarily occupying the White House is some kind of holy icon more important than the Constitution or the nation. What I think the country cannot stand is failed justice and failure to demand that officials uphold their oaths of office.

The Reagan Revolution that bypassed congressional authority also left its mark on the federal courts, where Reagan and Bush named a large majority of the judges. And the effect became apparent in Iran-contra court cases.

Despite the partial immunity given by the committees, Special

Prosecutor Lawrence Walsh succeeded in getting a three-count conviction against North. But this was later overturned by appellate and Supreme Court majorities dominated by Reagan-Bush appointees.

North claimed to have been cleared. He was not. What saved him from the felony sentence was the limited immunity granted at the congressional hearings and the courts' interpretation of that as almost unlimited immunity.

Who says crime does not pay? North cashed in handsomely with speaking fees and royalties; and several convicted Watergate figures who served time in prison emerged to profitable celebrity status.

Under constant attack by the administration and its allies, Walsh nevertheless secured guilty counts against several other people—including former National Security Adviser Robert C. (Bud) McFarlane.

If the last refuge of a scoundrel is patriotism, the last refuge of scoundrel protectors is the cost of justice. Officials and commentators who wouldn't blink an eye at a billion dollars for one non-working and not-needed bomber moaned and groaned about the time and *cost* of continuing the Special Prosecutor's Office. Of course, much time could have been saved if high officials had not continuously stonewalled. It took five years for Bush to begin complying with the special prosecutor's request for his personal notes.

Iran-contra could have been called the Amnesia Scandal. The highest officials—president and vice president—had trouble recollecting things. Even after Oliver North said that President Reagan knew and approved of his actions, Reagan had memory trouble.

Vice President Bush said he was "out of the loop" on arms-for-hostages discussions, and he would have opposed such deals had he known. Though other officials referred to the presence of Bush at these meetings, he couldn't remember much. His performance may have been best summed up in a Jackie Mason comedy routine that went something like this: "Mr. Bush, were you there when these matters were discussed?" "No, I was in the bathroom." "How long were you in the bathroom?" "Oh, maybe three or four years."

Reagan's passive statement on anything amiss in the whole scandal was that "mistakes were made." As for Bush, his denials may have been his biggest mistake—deceptions that proved a tangled web for him. It finally turned out that Bush was indeed "in the loop."

Many of us had hoped that Watergate would provide an example that

297

"IS THIS A GREAT COUNTRY OR WHAT"

Oct. 23, 1991

©1991 HERBLOCK

298

would deter future scandals. It only seemed to instruct future administrations in how to avoid being caught. The Reagan administration apparently heeded Nixon's advice to co-conspirators that nothing can be done to you for what you don't remember. When Reagan was finally questioned under oath, after he left office, he couldn't remember.

The other impression left by Watergate was that there had to be a "smoking gun"—in that case, the incriminating tapes. Now, almost nothing less than a tape or video of a conspiracy or crime in progress might do—perhaps not even then. If there had been a smoking gun, surely Reagan or Bush would have explained that the gun was unfortunately addicted to cigarettes.

One of the differences between the Watergate and the Iran-contra scandals was the fact that Nixon was not as well liked as Reagan. With this president people were willing to share in the general amnesia. Perhaps more importantly, the public had taken a long time to accept the facts of Watergate and now seemed to suffer from scandal burnout.

Toward the end of the Reagan administration, a final fillip added to the effect that his whole presidency had been scripted in Hollywood. Former Chief of Staff Don Regan disclosed that Reagan often acted only after his wife, Nancy, consulted an astrologer. Astrology may have dictated the timing of his trips, including one to a cemetery containing Nazi graves at Bitburg, Germany. Astrology may even have played a part in his post-presidential trip to Japan, where he made a speech and remembered to pick up his check for $2 million.

Of course, it might be argued that Reagan's political success as president showed that there must be something in that astrology stuff. But I think the fault was not in the stars but in ourselves, or those of us who were star-struck viewers. Promoters of the movie-man presidency could describe it in the meaningless way other products are sometimes advertised in stores: as seen on TV.

May 30, 1982

June 3, 1984

"IN THIS SCIENTIFIC EXPERIMENT, JONAH..."

Dec. 11, 1981

Aug. 29, 1982

"ON TO CENTRAL AMERICA!"

March 13, 1984

"...TRAGIC EVENT...COWARDLY TERRORISTS... OUR BRAVE MEN ... STAND TALL ...WE'RE DOING EVERYTHING WE CAN..."

Sept. 21, 1984

SHOWING THE FLAG

Oct. 30, 1983

UNDERCOVER OPERATION

Jan. 6, 1983

"YOU CALL THIS A BILL OF RIGHTS? WHAT ABOUT THE FOUNDING FETUSES!"

Aug. 5, 1981

"THE FOUNDERS WOULD HAVE LOVED IT IF THEY'D THOUGHT OF IT"

Jan. 24, 1985

"WELL, WHEN YOU WERE DRIVING YOU DENTED THE FENDERS"

May 31, 1984

SPECIAL ASSISTANT FOR VOODOO AFFAIRS

May 4, 1982

"YOU FIRST, SON"

Jan. 3, 1984

**♪"..WHEN YOU WISH UPON A DREAM
NO REQUEST IS TOO EXTREME..."♪**

Dec. 31, 1986

DUMP

Feb. 10, 1983

"WOW!"

July 16, 1989

"WHATEVER HAPPENED TO GOOD OLD KING KONG?"

Dec. 2, 1988

30

The Shore

The ocean has always had a special attraction for me, and on winter vacations I've looked for accommodations that travel agents identified as OTW—On the Water. There is probably nothing unusual about this, except that I am no John Masefield, who must go down to the sea again, with the ships and voyages and all. My situation was summarized by friend Freddie, after I finally acquired a small summer place on the ocean. He smilingly told a mutual acquaintance in Washington, "Herb doesn't drive and he doesn't swim and he has this very nice place on the Delaware coast." It was true. And he might have added that my landlubber's only qualifications for deep-water activities was that during a few times on boats I avoided getting seasick.

As for swimming, this Chicago boy was taken as a small child to a Lake Michigan beach where other kids were happily splashing around. In my case, the cold water had a kind of litmus effect, causing me to turn blue. My folks bundled me up and took me back home; and without other swimmers in the family, the experiment was not repeated.

Later I made attempts in YMCA pools; and in the Army I responded to a bulletin board notice of a swimming course. But I was the only GI who signed up and the instructor did little for one pupil.

The last attempt in a pool was made when a friend who'd had remarkable results in making water babies out of dry small fry assured me that she could do the same for me. She got me to take a horizontal position in the water and held up my legs to help me resist my instinctive desire to touch bottom. What she had not taken into account was that this method, which supported the entire bodies of small children, did not work when applied to a nearly six-foot, 175-pound man— especially one with a tendency, even in water, to prove the law of gravity. While she was focusing on keeping my legs afloat, she did not notice that the other end, which included my head, was now below water. In that position it is not easy to say, "Wait a minute," or, in fact, anything else.

As she struggled to keep my feet at water level, I struggled to bring to her notice what was happening to the upper body. I finally succeeded only by clutching and pulling down the bottom part of her two-piece suit. While this is not recommended for a get-acquainted ploy, it was a real attention-getter, and one that enabled me to right myself and spout water. That experiment also was not repeated.

But the ocean retains its fascination, even though I get no farther into it than sloshing along the water's edge; and I never tire of watching it, whether it is serene or savage.

In early morning, the beach is empty save for a solitary fisherman standing almost silhouetted against the sunrise sky. After a while an early jogger runs by. A little later from the other side of this shoreline stage, a woman walks purposefully with arms swinging in exercise fashion. After the walkers and the joggers come a couple, with small children trailing behind, carrying their folded beach chairs, towels and blankets, as they decide on the best place to stake out. Then comes the planting of the first brightly colored beach umbrella. Then there is another. And soon the beach is in full bloom with quiet explosions of colors in umbrellas, bright chairs, swimwear and towels. The shore is alive with people, a few making forays into the waves, others standing, sitting, walking, tossing balls and spinning disks or just stretched out inert and tanning. A couple of kites dart around the open sky they share

306

with the gulls. Occasionally, a motorboat slices a white streak in the water. Sometimes in the distance you can see the shining curves of sporting dolphins.

As the afternoon wanes, the beach activity decreases. The umbrellas begin to fold like morning glories. There is a shaking out of blankets and a gathering together of gear and children. Couples and kids trudge up through the soft sand with their impedimenta, a little slower than in the morning.

Then a fisherman sets up his pole again. Some gulls hover around, possibly attracted by the bait or hoping to share in the catch—or maybe just figuring this guy with the fishing pole must know something. After a while they fly away. A couple of dogs appear—unleashed by their masters to race around the shore and dare the waves. Occasional couples stroll along the water's edge. A woman and child stop to examine a shell and to watch a sandpiper hurry back and forth on the wet sand. And finally the beach is empty again save for a couple of beach chairs and the patient fisherman. And then, on some nights, the moon touches up the white spray along the shore. Every day is an unfolding spectacle. And the natural beat of the surf is soothing after the city noises and the sound of sleep-destroying jets.

I don't mean to go on too much about the deep and dark blue ocean, which, over a few centuries, has already had some good write-ups. And I remember a story told about Joseph Conrad and H. G. Wells at a beach. Conrad, eager to show off his specialty, asked, "If you were writing, Mr. Wells, how would you describe the sea and the sky just as they appear now?" To which Wells replied, "Unless they had something to do with what I wanted to say, I wouldn't mention them at all."

They have to do with what I want to say. For a fellow who has spent all his life among city streets and buildings, on every trip to the shore I am one of the men with Cortés—or maybe it was Balboa. There is, besides the constantly moving water and constantly changing colors and the sea air that blows the cobwebs out of the head, the feeling of infinite *space*. There is also the feel of a small community, where you walk or bike a few blocks to get the papers and groceries from people who know you as a neighbor.

When I first got the little house on the water, I stepped out on the porch—I mean the deck—and surveyed the sandy back yard—the dune, that is—which obviously needed weeding. As I set out to tidy it up, a neighbor saw me pulling up the green stuff that sprouted here and there, and asked what I was doing. When I told him, he explained that the grass, or weeds, kept the dune from eroding; and each blade—sometimes the result of plugs of grass planted at considerable cost—was to be regarded as something like gold leaf. So much for my tidying up.

I am still a city boy and still look forward to every trip to the shore. Even on Brigadoon visits to open the house one day and close it the next, even when the trip is long and the highways are choked with cars that sometimes scarcely crawl, even when I finally arrive tired from a long trip for a short stay—when I draw aside the curtain and look out at the ocean, I think, It was worth it.

I love it. I absolutely love it.

31

Fighting Words

For a person who works mostly in drawings (one picture is supposed to be worth, you know) I'm fascinated and awed by the use and power of words. In politics, words can be marshaled in great causes, or used to stall, duck, weave, evade, retreat, hide, confuse and deceive. Sometimes they require "news analysis"—or translations of what the speaker is actually saying and not saying. Words are also used like battering rams to pound home ideas, true or false, through repetition. I try to listen and read carefully, though more slowly than I'd like. And I envy people who can catch all the details with their eyes on fast-forward.

Sometimes the cartoonist is up against a torrent of words—fighting the phrases. It was that way during the presidency of George Bush, which proved to be an exercise not only in frenetic play and travel but also in the flinging around of words. "Read my lips" was an effective campaign statement and also a delineation of a presidency, in which words too often triumphed over deeds.

In 1988, with the aid of speechwriter Peggy Noonan, Bush found

309

that words—well timed and spoken forcefully—could overcome all. In his convention speech, Noonan threw in regular-guy and tough-guy phrases; and Bush delivered them strongly enough to make the wimp image become "history."

One could hardly guess that this mucho-macho Bush was the same man who earlier that year in New Hampshire groveled before the *Manchester Union Leader* owners who had savaged and ridiculed him. Then there was the "kinder, gentler" phrase that took wing and soared, even as Bush descended to a low road against his opponents.

What amazes me is the way a few words and phrases can keep moving on with no obvious grounding in fact—like the animated cartoon characters that keep walking on air after they have stepped off a cliff.

The words "education president" kept reverberating even as schools shortened their hours and libraries closed because of sharp cuts in federal aid to cities. And the "environmental president" seemed kinder and gentler to timber miners and polluters when he approved the cutting back of protected wetlands, the overcutting of trees and the undercutting of clean air standards he had previously approved.

The relationship between words and deeds recalls the scene in *The Mikado* where Koko explains to the emperor his lying about having performed an execution: "When your Majesty says, 'Let a thing be done,' it's as good as done—practically it *is* done. . . . Your Majesty says, 'Kill a gentleman,' and a gentleman is told off to be killed. Consequently that man is as good as dead—practically he *is* dead—and if he is dead, why not say so?"

During the Reagan administration we had already learned that tax increases were not really taxes—they were "revenue enhancers."

In the Clinton administration, with the emphasis on burden-sharing, taxpayers became "contributors."

Under Reagan and Bush, other words took on new meanings. "Special interests" no longer referred to what Theodore Roosevelt called "malefactors of great wealth"—like the tobacco companies and other big-business contributors who supply corporate jets and put on lavish tax-deductible "hospitality parties" for government officials.

"Special interests" became the term for different lobbies—some very influential but essentially organizations of the non-wealthy—

310

representing environmentalists, consumers, teachers, veterans, senior citizens and labor union members.

New terms became accepted just as the McCarthy-era term "Democrat Party" became widely substituted for Democratic.

An example of how phrases and characteristics gain their own momentum was the description of vice presidential candidate Dan Quayle as a Robert Redford look-alike. Compared to Godzilla, yes. Otherwise not so much. The comparison originated in Quayle's own congressional campaign literature. But it gained currency as if based on actual observations. We might be grateful that his early campaign material did not describe him as an Abraham Lincoln think-alike.

In Bush's re-election campaign, words could fit any political occasion. When Ross Perot's independent candidacy first seemed a threat, he was denounced as being, among other things, an authoritarian with no respect for the U.S. Constitution. But when Perot's supporters seemed up for grabs, he just as suddenly became a "wise" and "courageous" man.

When the bills for Reagan-Bush policies came due in the form of a recession, Bush insisted that it did not exist. As the recession dragged on, he decided that there *had* been a recession, but that it had gone away.

In the fourth year of his administration, whenever his staff felt a need to drum up interest in a speech, they would describe it as a "defining moment" in his presidency. I think the real defining moments came in his political campaigns. In 1992, when he told interviewer David Frost that he "would do what I have to do to be re-elected," he seemed to me to have defined most of his career.

In the 1988 presidential campaign, the Bush staff combined a soft-on-crime charge with racial overtones to defeat Gov. Michael Dukakis. Bush made famous Willie Horton, a black convict who had stabbed a man and raped a woman in Maryland while out of jail on a Massachusetts furlough program. TV commercials featuring Horton's dark and bearded face suggested that Dukakis had no interest in keeping such criminals under control. For emphasis, another commercial showed actors portraying criminals entering and leaving prison via a revolving door.

Bush also painted the Democratic candidate as unpatriotic for upholding a conscientious objector's right to refrain from reciting the Pledge of Allegiance. As one display of his own patriotic devotion to the national emblem, Bush visited a flag factory. An inept and inert Dukakis responded by joining in a recitation of the Pledge of Allegiance.

It was a campaign in which Bush, who described himself as a "proud member" of the NRA (National Rifle Association) gun lobby kept referring to a statement that Dukakis was a "card-carrying member of the ACLU" (American Civil Liberties Union).

In one of the kinder, gentler cartoons that summer, I showed two men at a bar approving Bush's "thousand pints of lite." In a couple of speeches where Bush got in some lighter moments, he referred to this cartoon. But his tactics and policy switches turned me off. The "thousand points of light" cartoon shown here was drawn in 1992—when the tough-on-crime president and proud member of the NRA could not ignore the crime and gunfire increasing across the country. He blamed Congress.

I give more than a passing reference to the 1988 campaign, not because I'm a political junkie (which I am) or because I did not hold Bush in highest esteem (which I did not), but because I saw it as the real prelude to his presidency.

The Bush who opposed the ACLU in the campaign became the president who vetoed civil rights legislation because it would have established "quotas" and who, when he was finally forced to accept a bill, meanly kept an active ACLU member from the signing ceremony.

He refused to limit the American manufacture and sale of assault weapons, and went along with the NRA in opposing any form of gun controls. The Brady handgun waiting period bill was kept waiting during his term in office.

The same man who petulantly protested because speakers at the 1988 Democratic convention poked fun at him became the president who said that civil rights advocates were trying to "grind me into the political dirt." And when the subject of Middle East policy came up at a press conference, he complained that he was just "one lonely little guy" against a powerful pro-Israeli lobby of thousands.

Bushtalk won the 1990 Doublespeak Award of the National Council of Teachers of English. It is conferred for public statements that are

A THOUSAND POINTS OF LIGHT

July 5, 1992

"grossly deceptive, evasive, euphemistic, confusing or self-contradictory." Among domestic examples cited were "no new taxes," followed later by "tax revenue increases"; campaign statements favoring maternity leave, followed by veto of the paternal and medical leave bill; and in the foreign field, his insistence that we did not invade Panama—what we did was "deploy forces" there. Another prize-winner could have been his statement that Supreme Court nominee Clarence Thomas was "the best man for the job on the merits"; and race was not a factor in his selection.

When Bush ran against Reagan for the Republican nomination in 1980, he described Reagan's policies as "voodoo economics." But after he adopted these same policies, he didn't want to be reminded of his earlier view. Under the impression that no tapes of that statement were extant, he asserted that it had never been made—he had never used the phrase. But he guessed wrong—a network found and aired a tape of Bush saying exactly what he had said.

On another occasion, in a televised address from the Oval Office on drugs, Bush held up a little plastic bag of crack. He said it was purchased right across the street from the White House. A crack dealer not familiar with Lafayette Park had been lured there to enable Bush to use that line in his speech. Bush could have said that crack could be bought a few blocks from the White House and that would have been the truth. But he had to go a misstep beyond.

As vice president, Bush, in carrying out Reagan's Iran-contra policy, made a trip to Honduras to arrange a deal of $174 million in aid to the Honduran government in return for its support for contra guerrilla activities. Later, established in the White House, he asserted that "the word of the president of the United States, George Bush, is there was no *quid pro quo!*" But testimony from Iran-contra witnesses clearly showed there was. Like "no new taxes" and the denial of the "voodoo economics" statement, the word of this president of the United States, sad to say, was not worth the tape it was recorded on.

After the Chinese government snuffed out its citizens' movement to freedom at Tiananmen Square, Bush said we were suspending "U.S. participation in all high-level exchanges of government officials," implying an expression of great displeasure.

A short time later, we learned that National Security Adviser Brent Scowcroft and Deputy Secretary of State Lawrence Eagleburger had been sent to China. When this was disclosed, Bush said that no *exchange* of officials had taken place. And far from rebuking the Chinese government, Bush moved to give it most-favored-nation trading benefits.

In renewing that status in 1992, his use of words again proved curious. Responding to criticism of his failure to stand up for human rights in China, he asserted that his policy toward that government was the ''moral'' thing to do. This was even stronger than his usual defense of questioned policies—that they were ''the right thing'' to do. Who would want to do ''the wrong thing''?

On the ''moral'' front, another level was reached in 1992 when British author Salman Rushdie, targeted for assassination by the Iranian government because its ruler had found one of his novels offensive, surfaced to make a speech in Washington. One translator of his *Satanic Verses* had been killed and another was wounded in assassi-

Aug. 5, 1987

Nov. 1, 1991

nation attempts in foreign countries; and Rushdie had already spent years in hiding, under the protection of the British government.

Both the State Department and the White House declined to see him, and this time left the words to political spokesman Marlin Fitzwater. He explained that the president couldn't see all the authors who traveled around promoting their books. I did a cartoon of Bush and Secretary James Baker hiding under a desk. To me there is something indecent about even tacitly accepting any government's "right" to murder someone who has displeased it wherever in the world it can find him. The Rushdie case required nothing more courageous than a brief meeting. In the absence of that, the White House could at least have skipped the insulting-to-everyone "explanation" about book-promoting writers. But with that administration's feelings about the press, perhaps it considered writers fair game.

The press—or the media as it is called since the growth of broadcasting—is a favorite target of politicians who hate to see or hear words that don't mesh with their own. Bush frequently griped about the "media" that gave much time and space to his own words. He even complained about the "weird talk shows, crazy groups every Sunday telling you what to think." These weird Sunday talk shows generally featured administration members or others supporting Bush's views.

For many years there has been a myth that the national dialogue is dominated by "the liberal press," which is constantly denounced by illiberal politicians. But the accusation doesn't seem to be supported by facts. And the myth skips the strong "press" criticism of FDR, Truman, Carter, Clinton and others opposed by the illiberals.

Franklin Roosevelt was opposed by most of the leading publishers with widest newspaper and magazine circulations. From his day to this—from Col. Robert R. McCormick and Henry Luce to Rupert Murdoch and a number of far-out but far-reaching columnists and talk show hosts—the major and often the most raucous voices in the media have not been identified with anything to the left of first base.

Words are freighted with political overtones and are carefully selected to give impressions. "Conservative" sounds nice but is not a one-size-fits-all term for many who wear it. Some "conservatives" are not even in right field but over the wall, and they might better be called

316

by some other term—maybe "radical right" or "conservakooks." And what is "conservative," "radical" or "liberal" on what specific issues at a given time? As labels, the words have become meaningless.

In 1988, Bush assailed Dukakis with what he called "the L word"— almost too dreadful to pronounce in full. The "L" stood for "liberal," but he never explained what liberal stood for. The connotation was that it referred to being liberal with money—although it was Reagan and Bush administrations that ran up an additional two and three trillion in the federal debt. "Conservatism's" relationship to conservation was never defined either. During the Persian Gulf crisis, when Bush was asked at a press conference if he would now call upon the American people to conserve energy, his mechanical reply, "I call upon the American people to conserve energy," made clear that he barely tolerated the question.

On subjects like civil rights and civil liberties, on the rights of women and minorities, you could read his lip service.

A visiting editor told me he wondered why he had less regard for Bush than for Reagan. I think it was because Reagan, however unreal his policies or anecdotes, had real convictions.

When Bush was eager for a place on the Reagan ticket in 1980, he had a political epiphany. He not only discovered the merits of Reaganomics, but of the Reagan social policies as well. The Bush who had supported Planned Parenthood and abortion rights became an all-out right-to-lifer. As president, he enforced the "gag rule" at many clinics, effectively curbed U.S. efforts at world population control and hindered the use of fetal tissue in medical progress to help victims of Parkinson's disease.

In 1992, when Bush was asked about the total anti-abortion plank in his own party's platform, he said that he hadn't read the platform. And when he was asked if he regretted having made the "no new taxes" pledge in his 1988 campaign, his answer was interesting. He didn't regret it because it wasn't true, but because he got so much political flak for it.

He escaped a good deal of flak on the savings-and-loan scandal. Neither side mentioned it before the 1988 campaign because the thrifts debacle reflected on the executive branch, the regulators and members of both parties in Congress. Under Reagan, Bush had been active in deregulating the savings and loans. As president, he was given credit for starting to clean up the S and L mess, which he actually prolonged.

It could have been settled for a relatively small sum during the Reagan administration. In 1989, Bush still could have handled it for a fairly low amount. But he played down the problem, understating the cost until it increased the burden on U.S. taxpayers by hundreds of billions of dollars. One billion could be chalked up to the Silverado Savings and Loan, of which Neil Bush, the president's son, was a director. The Office of Thrift Supervision let young Neil off with the lightest reproach it could give him—an injunction to avoid *future* conflicts of interest.

The scandal surrounding BCCI—the Bank of Credit and Commerce International, sometimes called the Bank of Crooks and Criminals— also involved members of both parties. But again, regulators didn't regulate and the Justice Department was reluctant to move.

Scandals, as well as depressing economic news, were for some time overshadowed by Bush's foreign forays. In Panama, his first attempt to oust dictator Manuel Noriega resulted in a fiasco. On the second try, with full military force, Noriega was captured and civilian leadership was restored to Panama. This success was marred by the loss of uncounted civilian lives and the destruction of neighborhoods. In the waning days of Bush's presidency, he received wide support when he sent armed forces to get food to the starving in Somalia. But the Persian Gulf war was Bush's great military triumph—the high point of his presidency and of his standing in opinion polls.

Following Iraq's conquest of Kuwait in August 1990, Bush's outraged words were "It will not stand." Unfortunately, the wartime victory did not stand alone—it was like a good second act in a three-act play.

Up until the time Saddam Hussein's army crossed into Kuwait, Bush had contributed to his enormous military buildup by giving him almost everything he could ask for—high-tech equipment, intelligence and trust. Iraq was taken off the State Department's list of terrorist states. And when Saddam's brutal regime slaughtered many of Iraq's Kurdish minority, our government not only paid no heed but continued to fight against sanctions proposed by Congress. Shortly before the invasion, with Iraqi troops massed at the edge of Kuwait, our ambassador in

BOY AT THE DIKE

April 10, 1990

319

Baghdad had assured Saddam that our government took no part in Arab-Arab disputes such as Iraq's border quarrel with Kuwait. Even after the invasion of Kuwait, Bush's first words indicated that we would take no action. But then, perhaps after some spine starching by British Prime Minister Margaret Thatcher, he suddenly found Saddam to be "worse than Hitler."

With Saddam, as with Noriega, who had been on the CIA payroll and was a known drug dealer when Bush was head of the CIA, Bush's outrage seemed personal. These men had bitten the hand that fed them. They were not merely bad—which they had been all along—they were *ungrateful*.

Despite what we knew even then about policy errors, when Bush came to shove, I was for armed force to stop Saddam. This was not for the various changing reasons (including "jobs") put forth by the administration, but because a ruthless Saddam with missiles, possible biological weapons and a nuclear program was a threat to the entire region.

The war, in which Bush skillfully organized an alliance of U.N. countries, was conducted with remarkable success. But it was not as beautifully precisioned as might have been supposed from the manipulated news. This was so complete that when bodies of Americans killed in the war came back to Dover Air Force Base, TV cameras were barred "out of consideration for their families."

The sweet victory had a sour aftertaste.

Even with no accurate count, we knew something about the large civilian losses in Iraq and Kuwait. Gradually we learned the larger picture beyond the official film of supposedly pinpoint-perfect bombs dropped down chimneys—the American losses by "friendly fire," the misfired weapons and the missed targets.

Patriot missiles were originally declared to be 100 percent effective. Nearly two years later the Pentagon revised its estimate sharply downward. And the General Accounting Office put the *known* success rate at a mere 9 percent.

We learned of Scud missiles and launchers "knocked out" but still in place—along with Saddam, still in power, and still with the capacity to wreak damage on victims.

The official reply to criticism of the way the war ended was a False

Alternative. The choice, we were told, was between stopping when we did or going "on to Baghdad," where we presumably would be bogged down indefinitely while conducting a national house-to-house search for Saddam. But the Baghdad Express was only one option. We could have destroyed the capability of Saddam's army and immobilized all his aircraft. Gen. Norman Schwarzkopf acknowledged that he had been "snookered" in allowing Saddam's forces to keep helicopters, supposedly for civilian use. They were used soon enough, with other military force, in killing more Iraqi minorities.

Two years after the Desert Storm victory, Saddam was still defying U.N. teams trying to inspect his nuclear capacities and plants. And as Bush was leaving office in January 1993, both sides were in a state of hostility.

By the summer of 1992, Congress knew enough about the methods used in Iraq's pre-Gulf-war arms buildup and the possibility of perjury and malfeasance in this executive department operation that it called for another special prosecutor. For the first time an attorney general, William Barr, refused a congressional request for the appointment of such a prosecutor. Congress was again accused of being "political."

Under President Clinton, Attorney General Janet Reno called for reinstating the Special Prosecutor's Office.

If the 1988 campaign tactics foreshadowed Bush's presidency, the 1992 campaign provided a darker end. The progress of that campaign can be followed in a few key words. "Family values" was an early starter—distinguishing Bush and Quayle from candidates who were supposedly anti-family. The term sounded like Dad working, Mom making apple pie for the kids and Grandma helping to look after them. But in a time of two-worker households, single parents and second mortgages, the family values issue didn't quite catch on. When Quayle attacked TV fictional character Murphy Brown, single mother, he got himself boxed into a television sitcom. And prime-time Republican convention speakers who talked of "religious wars" and suggested "cultural wars" did not strengthen family ties—or political party ties.

"Character" was another word supposed to reflect on the presidential opponent. But this shot had a recoil. To people remembering the no-new-taxes pledge and other non-truths, the incumbent had a character problem. George Bush was no George Washington (if the

Democrats didn't chop down that cherry tree, then they made him do it). And his attempt to campaign as another Harry Truman was also a piece of miscasting. It brought hoots from people who recalled the original straightforward HST, who had ordered the integration of the armed forces—a move, incidentally, opposed by Eisenhower. Truman also had proposed national health insurance (which the GOP called "socialized medicine") 47 years before Bush finally caught up with the idea during his re-election campaign.

Bush almost burlesqued himself when he said that in the Democratic platform he could not find the three letters G-O-D. Like any incumbent, he leaned heavily on "experience." But in a debate with the two other major candidates, this word lost some of its steam when candidate Ross Perot confessed that he had no "experience" in running up trillion-dollar debts.

Realizing the desire for "change," which his opponents called for, Bush tried to present himself as the best agent for it. But this was a little like a candidate promising that on day one of his 209th week in office, he would get up from the ground running. And the promise of tossing out his economic advisers sounded like a losing coach blaming the team.

In the same campaign Bush was willing to take credit for ending the Cold War. More accurately, it was during his term in office that the people of the Soviet Union ended dictatorship and the Cold War. Presidents of both parties could share credit, and Truman and Kennedy had faced some of the hardest decisions. Bush was actually somewhat behind the curve in recognizing the changes in the Baltics and Eastern Europe and notably slow in aiding Russian democracy and in calling for action to stop the slaughter in Bosnia.

In an era of political "spin," one of the dizziest turns occurred in the 1992 campaign. A chief Bush strategist denounced Clinton for spending "taxpayers' dollars" to defend himself against character charges—many of them traced to Bush campaigners. Presidential campaigns are supposedly financed by taxpayers' dollars.

I've thought back to the first presidential campaign that reached my consciousness, Wilson vs. Hughes, when my dad punished my brother Rich for using a word in a political jingle. Not only was "the word" milder than much of what we hear in movies and on TV, but the campaigns themselves, during fourteen or so presidencies, have descended to lower levels. True, partisans always get worked up and some activists see each campaign as Armageddon. But what used to be called "whispering campaigns" are now the stuff of broadcast commercials and of innuendos and charges that hit the nation's TV screens in time for the evening news.

In the words department, people who practice character assassination don't call it that. The sanitized term for opponent destruction is "raising the negatives." This is something like the CIA's termination "with extreme prejudice," the Vietnam War term "wasted" or the more descriptive mob term "whacked."

In an attempt to drive Clinton's negatives through the roof, the State Department rummaged through his passport files, leaving no rock or file folder unturned. It even went through travel files of his mother.

Rep. Robert Dornan (R-Calif.), who sat in on a campaign meeting in the Oval Office, suggested—on the basis of nothing—that when Clinton visited Moscow as a student, he may have been the guest of the KGB. A rumor was also floated that Clinton had considered renouncing his U.S. citizenship—rather odd since he was also accused of being politically ambitious almost from birth. "Ambitious," incidentally, is a word with two faces. We hope young people will be ambitious—perhaps to become president (praiseworthy). But "Caesar was ambitious . . . a grievous fault." So were most of our chief executives (praiseworthy). One GOP stalwart declared that Clinton had spent years "plotting" to become president.

After the election a fired State Department official said that the White House had wanted the renouncement-of-citizenship rumor checked out. The government search activities were "known to" Secretary of State Baker, White House chief of staff during the 1992 campaign.

The separation of words from fact became complete in attack commercials and Bush-Quayle speeches that falsified their opponents' statements. For example, Quayle said that Clinton and Gore maintained you couldn't have jobs and help the environment at the same time—the exact opposite of what they had said. In a startling fabrication Bush claimed that Clinton had condemned the entire U.S. military as "immoral"—this supposedly in a letter that proved to be nonexistent. At the same time Bush continued to deplore campaign sleaze, and

323

he mixed attacks on his opponents with continued assaults on Congress.

Congress is itself hardly at a loss for words. Members not only fill the *Congressional Record* with words, but also fill the mails with franked reports and fill the various districts with taped messages. I've criticized Congress a lot in pictures and words, but generally on its perks, privileges and pensions—and on the actions, inactions and misdeeds of members.

I did cartoons about the financial hanky-panky of Speaker of the House Jim Wright (D-Tex.). He might have been a great Speaker if he'd kept his nose clean. When tempted to increase his income with questionable deals, he would have done well to recall what a previous Speaker, Sam Rayburn, is said to have considered the three most important words in the language: Just a minute.

But I do not care for cheap shots at Congress, especially by administrations that have their own irregularities. The persistent downgrading of Congress by an executive serves a sinister end—to make it seem like no big deal to lie to Congress, to withhold information the executive is required to share with Congress and to disregard the laws it has passed. Under our form of government, it's a very big deal and that's why special prosecutors are needed.

Bush was hardly up against the kind of "do nothing" Congress that Truman was. Congress had cooperated with Bush on legislation until halfway through his term he decided to make it a target. Even during this political cold war, it passed legislation to clean up its own campaign financing, although a sure veto gave some members a free ride. By the end of 1992, Bush's take of public financing came to some $200 million. But he opposed any public financing to reform congressional campaigns, piously claiming that it would put the congressmen's hands in the taxpayers' pockets.

Closer to home (mine), Bush didn't support voting representation—for us taxpayers in the predominantly Democratic and predominantly black District of Columbia. It's one thing to oppose Democrats; it's another to oppose democracy.

The final key word in the Bush reelection drive was "trust." Unfortunately for him, that did not describe the feeling of many in his own party. Some Reagan supporters thought he had betrayed the

324

master and dropped the torch. "Moderates" were dismayed by his coziness with the "religious right." That segment, in turn, persisted in regarding him as a closet moderate. There was a widespread impression that if someone asked, "Will the real George Bush stand up?," nobody might stand at all.

During the closing days of the campaign, the "trust" issue received another blow when the Iran-contra Special Prosecutor's Office disclosed a memo by former Secretary of Defense Caspar Weinberger. It clearly showed Bush had made false statements about his involvement in the Reagan Iran-arms-for-hostages policy, and that he had actively supported it.

As the strange 1992 campaign ground to its conclusion, some of Bush's own people were a little surprised by his use of other words—like calling his opponents a couple of "bozos." Gov. Clinton and Sen. Gore seemed more "presidential" than the president.

Readers didn't have to be clairvoyant to know that I preferred Gov. Clinton. From September until November 3, nearly all the cartoons were on the campaign. Some were on out-again, in-again billionaire candidate Ross Perot, most of the others on the Bush campaign and record.

When the election was over, my feeling was one of total relief. An almost completely negative campaign had not worked this time. The voters may have made their choice more on pain in the pocketbook than on assaults to their sensibilities, but they opted for Clinton's word, "Change." Many journalists were happy to find in Clinton a president who spoke in complete sentences, something often lacking in Bush's answers to questions.

Bush's waywardness with words did not end with the election. It reached an apex—or nadir—with his 1992 Christmas Eve pardon of Weinberger and five others involved in the Iran-contra scandal. Despite the fact these five had already been indicted or convicted or had pleaded guilty, in Bush's words their acts represented "patriotism," and admitted or proven crimes were magically transformed into mere "policy differences." After deploring what he called "the criminalization of policy differences," Bush—whose personal involvement in Iran-contra was at issue—said of his pardon actions, "I am doing what honesty, decency and fairness require."

Saying is believing.

Bush made another scathing attack on Special Prosecutor Lawrence Walsh. Bush could at any time have fired Walsh, but probably thought this would have been too reminiscent of Nixon's "Saturday Night Massacre." It certainly reminded me of that earlier presidential surprise though. This time, instead of cutting short a weekend at the shore, I gave up part of Christmas and the next day to do the cartoon of the Bush pardons and Justice. I felt as if our government of laws—and I—had been politically Pearl Harbored.

A final word about words—those in the Constitution. That document is subject to revision, but I have strong feelings about people playing politics with it.

When Bush made his 1980 U-turn on the abortion issue, he decided that the Supreme Court's *Roe* v. *Wade* ruling was wrong. But as president, he went further. He proposed riveting his policy change into the Constitution by calling for an amendment to make abortion illegal. He also wanted an amendment to require a federal balanced budget (never mind how). Like Reagan, he wanted an amendment to bring organized vocal prayer into the public schools. And he called for an amendment to make "desecration" of the flag a crime.

These don't have the same ring as "We the people of the United States, in order to form a more perfect Union . . . and secure the blessings of liberty to ourselves and our posterity"—or an amendment like "Congress shall make no law respecting an establishment of religion, or prohibiting the free exercise thereof; or abridging the freedom of speech, or of the press. . . ."

The idea of the freedom-seeking founders was not to establish criminalities and prohibitions upon the people but to ensure protection for individuals against the power of government.

The words and music don't sound as good played backward.

THE SORCERER'S APPRENTICE

Oct. 7, 1990

©1990 HERBLOCK

"WHICH LIPS ARE WE SUPPOSED TO READ?"

Oct. 4, 1988

Oct. 12, 1988

Dec. 22, 1991

"BE ALERT, MEN — LET ME KNOW IF YOU COME ACROSS ANYTHING AMISS"

May 6, 1988

"DR. BUSH AND DR. REHNQUIST WILL SEE YOU NOW"

©1991 HERBLOCK

Nov. 21, 1991

PUBLIC LIBRARY

TODAY'S QUOTATION:
"Dollar bills don't educate students"
— George Bush, "Education president"

CLOSED

©1991 HERBLOCK

May 23, 1991

"CAN'T SEE ANY OF THEM? VERY WELL
YOU'RE HIRED"

BCCI
IRAN-CONTRA
SAVINGS-AND-LOANS
SCANDALS

DEPT. OF
JUSTICE

©1991 HERBLOCK

Nov. 13, 1991

"I GOT IT FOR FREE WHEN I INSURED THEM"

Fastbuck Savings & Loan

©1988 HERBLOCK

Nov. 30, 1988

GIFTS AND OIL DEAL

BOOK DEAL

S&L POLICIES

REFLECTIONS OF A PUBLIC MAN

©1989 HERBLOCK

April 25, 1989

BLOOD BROTHERS

Aug. 7, 1990

"TODAY KUWAIT, TOMORROW—"

Aug. 3, 1990

"PEOPLE'S REPUBLIC"

June 6, 1989

FORTUNE COOKIE

Aug. 24, 1991

IRAQI FREEDOM FIGHTERS

VICTORY PARADE

©1991 HERBLOCK

April 5, 1991

332

"DON'T ANYBODY LEAVE — IT MIGHT RAIN AGAIN SOME DAY"

Feb. 8, 1990

"THAT'S NOT OUR PROBLEM"

Dec. 6, 1991

"OR YOU CAN ALWAYS DEAL WITH ME AGAIN"

Nov. 25, 1992

BOAT PEOPLE

Feb. 7, 1992

Nov. 19, 1992

June 2, 1992

HEALTH COVERAGE

May 3, 1991

THE CALL

Oct. 2, 1992

"MY OPPONENT SHOULD COME CLEAN"

Sept. 23, 1992

©1992 HERBLOCK

335

"AH, INDEPENDENCE DAY — THE GLORIOUS FOURTH! DO SEE THAT THE NATIVES GET A NICE FIREWORKS DISPLAY"

June 30, 1978

SOFT MONEY

Nov. 18, 1988

"FOUR YEARS AGO THEY SAID THEY'D ALL BE HERE"

Oct. 18, 1992

"IT DIDN'T FLY"

Oct. 20, 1989

"REALLY? HE'S BEEN MY DOCTOR TOO"

©1991 HERBLOCK

Nov. 14, 1991

"KEEP HANGING IN THERE, FELLA"

US

RUSSIAN DEMOCRACY

©1992 HERBLOCK

Dec. 13, 1992

BOSNIA

MILOSEVIC SERBS

WORLD LEADERS

©1993 HERBLOCK

Jan. 13, 1993

NOT GAYS!

NOT WOMEN!

NOT NEGROES!

©1993 HERBLOCK

Jan. 28, 1993

DESERT NORM

U.S. PROBLEMS =

©1992 HERB

March 29, 1992

338

GETAWAY

Dec. 27, 1992

©1992 HERBLOCK

339

"YOUR NAME CLINTON?"

Nov. 6, 1992

340

"ARE YOU GONNA LET THIS ADMINISTRATION MAKE ME PAY TAXES ON THE MONEY I SPEND TO INFLUENCE YOU?"

Feb. 24, 1993

Feb. 17, 1993

"WE'RE DOING GOD'S WORK"

March 12, 1993

"WHAT WE WANT TO DO, AL, IS STREAMLINE IT"

March 4, 1993

32

Two-Way Communications

Everyone in the opinion business gets mail. Columnist Mary McGrory has a favorite letter. It came from an enthusiastic admirer who ended by saying, "I hope to make the name of Mary McGregory a household word." Ever since then she has been Ms. McGregory to me.

All kinds of mail comes in—pro and con—junk mail and handsomely printed material that falls into a category of its own. This includes engraved announcements from law firms you don't know, advising you that someone you don't know is now joining with four other people you don't know to send out these steel-plate cards to recipients they don't know.

Those of us who do unflattering pictures of officials get a good deal of feedback. Much of this comes in the form of letters to the editor. But face-to-face meetings rarely bring unhappy responses from the subjects themselves. Most politicians probably get used to give-and-take and have made progress in politics by knowing how to be politic.

You might expect a Strom Thurmond to be rather hostile, but he has been not only agreeable but complimentary. And you can hardly be offended by an occasional politico who says he wishes you were on his side—almost as good as Alice Longworth's smiling greeting, "Your cartoons are deliciously wicked." But this does not always apply to their supporters. About once every two or three years at a large party, someone—usually a young fellow I don't know or recognize and who has not introduced himself—wants to let me know he doesn't care for what I do. It is the stand-up equivalent of an anonymous letter. But it gives the guy a chance to say, "I told *him*."

I used to suppose that people of all political views must have the same experiences, and perhaps they do. But I think there is a certain fanaticism about right-wing extremists. And one of the things that distinguishes so-called liberals from illiberals (not real conservatives) is the liberal belief in the other guy's rights to his opinions. Editor J. R. Wiggins remembered the Oliver Cromwell quote, "I beseech you, in the bowels of Christ, think it possible you may be mistaken."

There have been a couple of exceptions to the rule of anonymity—times when I've been surprised by a reaction. One of the oddest was an encounter with a politician I had never cartooned. At a New Year's party in the late 1950s or early '60s, I was introduced to Robert E. Merriam, who had earlier been a nominee for mayor of Chicago. I knew who he was and was glad to meet him. He took me aside to talk and suddenly seemed to be blaming me for his loss to the other aspirant for the job, Richard J. Daley.

I thought he must be joking, but he was not. The connection was this: In 1953 the Independent Voters of Illinois had invited me to Chicago to give a talk. The speech, which was not on the mayoral election at all, was critical of Eisenhower administration policies, and got a good reception. But Merriam had apparently hitched his wagon to the five-star president, and he contended that my speech had cost him the Independent Voters' endorsement and consequently the election. I never met Daley, who was later the subject of critical cartoons I did, but I'm sure he'd have been as amazed as I was at the notion that I was responsible for his becoming mayor of Chicago.

Years later, during the Ford administration, I was joined at the bar in a friend's home by a cabinet member who was unhappy about a cartoon in which he figured. He warmed to the subject, claiming that

I had never read his entire speeches. Of course I hadn't, but I've always tried scrupulously to verify quotes and to make sure I have the real thrust of officials' statements. I pointed out to him that while I had not read every word of all his speeches, I had seen him on television, live and unedited, and knew what I had heard him say. Our little contretemps ended there and we had no further problems. Perhaps he thought it was always worth a try for a politician to suggest that he had been misunderstood.

At another friend's house—this time in London—when the guests ambled into a sitting room after dinner, a lady joined me and sat down to talk. She indicated that she was familiar with my work, which was nice. She then began berating me non-stop for my cartoons about the military junta then in power in Greece. After I finally disengaged from her, I learned that she was a special friend of one of the Greek colonels in that ruling junta. She was quite a spirited talker.

Most complaints from abroad have not been delivered in person. But they have had in common a misunderstanding of how a free press works, as well as a misunderstanding of how *The Washington Post* operates.

At a 1961 conference in London, USSR official Georgi Zhukov was unhappy about a cartoon I had done of Khrushchev that was reprinted in the *London Times*. He said, "We do not disseminate newspapers that carry such cartoons, for example, as was printed in the *Times* on the opening day of the conference. . . ." He said that if such were turned loose in the Soviet Union, "We would have to strengthen the guard on the British Embassy to protect them against the just wrath of the Soviet public. . . ." Time marches on. The *Times,* the Brits and I survived the wrath of the Soviet public better than communism did.

The South Korean government of Park Chung Hee had a more direct approach. In 1978, when scandals involving its government and U.S. congressmen were in the news, it issued an order to the U.S. public relations firm it had hired to improve its image. It instructed the firm to have me fired for depicting Park Chung Hee in an unfavorable light. Said one of the PR people, "They have a fairly basic lack of understanding of the American news media."

Since his earliest days of prominence, I had done cartoons about Spanish dictator Francisco Franco and his government. And when he was trying to pass himself off as being on a par with leaders of the European democracies, I drew him as a scruffy character—sometimes with a few flies around him. His embassy frequently complained to *The Post*. But it went further.

Since that regime controlled everything including Spain's travel bureau, one of its representatives called on *The Post* management with a threat to withdraw its advertising if they did not tell me to curb the cartoons. *The Post* executive replied, "If you insist that we speak to our cartoonist, we will—but then he'll put those flies back around Franco's head."

This happened at a time when *The Post* was still a lean and struggling newspaper and every inch of advertising was precious. But best of all, this incident—along with newspaper cancellations from time to time—was something I didn't hear about until long after. *The Post*'s separation of advertising and circulation from news and editorial policies was so complete that I have also heard of incidents where it suffered more important ad losses without a peep to the newsroom writers or editorial departments. The same separation has applied to investigative and critical pieces about people who are personal friends of the editor or publisher. This is the kind of policy that has made *The Post* a great newspaper.

In a conversation with Bob Lasch, when he was editor of the *St. Louis Post-Dispatch,* we discussed problems of newspapers and editorial policies in general. He observed that most newspaper owners pointed with greatest pride to the things their papers had done in the past—which they had fiercely resisted doing at the time. I think this was a cogent observation. But *The Post* would be an exception to that generality.

More people complain to the editors and publisher than to me, but we all get a share. And because the cartoons are also published in other cities, I sometimes get letters *from* editors as well. When I sent out a Christmas cartoon that pictured Santa Claus with a small child and a large ribbon bearing the legend, MERRY CHRISTMAS! one New York State editor urgently wanted to know why there was no caption on the cartoon.

But this is less of a problem than editors who used to tinker with titles to fit space or to say something a little different from the original.

One day a bilingual friend showed me copies of a Spanish-language paper in this country that subscribed to the cartoons. He asked if I knew about them. I said I did. He asked if I understood the translations into Spanish of the titles and labels on the cartoons. I did not. He explained that, in one form or another, they all said "Down with the Government!" A definite no-no.

An example of official editing came in 1991, courtesy of our ambassador to Kuala Lumpur. He sent on a copy of a cartoon reprinted in the *International Herald Tribune* that the Malaysian authorities had partially blacked out. I had drawn Gorbachev as the sculptor Pygmalion dueling with an emerging nude Galatea (Freedom). They found her too sexy and obscured most of her body.

At *The Post,* the letters to the editor all get read, and the people who handle them try to print a fair representation of the large volume they receive. To get extra attention, some letters contain real eye-catchers.

Before the "foreign invasion" of autos, I did a number of cartoons on mistakes of the U.S. auto industry, sometimes using the made-up company names, Monster Motors and Moron Motors. The General Motors public relations director wrote a letter to the editor about these and had someone draw a cartoon in reply, which *The Post* ran with his letter. It showed me wearing blinders and, in witch-doctor fashion, sticking pins into a little model of a car. Okay. But it was too bad the ingenious PR man was not working in the planning department. Only three years later GM came out with a masterpiece of Idiot Design: the '79–'80 four-door cars—mostly Chevvies—in which the rear windows were designed not to open at all. Once in a while I still find myself riding in some old taxi with non-opening windows and the driver verifies the make and vintage.

On the same subject, I did a cartoon during the recession of the early 1980s that was a comment on the rug-bazaar method of haggling over the price of new cars (in which the salesman generally says he has to go to another room to talk to the manager). I drew a car salesroom with a worried dealer saying that if things get any worse he might even resort to listing the actual sales price on cars. In 1992, when car sales were flat, I flipped on the TV one evening and saw a segment about some car dealers who were trying a daring new sales method. They were listing a one-and-only take-it-or-leave-it best price on their cars and found that they had more buyers. Once more, satire turned out to be no joke.

General Motors was not the first to reply to the drawings with a drawing of its own. Earlier *The Post*'s arch rival, the *Washington Times-Herald,* had run a front-page cartoon picturing me at the drawing board with my head shaped like a cube or block—certainly a clear representation of that paper's opinion. Most rebuttals don't contain original artwork, but the mail brings me a number of envelopes, each containing a clipping of one of my cartoons. And on each the correspondent has changed the labels, altered the figures or written comments in the margins. These also do not come under the heading of "favorable."

Some readers will carefully count the stars in the flag or give stern instructions on its proper display. After I did a cartoon showing the flag being used as a cover-up, *The Post* ran a letter from a U.S. senator expressing shock at this "desecration." Discovering the American flag's connection with a public nerve did not begin with the 1988 Bush presidential campaign. George M. Cohan, as American as Mom, apple pie and the flag itself, could have told us about that early in the century. When he wrote, "It's a grand old rag, it's a high-flying flag," the superpatriots were so horrified that he abandoned the rhyme and in the next version simply duplicated the word "flag." The words "grand old rag" had reportedly been said by a Civil War vet and Cohan was moved by them. Not so the flag-wavers who had never seen it in battle.

The gun lobby is always firing off letters, not surprising since I've done lots of cartoons on guns and the lobby. Other lobbyists do their thing on whatever subject involves their interests. And some outfits are well organized for letter-writing.

I've drawn quite a few cartoons about the Postal Service, usually putting the second word in quotes. When the government set up the present corporate system, it could hardly visualize that this "Service" would get into such unrelated and unprofitable business activities as becoming a sponsor of the 1992 Olympics in Barcelona—where it lost millions of dollars on ventures completely unrelated to U.S. mail delivery. First-class mail service, which often takes a week to get a letter across town, certainly sets no Olympic records for speed.

But the USPS is quick and efficient when it is criticized. In the late

"IT'S NICE TO SEE THE KIDS LEARNING THE AMERICAN WAY"

"TOTE DAT BILGE! LIF' DAT MAIL!"

Jan. 7, 1988

Aug. 6, 1967

summer of 1992, a friend sent me a copy of the "Postal Service's Competitive Services Task Force Status Report," an impressive document that charts actions on the problems it faces and how it takes action to cope with them.

On one page it lists ITEM DESCRIPTION PRIMARY CONTACT. Item #1: Send letter to *Washington Post* re: Herb Block cartoon.

Under the heading WHAT ARE THE KEY ACTIONS THAT WILL BE TAKEN TO IMPLEMENT THIS ITEM? it says, USPS letter to editor of *Washington Post*. Jean Li. Rogers.

Next: WHAT IS THE CURRENT STATUS REGARDING THESE ACTIONS? Letter signed by John Wargo, appeared in *Washington Post* on 4/30/92.

And in the final column, under the heading ANTICIPATED COMPLETION DATE: Completed 4/30/92.

Mission accomplished! The U.S. Postal Service gets its complaint off in efficient businesslike, even military fashion. It proved itself well organized for writing letters, if not for delivering them.

Don Graham, publisher of *The Post* and a man of great humor,

348

always knows he can expect a complaint from the Postal Service verbally or in writing each time I do a cartoon on it.

Other drawings produce critical letters from people who consider themselves experts on some subject or other. Maybe it was the Hemingway influence, but for quite a while anytime I drew a bull or steer, this was enough to bring letters from aficionados who had been to Spain and knew all about thee bools and thee boolfights. I could hardly draw a cow or a calf without hearing from some traveled American about what it was like to see the bools, and how they should be drawn.

Then there are boats. Lifeboats are built with a bow at both ends. But if I draw one leaving a sinking ship, I am sure to hear from some reader who has rowed a boat on a lake, explaining that boats always have a flat end.

Jimmy Durante used to say that *every*body wants to get into the act. And well they might. Everybody has something to say but is not lucky enough to have an outlet. A lot of letters and phone calls come from people who have "ideas for cartoons." Some of these ideas may be very good, but I don't use them or want to hear or read them. This is simply because it's easier for me to start from scratch, figure out what to say and how to say it—without trying to remove from the mind a suggestion that's been tossed to rattle around in there. That's like trying to not think of an elephant.

Most people with suggestions simply want to get something off their chests. But at least one correspondent seemed to regard his thoughts as matters of personal pride. When I wrote explaining that I didn't use ideas, he shot back another letter saying that Shakespeare used other people's ideas, many great composers and writers used others' ideas, and who was I not to use them?

Late one day when I was alone in the office a phone call came from a man who said he had an idea for a cartoon. I explained that I appreciated his calling but I didn't use them. He said, "You don't understand, this is for free." I explained again that I understood but really didn't use ideas, and he said, "You can at least *listen*." I said that I was sorry I couldn't, I was right on deadline and was going to have to hang up now but thank you anyhow. I finished the drawing with just enough time to run it downstairs when the phone rang again.

349

The voice said, as rapidly as possible, "You-show-Uncle-Sam-standing-behind-this-guy-in-the-White-House-and-lifting-up-his-foot-to-give-him-a-kick-in-the . . ." (click).

One cartoon produced phone calls to people having nothing to do with the subject. During the 1992 Democratic primary campaign, when former California Governor Jerry Brown kept plugging his 800 fund-raising phone number, I drew him in a race in which I incidentally had him carrying a sign reading Dial 1-800-NUT-CAKE. People who dialed that number found themselves in touch with the Continental Baking Company, which explained that it made Twinkies but not nut cakes—at least not yet.

This is also an example of the Unintended Effect. From time to time I have *tried* creating words—like MARXET ECONOMY during the USSR partial transition to a market economy—and these have produced not a ripple. But I heard and read everywhere about NUT CAKE.

There are many phone calls and letters requesting copies of cartoons. The only ones that make me feel like complaining are those that come from press secretaries (or second or third assistant deputy or assistant press secretaries) to government officials. My taxes go to support these fellows, and some of them apparently have little to do but butter up their bosses by writing and phoning people like me to send things they want for their employers. That's too much.

There are also requests from collectors who are obviously *not* public relations people. The writer tells you he has work by 95 other current cartoonists in his collection and is now ready to include lucky you. Please send something as soon as possible.

Many journalists have found that for happy-talk mail nothing beats news of an award. This produces a flood of letters from colleagues, strangers and people you haven't heard from since childhood, and maybe a few from politicos and salesmen. A fellow cartoonist used to declare that every single letter should be answered promptly, and he chided me if I did not respond to a note from him by return mail. Then he hit the Pulitzer jackpot, and the letters poured into his lap. His reaction was "If all those people think I'm going to stop work to answer their mail, they're crazy."

Every published cartoonist must also get letters from kids who want to draw—and from parents who say their kids like to draw cartoons and what should they do about it? I guess just let them keep it up unless they're doing it on the living room walls.

It's hard to know what to tell interested youngsters except that it's a lot of fun if you really like it; some art instruction might help; school publications and small papers are good places to start; and if you're really interested in what's going on in the world, editorial cartooning is a dandy line to be in.

It would be impossible to write critiques on all the samples sent in. A colleague tells me that he responds to all aspiring cartoonists by writing that their work is wonderful, which, he says, is all they want to hear. But that doesn't seem fair either, and it can also be impractical. At times I've written quite encouraging notes about work that looked promising. But these have often been interpreted as encouragement not to do more and better cartoons, but to write more and more letters.

The most memorable advice to cartoonists that comes to mind was given by Chic Young, who created the strip "Blondie": (1) You can tell if the ink on a drawing is still wet by rubbing your hand over it (how unfortunately true); and (2) If you spill drawing ink on the carpet, it can be removed with a pair of scissors (true again).

I try to comply with as many requests as I can, even knowing that these efforts usually don't bring acknowledgments. But there are occasional bright thank-you notes. The all-time nice-guy record holder in this regard was Meredith Willson. When I did a cartoon of President Johnson as *The Music Man,* Willson, creator of that musical, wrote to ask for a copy. I mailed it to him and he wrote a handsome letter in reply. Then, almost a year later, he wrote again to say that he found it a daily joy and "I'd be a pig not to tell you this." He must have been as charming as his songs and shows.

Whenever I'm tempted to grumble about some lack of response, I'm chastened by remembering some delinquency of mine—one in particular. Screenwriter Dudley Nichols and I had corresponded a good deal and sent each other books. When I visited Hollywood, he laid out the red carpet for me and had it rolled out at studios. He was a kind, generous and highly principled man and the perfect host.

The curtain now descends to denote the passage of more time than

I like to think about. In the next scene we see me trying to clean up a messy office. Here I find a nice long letter to Nichols, thanking him for a very enjoyable visit and telling him that I am enclosing a cartoon he might like. The letter was never mailed. It had been put aside briefly until I found just the right cartoon. But I evidently remembered only that I had written the thank-you letter. Guilt! Shame! I never heard from him again, and with this discovery realized why.

Well, I learned something. A brief note on its way beats the ideal gift or perfectly worded letter that is never sent. At about the same time I found the unmailed letter, Nichols died. I talked a colleague into writing an editorial about him—not the same, though, as a live letter would have been.

One more item on the matter of requests has unfortunately become the fax of life. People who used to assume that letters took a reasonable time to go back and forth now make their requests by instant faxing and phone to demand instant action. To a guy trying to beat out the daily work, the only possible instant response is "No!" Such fax attacks almost soften my feeling toward the Postal Service, which does not strike like lightning and does not jam up the office machinery.

Still, even the fax messages come under the general category of "favorable" reaction. About the others—

The dear-sir-you-rat letters are easiest because you don't have to answer them. Sometimes you don't even have to open them. When the envelope has more flags on it than a national campaign rally and the address is to Commie-loving knucklehead cartoonist, you can do the kind of thing Johnny Carson used to do while wearing a turban: You can hold one of these envelopes to your head and guess that what's inside may not be entirely complimentary.

Among the letters that *are* complimentary, there's one kind that is a little hard to answer. It goes like this: I read your work every day, and it is splendid. Thank goodness there are people like you upholding our liberties. Because otherwise the Mormons would be taking over this country and putting all our women in their harems, and I think I saw some of those fellows following me at the Safeway last Saturday . . .

You can write in reply: "Dear Sir—Thank you, I guess . . ." No. How about, "This is to acknowledge your interesting . . ." Nah. Maybe we'll answer that one later.

33

Personally

There are two kinds of people—savers and throw-awayers. Savers generally mate with throw-awayers because this is nature's way of keeping the world from turning into a total dump. When two savers are under the same roof, you get something like the Collyer brothers, a couple of very wealthy men who collected and saved everything. When they did not emerge from their mansion for a long time, they were eventually found beneath a couple of their collected wall-to-wall grand pianos.

Being a saver has its advantages and disadvantages. One of the advantages is that after you have finally managed to open the adult-proof, safecracker-proof bottles in which aspirin and vitamins are now packaged, you can transfer the contents to the good old user-friendly screw-top bottles you saved to clutter up your medicine chest. Other bottles and jars are good too—sometimes just the right size to hold pencils and pens or flowers that don't look quite right in any of the assorted vases. If you save the lids too, bottles can come in handy as replacements for the orange juice cartons that get torn apart or bashed in when you try to open them.

Boxes are also good to save. You can always put things in them, although later you may forget what's in them or even lose track of the filled boxes themselves. But there is always the possibility of coming across an interesting old letter or magazine article or some good old gadget that they don't make anymore because it worked too well. This is also why you have to buy several of anything you like before the product is pulled off the market. Of course, that also contributes to making your living quarters Home Sweet Warehouse.

The disadvantages are that you can't generally find those good old things because you live in an accumulated mess where a good deal of your time is spent looking for things or just trying to keep piles of old papers and magazines from caving in on you. Slick magazines are a special hazard and need to be kept in boxes because they provide too slippery and unstable a foundation for stacks of papers and other magazines.

If you read in bed, as I do, a slick magazine dropped at bedside as you turn off the light and head for slumberland will lie in wait for you in the morning. When you first set foot down it will send you scooting out the bedroom door and down the steps with record-breaking and bone-breaking speed. The same principle applies to papers and magazines on the floor where you are drawing or writing. Here they can menace you when totally awake but in a hurry to turn in some work.

The trouble with magazines—aside from the fact that they begin sending you renewal notices the moment you subscribe—is that there are always more interesting things than there is time to read. I once tried a speed-reading course in an evening class. But it started the same time I finished work, when I was ready to try some speed eating. And even under better circumstances it might not have helped anyhow. What I could use is something to paste on the forehead serving the same purpose as the small glass plates that translate bar codes as items are slid across them by the grocery cashiers. But that hasn't been invented yet, and so unfinished reading matter continues to pile up.

With the march of progress, something else now piles up—tapes of TV recordings. Unlike many of my friends, I have a VCR that is easy to program—perhaps too easy. I record lots of things, but neglect to write down identifying names and dates. The result is that I have one of the world's great collections of mystery tapes. It is like having kitchen shelves loaded with canned goods—many with no labels on them.

But the march of progress has at least saved the accumulation of used cooking utensils. My answer to the question, "Do you cook?" is: "I warm." That is, I toss into the magic microwave previously prepared meals that are brought home from the office or delivered, and the microwave asks for little more than paper or plastic plates.

At the office three indefatigable helpers serve as good fairies to keep the floors clear, the papers and magazines and clippings and letters and pictures sorted. But there are never any fewer cartoons, books, clippings, letters and whatnot. And after every square foot of file and cabinet space is filled, the next step is a larger house, rented storage rooms or a good, slightly used pyramid.

In an extension of Parkinson's law, I not only fill all available time but also all available space.

In early days at *The Post*, the management wasn't much help in the neatness department. There was a succession of men who were apparently transferred from other positions to building managers on the way to out-of-the-building-completely. They had reached a remarkable level of incompetence. Whatever attempts I made to get organized would come to naught when one of these managers decided, sometimes with no notice, to move my working area. At one time, many offices were enclosed by metal walls designed for easy assembly and reassembly to create new spaces. One day I arrived at my office to find it wasn't there. The contents were there, scattered around, but the walls were gone. The building manager had decided to borrow the walls for use elsewhere.

A variation of this maneuver took place later when I outgrew a small office and stored old drawings in an assigned space on another floor. One day an artist on that floor suggested that I come upstairs to retrieve my drawings, which were strewn along a hall when some building official decided that room was needed for other storage. At that time I was shading with a soft graphite stick, which produced nice dark areas and beautiful gradations. There was only one problem—the drawing would smear if anything touched it.

Tossing the cartoons into the hallway didn't improve them any, even with tissue sheets over them. And some years later when I gave a Pulitzer speech at Columbia University, it was suggested that I might contribute a certain prize cartoon to its collection. I mumbled something, but couldn't bring myself to explain that it existed but had been smeared almost beyond recognition.

When the graphite sticks became harder to come by, I finally turned to crayon. This helped solve the cartoon-storing problem but did nothing to improve my saving and storing habits. When I finally got a nice office with permanent walls—and the succession of rotating building managers had come to an end—the rest of the messy situation was all of my doing.

In 1972, *The Post* built an addition to its building at a cost of around $30 million, and I was given an office in the bright new section. My secretary and I got everything moved there, although the quick transition left the office contents in more disarray. Eager to see how things were working out for everyone in the expensive new quarters, Ben Bradlee came by. He looked around at all the old accumulations and the piles of papers now even less orderly than before, and said, "Jeez, it makes you feel it was all really worthwhile."

At home, the good fairies are a couple of intrepid housekeepers who make visitations to perform the almost impossible task of keeping the place clean while following strict instructions to move nothing. Worst of all about being an incurable saver: I don't enjoy it. Visitors smile and say this must be the way I like it. It is not. I wish each thing was in its tidy place. I'd feel better about the surroundings and could save all kinds of time trying to find things. But the books don't get put back on shelves, there is always more to read—*later*—in magazines and papers and always new stuff coming in and piling up.

I have one excuse, lame though it may be. In my line of work sheets of drawing paper, file pictures, photos and other material take up more space than, say, a word processor and software. So do all the papers and notes connected with using an old-fashioned typewriter.

So *part* of the problem is job-related. I used to feel flattered when other cartoonists dropped by with their wives or girlfriends—until I realized that on the way out they were triumphantly telling their companions, "You see, you thought *I* was messy."

Okay, I'm a pack rat. But someday I'm really going to get things straightened out. God knows when.

Besides savers and throw-awayers there are two other kinds of people—Earlys and Lates. I'm a Late. Let me explain—I don't mean late to dinners or appointments. Unless they are scheduled before I finish work, I am Mr. Punctual. I'm the guy who tries to make every appointment as if the time schedule is written in blood. I'm also the guy who gets to train stations and airports an hour or so earlier than they want me to *start* waiting. This is after spending several evenings packing for an overnight trip as if I were planning a D-day invasion or at least a trip abroad. And I generally take along everything, except some item I could really use or wear. We are also talking here about a fellow who has never gone hungry in his life, but who takes to a hotel room a supply of food in case Starvation should strike in the middle of the night—and who can scarcely sleep for fear of being delinquent on meeting the hotel check-out time.

I'm not the tardy kind of a Late. I mean *Late* as distinguished from an *Early,* who is up with the birds, singing, chattering, packing in a big breakfast and ready to face the world before the world has washed its face. I'm not even up with the more sluggish birds. My bedroom blinds are drawn tight, the phone turned off and door closed to keep out anything or anyone intrusively sunny. I do get a 7 A.M. temporary wakeup from National Airport planes—filled with *real* Earlys—that fly over my house, trying to buzz it as closely and noisily as possible. In the days of the quiet old prop planes I never even *thought* of how to go about buying an ack-ack gun. Flights are supposed to stop at 10 P.M., a nice wide-awake time, so they can accommodate those Earlys.

These regulations are undoubtedly set by government officials—the kind I read about in the papers who conduct breakfast meetings. Breakfast meetings! This is to make voters feel their officials are working like crazy. But they probably knock it off for the day while we Lates are hard at work.

There must have been a time when I rose early enough to perform a boy's function of keeping his parents from getting enough rest, and later there must have been eight or nine o'clock classes at school. I can even remember a time when I woke up to tune in a radio program called "The Breakfast Club"—anyhow the part where they were clearing the table. But that was quite a while ago.

I'll confess to being up early to appear on morning TV programs when promoting a book. You do things for a new book the same as you would for a new child. I get to the studios promptly, even if the makeup person has to paint eyeballs on my lids. ("They're blue, ma'am.") I know these programs have big audiences, but I always wonder who is watching. Being up at that hour is enough; it is okay for shaving or making coffee but not for eye contact with a screen. Well, that's because I don't know how the other half of the Earlys and Lates live.

Being a Late is not to be confused with being lazy, although when we were a rural country and the cows were beating on the door to be milked before dawn, the two were considered synonymous. There is a difference in internal clocks and mechanisms. Some of us take a while to get revved up, but are just going full steam when the whistle is blowing for others to call it a wrap and start with cocktails or dinner. That's when they begin phoning me to chat as I'm working like crazy.

I generally don't get to the office until 11 A.M. or noon, but going through the morning papers at home over a leisurely pot of coffee is not wasted time. Brunch at the desk doesn't take long, and as the day wears on, the pace picks up. By five o'clock and sometimes even a little later, I stop cranking out sketches and start on a finished drawing. And whatever the drawing is, simple or complicated, it seems to take about the same amount of time. Occasionally I've accidentally spilled a little water on an unfinished drawing, and have often thought about what would happen at almost-deadline if it was a bottle of ink that spilled. I hope I never have to find out. I don't usually get out of the office until after 9 P.M., sometimes later. And not long after that, it's time to start reading the early edition of the next morning's paper.

I think it was some essayist like Charles Lamb who once wrote a piece on Lying Late Abed. The title, like Irwin Shaw's "The Girls in Their Summer Dresses," calls forth delightful thoughts just in itself. At the end of a long day, I often wonder if it would be better to be on a schedule where I finished earlier instead of leaving the office with just about enough energy to hail a cab. But in the morning, when consciousness seeps in and I can just lie there dozing or giving things a quiet think, I realize that leaping out of bed to race downtown would be silly.

For me, not having the daily work or an office to go to would be awful. But not having to get there at some particular hour—ahhhhhhh! As I flip over in bed to take a sprawling position on the other side, I realize the full joy of being a "Late."

34

The Draw

Fellows who have had a bad evening at cards are inclined to say, as they watch another guy pull in the chips, "Some people are born lucky." It's true. I don't know about cards, but the sentiment is correct. An English statesman, well along in life, was asked how he would like starting all over. His reply was, "Heavens no—to be born again in the right country, in the right kind of family, with the right kind of education and opportunities—I wouldn't take a chance on being that fortunate again." I think the difference between someone like that and successful politicians or tycoons who think the answer to poverty and everyone else's problems is to say, "Pull up your socks," is that some think more about their own good fortune.

When Jim Dickenson was covering politics for *The Washington Post,* he told of asking a wealthy Republican governor, then trying for his party's presidential nomination, who or what he would like to be if he were not Pierre (Pete) du Pont. To Jim's surprise—or at least mine when I heard about it—the answer was that he wouldn't mind being in my shoes.

Perhaps I shouldn't have been surprised. What could be a more enviable or satisfying job than drawing a picture every day and getting in your two cents' worth on whatever is going on in the world?

People who are lucky enough to be college graduates often face the question of what next—what occupation they will follow or where they will fit in. Luckier still is falling into a happy occupation, as I did, even before leaving school.

Does that mean that life is an unending song and ha ha, somebody has screwed up again, but no matter? Of course not. Don't we all have our downs as well as our ups? For example:

In the spring of 1936 I got exciting news. Shortly before the Pulitzer Prizes were to be announced, the names of some of the recipients leaked, as they often did then. Walter Winchell's column listed me as a winner. The Columbia University paper ran one of my cartoons—apparently also part of the annual award custom—and there were wire service reports that brought congratulations from out-of-town friends. I was bursting to tell my folks the good news, but thought I'd better wait until it became official. It didn't. No award was made in the cartoon category. After all the unofficial "announcements," it was a great let-down, and there was no satisfaction in hearing later that another cartoonist and I had been in a dead heat.

In unhappy moments, as time went by I visualized myself someday being awarded The Prize and declining to accept it, as Sinclair Lewis had done a few years before. Hah! Thanks but no thanks, I don't believe in awards—something like that. Hah!

In the course of a brilliant speech on these prizes, Russell Baker told of *his* dark feelings about the awards, until he was notified of *his* own selection. Then, as he put it, the scales fell from his eyes and he saw their merits clearly.

A few years after the non-award I forgot all about those fantasy statements pooh-poohing prizes. They may not represent the definitive word on what's good, and again luck is usually involved, but they certainly don't hurt the morale.

There is also the psychic return in words of approval. When people precede a compliment with "You must be tired of hearing this," the answer is No—really—not at all—please go on.

As for the non-approvals, they go with the territory.

What goes with the territory in any life are the personal peeves and the common irritations and annoyances. There are the telephone solicitations; gatefold ads in magazine covers; potholes; tailgaters; litterbugs; blood-and-gore ''entertainment''; stores and restaurants that patronize their patrons, and discourtesy anywhere; products designed to conk out one week after the warranty has expired; repair people who go incommunicado when they are due to arrive and make a mockery of the phrase ''service economy''—and how about the remote controls that we can't seem to control? As Jackie Gleason might have said, ''Don't get me started, Alice.''

Most frustrating are the misdeeds and failures of governments—*our* governments, *our* public servants—that infuriate us—the political outrages and scandals that make us want to shout, ''They can't *do* that!'' But there's the non-rub, the real point, the place where I have it good. I have my own reserved soapbox. I get to *say* it in published cartoons. And for creative pleasure, the little black ink bottle contains everything from a picture of a pompous politico down the street to a drawing of planets swirling around in space. It's the ideal occupation—always the same but always something new.

Of course, some days are better than others. When I turn in at night with the early edition of the next morning's paper, I open to the editorial page and sometimes think, I could have changed a pen line here or a word there. But even if a day's piece doesn't come out just the way I hoped it would, there's always a clean slate, a fresh sheet of paper, a waiting space, a chance to have another shot at it tomorrow.

Tomorrow!

Index

368